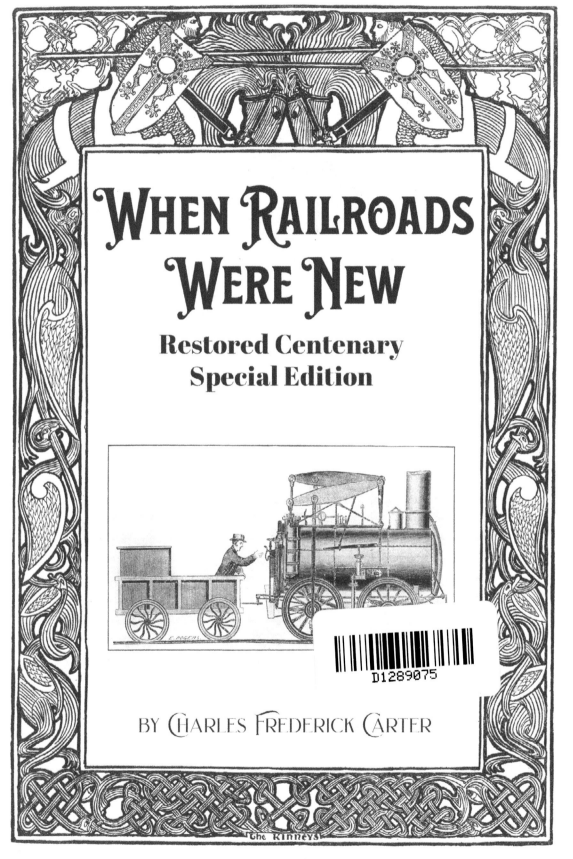

WHEN RAILROADS WERE NEW

Restored Centenary
Special Edition

BY CHARLES FREDERICK CARTER

When Railroads Were New:
Restored Centenary Special Edition

by Charles Frederick Carter

Copyright © 2021 Inecom, LLC.
All Rights Reserved

More books at
CGRpublishing.com

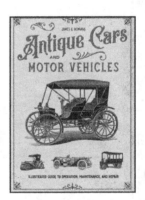

Our Iron Roads: Railroad History, Construction, and Administration - Illustrated Enlarged Special Edition

The American Railway: The Trains, Railroads, and People Who Ran the Rails

Antique Cars and Motor Vehicles: Illustrated Guide to Operation, Maintenance, and Repair

CONTENTS

CHILDHOOD OF RAPID TRANSIT, 1835-1836.

The New York Central on the Mohawk. Showing the Erie Canal near Little Falls. From a painting by E. L. Henry.

4

WHEN RAILROADS
WERE NEW

BY

CHARLES FREDERICK CARTER

CENTENARY EDITION

ILLUSTRATED

PREFACE TO THE FIRST EDITION

CONCERNING certain aspects of the railroad, such as its finance, both high and ordinary, its construction and operation from a technical viewpoint, its moral turpitude and its predilection for manslaughter, whole libraries have been published. The fact that more libraries are constantly being added indicates a sustained interest in the subject which is not at all surprising, considering how intimately the railroad enters into the life of everybody, from the hosts who look directly to it for their bread, to the farmer and the manufacturer whose products it takes to market, the baby who depends upon it to bring the daily supply for his bottle, and the millionaire who expects it to furnish him an income.

What is surprising is that the general reader might search in vain throughout the wilderness of words for any satisfactory account of how the railroad came to America; of how Smith and Jones and Robinson quarreled first about what a railroad was, then about its desirability, then about how to build and run it; how they struggled with poverty, ignorance, and other inevitable obstacles, blundered and struggled on again until they had at last developed a method of transportation that, measured by its influence in accelerating the march of Progress, is the greatest achievement in the annals of the race.

Such human-interest stories of the railroad as have been preserved are but disjointed fragments constituting a delirium of contradictions. It seems as if every statement ever made about the history of the railroad by any one has been disputed by some one else. For example, the honor of inventing the link motion of the locomotive is claimed for three different men. The invention of the four-wheeled truck is also claimed for three men. One of them obtained a patent for the device, then spent a fortune trying to protect it only to find out that he was not entitled to it.

The man who made the first trip on a locomotive in America gives a date for the event that contemporaneous data proves to be wrong.

The management of the greatest locomotive works in the world asserts that the first engine built by their founder ran only on fair days at the outset of its career, being replaced by horses on rainy days by its proud but prudent owners. On the other hand, the engineer who claims to have had charge of this first locomotive declares he ran it every day, rain or shine.

Dates that vary a whole year are given for so recent an event as the running of the first through passenger train over the Canadian Pacific Railway.

A former auditor of the Lake Shore in attempting to give the date of the Ashtabula wreck, in a historical paper presumably prepared with care, errs regarding the day of the month, the month, and the year. Yet auditors are popularly supposed to be the most distressingly accurate of men. Even this was outdone by a minister, who achieved the truly remarkable feat of writing a book about the same wreck without disclosing the date thereof or the number killed and injured therein.

In this volume an attempt has been made to gather

the floating fragments of railroad history having a human interest into a coherent narrative of the work-a-day trials and triumphs of the pioneers in the planning and the building of the railroad that would be neither a dry historical treatise nor a collection of anecdotes. It is not designed to be comprehensive in the sense of including details of all the early railroads, or even of all the important ones that have survived; for such a work would be as wearisome as it would be profitless. It is hoped, however, that it is sufficiently comprehensive to present a homely picture of the development of the railroad in America under various representative types of conditions.

Much of the material was published in a series of articles in the *Railroad Man's Magazine* by the Frank A. Munsey Company, New York, through whose courtesy it is reproduced here.

C. F. C.

New York, *March 2*, 1908.

PREFACE TO THE CENTENARY EDITION

THE eighteen years that have elapsed since this volume was completed have wrought many changes in the world. In these mutations the railroad has been an increasingly important factor.

One change of notable significance is in the attitude of the public toward the railroads in 1926 as compared with that in 1908. When the last chapter was finished public hostility toward the railroads, fanned by designing demagogues, amounted almost to fanaticism. A small part of this hostility was undeniably due to the misdeeds of deliberately dishonest promoters whose conceptions of right and wrong were delimited by the line beyond which prospects of prison outweighed chances of gain. Perhaps it would be more correct to speak of the memories of such misdeeds rather than of any crooked deals then current; for the progress of civilization, accelerated by railroad influence in providing means therefor, has steadily advanced the standards of common honesty. That which seemed all right in the 70's, provided one could get away with it, was distinctly off color in 1908; the things that were condoned in 1908 simply are not done in 1926. Only outright outlawry flourishes unabashed in these modern days.

Of one phase in the evolution of ethics railroads were the innocent victims. Railroads were the pioneers in America, and pioneers are ever poor and needy, as has been set forth in these pages. Since there was not enough traffic for all, big shippers could go shopping for rates; and the cleverest shopper obtained the lowest rates. Since civilization began, buyer and seller, regardless of the commodity involved, have each striven for the best end of the bargain. There was no violation of statutory law, nor infraction of the moral code, nor yet a lapse from the business ethics then obtaining in this former method of fixing freight rates. When a railroad accepted an unprofitable rate in order to secure business urgently needed to help pay operating expenses it consoled itself, like the apothecary in "Romeo and Juliet" by saying "My poverty, but not my will, consents."

In due time it became apparent that this immemorial custom of bargaining could not be applied to such a vital matter as transportation. Government regulation of rates was, quite properly, established as the next step in railroad evolution and one cause for popular discontent was removed, though the discontent, unfortunately, lingered.

In another way the railroads were the innocent victims of circumstances which they themselves created, or helped to create. Cheap transportation so stimulated the development of the nation that the concerted efforts of inventive genius and finance were not able to keep pace with it. The result was that the railroads could not at all times meet the current demand for the movement of freight. Embargoes were frequent at the peak of traffic movements causing great losses and greater exasperation on the part of shippers.

PREFACE

The depths of railroad inefficiency and consequent disfavor were plumbed when the railroads were struggling to recover from a government operation that almost proved fatal. But early in 1923 it became evident that the patients would recover. In three years more than three billions of dollars were raised for investment in additional equipment and other facilities though how it was done by an industry deep in public disfavor and having but slight appeal to investors the men who did it, perhaps, could not tell. This made possible the movement of the greatest volume of traffic on record in 1923. Responding to an enthusiastic encore the railroads established a new high record in 1925 and immediately set out early in 1926 for yet another high water mark. Meanwhile the railroads have learned to co-operate among each other and with the shipping public as they never co-operated before. The net result is that the railroads to-day are among the most efficient industries in the country if, indeed, they are not the most efficient.

Publicity about railroad affairs required by law also has proved to be a blessing both for the carriers and for the public dependent upon them for opportunities to live and do business. Things not understood have ever been objects of suspicion and distrust; familiarity with the deserving breeds friendship. Professional hostility toward railroads has almost entirely disappeared since the campaign of 1924.

Now that the railroads and the public are on such friendly terms that they can laugh together over their early struggles the present seems a good time to contribute to the discussion by offering a new edition of this account of the beginning of the railroad era in America.

Such an edition seems particularly opportune because the world is entering upon the centennial anniversary of the railroad. Centennial anniversaries are commonly associated with a specific date; but the railroad is so rich in anniversaries that the series of celebrations which began on April 23d, 1923, when the Delaware and Hudson celebrated the centennial of its original organization as a canal company, may quite properly be continued at least to November 7, 1985, which will be the centennial anniversary of the completion of the Canadian Pacific, the last of the great pioneers described herein.

Charles Frederick Carter

New York,
    June 11, 1926

CHAPTER I

THE DAWN OF THE RAILROAD ERA

ONE of the cardinal grievances of the Israelites in bondage was that they were obliged to make bricks without straw. Yet brickmaking as then practised was a craft demanding only rudimentary intelligence and skill. A limitless supply of raw material free of cost was right at hand, while the finished product which fulfilled the requirements of that primitive day was so hopelessly inferior that it could not have been redeemed even by the addition of straw.

If those discontented bondmen could make so small a matter the subject of a protest which has passed into a proverb for later generations, what would they have done if they had been called upon in the second quarter of the nineteenth century to lay the foundations of the great railroad systems of the United States without the technical training needed to solve the profound engineering problems involved, without material to work with or money or credit to buy it, and even without a remote conception of what a railroad should be?

It was under precisely these conditions that the first railroads were built in America. Our grandfathers tried to borrow a few ideas from the English at first, but the attempts were so discouraging that they were quickly discontinued. Of the first four locomotives imported from England only one ever made so much as a trial trip, which was never repeated; the others were so lightly esteemed that they were never permitted to turn a wheel, but soon disappeared so utterly that no man knows what became of them.

The Baltimore and Ohio, the first important railroad, which cost $31,000,000 by the time the rails reached the Ohio River, was begun by the people of Baltimore when all the earthly possessions of the entire city were worth barely $25,000,000. The promoters of the enterprise were so ignorant of the nature of their undertaking that they had to appoint a committee to go and find out what a railroad was before beginning operations.

In spite of all these difficulties those sturdy pioneers wrought cheerfully on, the only complaint they ever uttered being on account of their inability to build more railroads. Their disappointment in this respect was providential for their descendants; for if all the railroads ever projected had been built there would have been no room on this continent for anything else.

It would be difficult, indeed, to overestimate the transcendent importance of the part the railroad has played in making the Nation what it is to-day. Perhaps it would be within bounds to say that without railroads to bind the States into one homogeneous whole, the Nation never could have attained its present size and importance. But however exalted a place in the march of progress be accorded the railroad, no achievement that can be attributed to it is nearly as wonderful as the fact that the railroad itself was evolved from such seemingly impossible conditions.

Difficult as it is to realize, it is only a century

since the charter for the first railroad in America was drafted. Only fifty-six years had then elapsed since Watt had patented his steam engine, and only forty years since the astounded legislature of Pennsylvania had silently ignored the request of Oliver Evans for a patent on a steam wagon, as the hallucination of a disordered mind. Progress in engine building had been so slow that twenty-seven years before that pioneer railroad company was organized the Philadelphia waterworks were operated by a wooden boiler supplying steam at two and a half pounds pressure to an engine built chiefly of wood with a copper cylinder as large as a good-sized modern boiler.

In a nation of magnificent distances the need of transportation became urgent at an early period. But attempts to supply the need were resisted, as a matter of course, by that considerable part of every community which is forever under arms, ready at a moment's notice to defend established conditions against the encroachments of progress. Even a stage coach on a moderately good road was too advanced for the reactionaries. One of them took his indignant pen in hand to write to an Albany paper in 1823 that he had lately noticed with surprise the reckless speed with which a journey was made in a stage from Utica to Albany and return, the distance of two hundred miles being covered in seventeen hours and twenty-eight minutes. This was so remarkable a feat that it attracted the attention of seven citizens of Buffalo, who attempted to beat the record and succeeded in covering eighty miles in six hours and twenty-six and a half minutes.

" Why the necessity for this waste of horse flesh? " demands the letter writer. " Of traveling nearly thirteen miles an hour on a party of pleasure and at every moment in danger of running afoul of other carriages on the road? "

Despite all protests, means of communication were steadily improved until in 1811 there were 37,000 miles of post roads in the United States, including the great National turnpike, begun in 1806 and built from Cumberland, Md., to Steubenville, O., at a cost of $1,800,000, and afterward extended to Indianapolis. States followed the example of the National Government by appropriating money for highways, while turnpike and plank road corporations were financed by private capital. In time it became possible to travel from Boston to New York, a distance of 270 miles, in twenty-five and a half hours; and from Baltimore to Louisville by stage and steamboat in six days and eight hours, including twenty hours' detention at various places.

But a freight tariff based on a rate of a hundred dollars a ton between Albany and Buffalo was not calculated to foster trade. When the necessities of traffic became so urgent that they could no longer be disregarded the people at last turned their attention to the building of canals as a source of relief. Washington, while surveying in his younger days, had become deeply impressed with the possibilities of a system of canals and turnpikes to connect the waters of the Potomac with those of the Ohio, and the scheme was always a favorite with him. General Philip Schuyler, of Albany, who went to England in 1761 to settle the accounts of General John Bradstreet, was greatly impressed by the Bridgewater Canal, then just opened. On his return to America he was the first to propose a canal to connect Lake Champlain with the Hudson. In 1762 some citizens of Pennsylvania applied to the legislature for a charter for the Schuylkill and Susquehanna Canal to connect the rivers of those names. This canal, four miles long, finished and operated in 1794, was the first projected and the first chartered, while the South Hadley and Montague Canal, five miles long, around the rapids of the Connecticut River at South Hadley, Mass., opened in 1792, was the first operated in the United States.

After a conference with Washington on the subject of canals, Elkanah Watson made some explorations in 1788 which convinced him that a water route by way of the Mohawk River and a canal to Lake Ontario was feasible. By four years of hard work Watson, Schuyler, and a few other enthusiasts wrought public opinion up to a point which enabled them to secure from the New York legislature charters for two canals. From one of these schemes the Erie Canal was ultimately evolved.

The sentiment in favor of canals thus started spread gradually until the astonishing results accomplished by the Erie Canal fanned it into a furore. Immediately all sorts of possible and impossible canal projects were advanced, with the result that by January 1, 1835, forty-eight canals aggregating 2,617 miles were in use. At the climax of the canal period five thousand miles of these artificial waterways costing $150,000,000 were in operation. Public opinion, which had so reluctantly taken this step in advance, now assumed that the last word had been spoken on the subject of transportation; that the canal was the apotheosis of engineering skill.

The little band of advanced thinkers which accepted
the wonders of the canal with mental reservations, and
which had heard with eager interest of Richard Trevithick's experiments with a steam locomotive on a
tram road near Merthyr-Tydvil, in Wales, in 1804;
of Blackett's locomotive, modeled after Trevithick's
nine years later; of Chapman's endless chain locomotive, brought out about the same time, which saw
eighty years' continuous service before it earned honorable retirement to a museum hall, and of Stephenson's locomotive, "My Lord," which drew nine loaded
wagons up a twelve-foot grade on the Killingworth
Colliery road in 1814, therefore had not only to overcome the inertia of blind opposition to all progress,
but also to pry popular prejudice out of a settled conviction in favor of artificial waterways.

Even this task was trifling compared with the Her-
culean labor of converting the numerous class which
simply knew that railroads could not be built nor operated if they were built, and who were, therefore, not
open to conviction. These men were the fathers of
the statesmen whose witticisms, inspired by S. F. B.
Morse's request for government aid to demonstrate
the worth of that fantastic absurdity, the electric telegraph, are embalmed in the *Congressional Record,*
and of the Chicago bankers who told the promoter
who appeared before them with a proposal to establish one of Morse's patent telegraphs connecting that
thriving town with the East, intimating that in time
it might do a business amounting to as much as a
hundred dollars a day, that he was crazy, and ordered
him out of the room. Doubtless the ancestors of the
influential capitalists who thirty-five years later jeered

at Alexander Graham Bell's attempts to finance a scheme " to talk through a wire," and the heroes of many other exploits of a similar character were also represented.

Colonel John Stevens, of Hoboken, wore his life out in futile attempts to convince his contemporaries that railroads were the only satisfactory solution of the transportation problem. Colonel Stevens, with a grasp of the question wonderfully clear for that day, worked out a plan for a railroad with wooden rails supported on piles from Albany to Lake Erie, which he urged the National Government to take up. In 1812 Stevens published a pamphlet entitled " Documents Tending to Prove the Superior Advantages of Railways and Steam Carriages over Canal Navigation." He could see nothing to hinder steam carriages from attaining a velocity of a hundred miles an hour, but thought that in practice it might not be convenient to exceed twenty to thirty miles an hour. But Chancellor Livingston and Gouverneur Morris demonstrated conclusively that a railroad under any circumstances was impossible.

About the same time Oliver Evans, of Pennsylvania, " The Watt of America," inventor of the high-pressure steam engine, made this remarkable prediction:

" The time will come when people will travel in stages moved by steam engines from one city to another, almost as fast as birds can fly, fifteen or twenty miles an hour. Passing through the air with such velocity will be the most exhilarating exercise. To accomplish this two sets of railways will be laid, so nearly level as not to deviate more than two degrees from the horizontal, made of wood or iron, on smooth paths of broken stone or gravel, with a rail to guide the carriages so they may pass each other in different directions, and they will travel by night as well as by day. Passengers will sleep in these stages as comfortably as they now do in steam stage boats. Twenty miles an hour is about thirty-two feet a second, and the resistance of the air about one pound to the square foot; but the body of the carriages will be shaped like a swift swimming fish to pass easily through the air. The United States will be the first nation to make the discovery, and her wealth and power will rise to an unparalleled height."

Henry Meigs, a member of the New York legislature in 1817, a young man of fine talents, lost his influence, ruined his prospects, and came to be regarded as a proper subject for a strait-jacket because he expressed his belief that steam carriages would be operated successfully on land.

The most embarrassing feature of the situation was that these prominent citizens who knew railroads were but the impracticable dream of irresponsible visionaries, were the owners of what little capital there was in the country, and railroad building is distinctly an enterprise requiring funds. The character and extent of this opposition, which by no means was confined to Massachusetts, are admirably set forth in this extract from a speech by Henry Williams, a director of the Boston and Worcester Railroad, at the celebration in Worcester of the opening of the road July 6, 1835:

"A few years ago this project started. It had many warm and high-spirited friends and advocates; also many strong and powerful enemies. Strange as it may seem, these enemies were to be found principally among the rich and powerful—the very class of men who possessed the most ample means, and so might have been expected to be first and foremost in advocating and prosecuting an important, a noble public enterprise. True, there were honorable exceptions; but it cannot be denied that very many great men, very many rich men, refused all participation, scoffed at our project, pointed at some of us the finger of scorn and bandied such epithets as ' hare-brained enthusiasts,' ' visionaries,' who ' almost deserve to be sent to the mad-house.'

" All this was said—nay more; for when the first spade was stuck in the ground the directors were called ' fools,' ' idiots,' and ' knaves.' They were declared guilty of a high crime in commencing a work which must inevitably result in as total a loss as if the money expended were shoveled into the bottomless pit.

" All this was said and much more. Measures were actually taken to arrest work and cause an abandonment of the enterprise. But, thanks to the true friends of the project, they stood firm and, with warm hearts and just confidence in those who were chosen to prosecute the work, manfully and successfully resisted all attempts to crush the noble project.

" The road had a sorry beginning. At first some of our prominent men were willing to advance a few dollars to make examinations and surveys; but when called upon to take and pay for the stock for which they had subscribed, they flinched and vociferously cried out that it was madness to go on; that the road would cost three times the amount of the estimates, and that even if it should be built it would be next to worthless and could never pay half of one per cent on the cost.

" Here we are, my friends, in the hall of the heart of the Commonwealth. We came by railroad all the way from Boston, forty-two miles, in less than three hours. The road is finished, but who accomplished the work? Has it been done by the rich men, the great men of the times? By our quarter, half, and whole million men? No, sir! It has been accomplished by the bone and sinew of the community; by the middling interest people, by that class of men who have warm hearts, clear heads, and who possess almost a monopoly of generous public spirit."

Still another part of the opposition to the railroad was made up of a class which was unable to help, but which was able to hinder materially by playing upon unreasoning prejudice. Of this type was the Englishman who in 1830 assumed that the railroad advocates planned to dispense entirely with horses and drivers. He figured that earning power valued at a hundred million pounds a year would be thus utterly destroyed. What was to become of all the people thus deprived of a livelihood?

Another Englishman, a scientist, was much exercised over the doom of America after this unfortunate country had fed to its locomotives the last pound of its limited supply of coal.

Still another summed up the horrors and dangers of railroad travel thus:

" Reader, how would you like to be put in a box like a coach or a sedan and dropped out of the window of the fifth or sixth flat of a house? Sixty-six miles an hour is the highest velocity attained by falling bodies in one hundred feet, and forty-four miles an hour in falling sixty-four feet. Even supposing that means were found to abate one-half of the violent shock in stopping, enough remains to terrify considerate men from risking their persons in such species of conveyance. Till we have bones of brass or iron, or better methods of protecting them than we have now, it is preposterous to talk of traveling fifty or sixty miles an hour as a practicable thing."

Most remarkable of all was the discovery, also by an English genius, of a new disease superinduced by rapid travel on the railroad. He declared that it was a notorious fact that the brains of business men were so addled by the swiftness of the journey from Manchester to Liverpool or London, that they often forgot what they went for, and had to write home to find out. One elderly gentleman became so impregnated with velocity, as the result of a prolonged debauch in railroad rides, that he dashed head foremost into an iron post and shivered it into pieces, according to this veracious authority.

All these remarkable stories were duly brought across the ocean, to be gravely discussed, embellished, and reconstructed to give them a local atmosphere, and fed to the credulous to rouse their apprehensions and their antipathies. In 1836 the people of Newington, Conn., drew up a remonstrance addressed to the directors of a railroad that had been surveyed through the town, setting forth that they were a peaceable, orderly people, and that they did not want their quiet disturbed by steam cars and the influx of strangers. Dorchester, Mass., in town meeting assembled in 1842, instructed its representatives in the legislature to " use their utmost endeavors to prevent, if possible, so great a calamity to our town as must be the location of any railroad through it." A committee of Congress, in a report dated February 21, 1829, expressed the conviction that clauses in charters prohibiting any one but the owners of a railroad from using it " seem to render it obnoxious to the charge of a close monopoly."

But once a great idea has germinated it will grow in spite of all the powers of darkness. The theory of the railroad was so sound that it won its way irresistibly. When at last the Stockton and Darlington Railroad of England, which had been authorized by Parliament in 1821 after desperate opposition, was opened for traffic in 1825, the more reckless enthusiasts on this side of the Atlantic jumped at the conclusion that a new era of transportation had dawned. Almost simultaneously advanced thinkers in widely separated parts of the country, each in his own way, set about the development of the American railroad.

One of the first Americans to form a definite conviction that the railroad was to supply the transportation of the future was Horatio Allen, the son of a professor of mathematics at Union College, Schenectady, who had adopted engineering as a profession. At the age of twenty-three Allen secured an appointment as resident engineer on the summit level of the Delaware and Hudson Canal just about the time the Stockton and Darlington Railroad was opened. Young Allen was clever, energetic, and ambitious. He won the friendship of his chief, J. B. Jervis, and he had the best possible opportunity for advancement in the science of canal building, then the most highly esteemed form of internal improvement.

But he was shrewd enough to realize that his chances of a career lay not on the canal but on the dawning railroad. So he resigned his position in 1827 and prepared to go to England to study railroad building at first hand. His late employers had such confidence in Allen that they commissioned him to buy the iron for a railroad they were building from Honesdale, the terminus of the canal, to the coal mines at Carbondale, and four locomotives to operate it. As compensation they agreed to pay his expenses for three months, but not to exceed nine hundred dollars, while he was studying railroads.

About the time that Allen gave up his position to go to England, the first railroad in the United States was completed. It was built by Gridley Bryant, from the granite quarries near Quincy, Mass., to tidewater on the Neponset River, a distance of three miles. It was used solely to haul granite from the quarry to a point from which it could be conveyed by water to Boston. The granite for the Bunker Hill monument was transported over this first railroad. The gauge was five feet. The rails were pine timbers six by twelve inches, on top of which was an oak scantling two by four inches, faced with bar iron five-sixteenths of an inch thick and two and a half inches wide. The ties were of stone twelve inches square and eight feet long, laid on a foundation of broken stone three feet deep. Such substantial construction was expensive, costing $11,250 a mile, but it reduced the cost of transportation to one-sixth of what it had been. Being down-grade all the way, two horses could haul forty tons at a speed of four and a half miles an hour.

The Quincy Railroad, although it was never operated with anything but horses, and carried no traffic but stone, was regarded as one of the wonders of the age. Visitors came long distances to see it in operation. So great was the rush to see the railroad, in fact, that a thrifty citizen opened a tavern near where the highway from Boston to Quincy crossed it and did a thriving business catering to the sightseers. Daniel Webster drove over one day after attending a funeral in the vicinity, and after a critical examination hazarded the opinion that railroads would bear some study. But not until years afterward did the great lawyer and statesman concede that the railroad was a success. For a long time he inclined to the belief that it could not be operated with locomotives. He thought, for one thing, that the frost on the rails in winter would be an insuperable obstacle.

Shortly after the Quincy Railroad was finished the Mauch Chunk Railroad, the second in America, was thrown open to traffic and public admiration. Business on this line was also confined to a single commodity, coal, moving in one direction. The Mauch Chunk Railroad extended from the Lehigh River to the Summit Mines near Carbondale, nine miles distant and at an elevation of nine hundred and thirty-six feet above the river. From the river bank there was an inclined plane two thousand one hundred feet long, having a rise of two hundred and twenty-five feet. The entire nine miles was built in two months and three days at a cost of twenty-seven thousand dollars. The ties were of wood spaced four feet apart. The rails were of wood held in place by wooden keys or wedges and faced with iron a quarter of an inch thick and an inch and a quarter wide. Cars carrying a ton and a half of coal were taken down in " brigades " of six to ten, in charge of two men, to the top of the plane in thirty minutes. The cars were lowered down the plane one at a time, the descent requiring three-quarters of a minute. On the return trip one horse hauled three empty cars, making the journey in two hours.

These two railroads, such as they were, served as models for the construction of the first railroad designed for a general transportation business. The first act of the Baltimore and Ohio Railroad Company after organizing was to send Philip E. Thomas, Alexander Brown, and Thomas Ellicott to study these lines for ideas to be applied in building their own road.

Allen sailed from New York in January, 1828. Being provided with letters of introduction, he was able to begin his investigations without delay under the most favorable conditions. The state of the art of railroad building cannot be described better than by quoting the following letter to the board of directors of the Charleston and Hamburg Railroad. The letter is of peculiar interest because it was a link in a chain of circumstances which influenced the Charleston and Hamburg to become the first railroad company in the world to adopt the locomotive as a motive power:

" I have now the pleasure of communicating the results of some observations which I have been able to make since I last wrote you. With the exception of one or two small roads at some of the coal mines near this place the railroad at Leeds is the first of much importance visited after leaving Liverpool.

" This railroad, three and a half miles long, extends to a mine. It was constructed about fifteen years since. The rails are of cast iron in lengths of three feet, and mostly in bad order. Most of this road descends a little from the mine and about the middle the line has a self-acting plane three hundred yards in length. They use a locomotive from each end of the plane, which have been in use seven or eight years, and I think them preferable to animal power. These engines are not of the approved kind. They, however, travel with their train, consisting of fifteen or twenty cars weighing nearly four tons each, at the rate of two and a half or three miles an hour. I rode up and down the line on one of them, and find that they are easily managed and that their direction can be sooner changed than the time required to move horses for that purpose.

" The next railroad of importance that I visited was the Stockton and Darlington. This was the first experiment to apply railroads to the purposes of promiscuous traffic, and was opened about two years since. The whole extent of this road, including some branches, is about thirty miles; and although the general object was to open communication from navigation at Stockton with an extensive coal region, was also designed for a general trade with the interior. This road is a single track, and although the passings are two to three in the mile, the detention to trade is not very great.

" They use both horses and locomotive steam engines upon the road and I had a fair opportunity to test their relative utility. The result is much in favor of the locomotive, as a reference with which I was favored to the accounts of the company fully testifies. The locomotives on this road are used only in the coal trade, and run a distance of twenty miles from Stockton. The greater part of this distance descends towards Stockton, varying from one-sixteenth to one-third of an inch per yard; no part ascends in that direction and only about two miles is level. They use four locomotive engines on this road which lead from twenty to twenty-eight cars in train weighing each 5,300 pounds independent of the car itself, and travel from four to seven miles an hour. Three of these engines are of Losh and Stephenson's construction, as they are called here, and one of them of Hackworth's.

" I rode up and down on these different engines a distance of thirty or forty miles. Losh and Stephenson's engines usually carry twenty cars, Hackworth's twenty-four and sometimes twenty-eight with which it is capable of traveling six to seven miles an hour. The others travel five or six, which is as great a speed as I think prudent to move at when loaded. Hackworth's engine is capable of ten or twelve miles an hour when light. In returning with empty cars I found the greatest ascents required the whole power of the engines and reduced the speed nearly one-half. This road is of wrought iron rails in lengths of fifteen feet which weigh twenty-eight pounds to the yard.

" From this railroad I proceeded to Newcastle-on-Tyne. This place, with the neighboring coal mines upon the Tyne, is the birthplace and cradle of railroads and locomotive steam engines. It was in this vicinity railroads were first introduced and it was at Killingworth, about five miles from the city of Newcastle, that the steam locomotive was first used to advantage.

" Killingworth is the residence of Wood, the author of the treatise on railroads. Letters which the politeness of Stephenson furnished me previous to my leaving Liverpool introduced me to Wood, who treated me with the greatest cordiality and very kindly answered all inquiries that curiosity and invention could suggest on the subject of railroads and locomotive steam engines. The Killingworth railroad extends from a colliery of that name to the River Tyne, a distance of five miles. It was on this road that the plate rail was used at a very early period. The present road has been laid about twenty-two years and is yet in pretty good order. The rails are of cast iron with the exception of a small portion which was laid of wrought iron by way of experiment about eight or nine years since. They have used locomotive steam engines here about five years. It was here Losh and Stephenson made their experiments on locomotives and here Wood made most of the experiments recorded in his work on railroads, which, I am happy to find, is considered as good an authority in this country as with us. Wood is now preparing a second edition of this work, which will comprise a great number of very interesting experiments and facts which his continued attention to the subject has developed.

" I saw these locomotives at work upon this road. They performed much the same as those upon the Stockton and Darlington and are of much the same construction as the three on that road. I have the particular dimensions of these engines as well as those upon the Stockton and Darlington road.

" My next object was to visit the railroads in the vicinity of Killingworth, and they are as common here as coal mines, which are to be seen in every direction. The most interesting of these to visit are the Springville and the Helton roads. The Springville road is a recent work, and in very fine order. The rails are of wrought iron, which is now altogether used in place of cast iron. They use only one locomotive upon this road, which performs much the same as those described. The Helton road have laid by their locomotive engines on account of the line of road being unfavorable for them.

" At North Shields I saw a railroad which was laid about twenty years ago and in very bad order, though still used.

" Previous to parting with Mr. Wood he gave me letters to Buchanan and Granger of Edinburgh, my next object being to examine the railroads of Scotland. These gentlemen construct engines and Granger is superintendent of most of the railroads now constructing in that quarter. They are constructing a railroad from Edinburgh to the Dalkeith collieries, a distance of six or seven miles. This will be an expensive work in tunneling, cuttings, and embankments.

" After spending a short time in Edinburgh I went in company with Mr. Granger to Glasgow, where he is superintending several railroads and had the pleasure of traveling with him over the whole line of the Kirkintilloch railroad. The road commences at a canal about nine miles from Glasgow and extends into the coal region about eleven miles. Seven miles of this road have been in use eighteen months; the rest is just opened. They use animal power only on this road, but they are constructing one from Glasgow to connect with the farther end of this, eight miles in length, upon which they intend using steam locomotives. This is heavy work; part of the cuttings and embankments being forty to fifty feet in depth.

"These railroads, together with those described in my last, comprise all the railroads of importance in the Kingdom. Several others are projected, and some minor ones are in progress. Upon the whole the subject appears to be quite as popular here as with us, notwithstanding they understand so much better than we do the expense of constructing railroads."

More than a year before the famous Rainhill trial of October 14, 1829, which was to determine the fate of the locomotive and immortalize the name of Stephenson, this young American engineer, then but twenty-six years old, executed his commission for the Delaware and Hudson Canal Company by ordering the first four locomotives ever seen in the United States. Three of these were from the works of Foster, Rastrick & Co., of Stourbridge, the fourth was built by Stephenson. The first of these locomotives arrived in New York in January, 1829; the last one in September of the same year. One of these locomotives was blocked up so the wheels cleared the ground, there being no track available, and fired up for the edification of the " gentlemen of science and particular intelligence," who, according to the New York *Enquirer,* " unanimously attended."

The Delaware and Hudson Company having finished its railroad from the canal terminus at Honesdale to the mines at Carbondale sixteen and a half miles distant, early in 1829, one of these locomotives, the "Stourbridge Lion," was selected for trial. It was shipped from the foot of Beach Street up the Hudson to Rondout, and thence by canal to Honesdale. Allen, being at leisure at the time, volunteered to set it up and make the trial trip.

The Stourbridge Lion was so named because the painter who put the finishing touches on it detected in the rounded boiler head a far-fetched resemblance to the King of Beasts, and so painted in glaring red a lion's head thereon. The locomotive had four wheels coupled, all drivers, and two vertical cylinders of thirty-six inches stroke at the back end of the horizontal boiler. Motion was communicated to the drivers by two grasshopper beams. The wheels were of oak with iron tires.

Crowds as eagerly curious as those in New York flocked to see the locomotive, and the day of the trial trip, Saturday, August 8, 1829, was observed as a holiday. A cannon had been borrowed by the citizens of Honesdale to add noise to the celebration. It burst after a few rounds had been fired, shattering the arm of Alva Adams, one of the men who were handling it.

In after years Allen was very fond of telling the story of that first trip of a locomotive on American soil. Here is the story as he related it on one occasion:

"When was it? Where was it? And who awakened its energies and directed its movements? It was in the year 1829 on August 9 * on the banks of the Lackawaxen, at the

* Mr. Allen seems to have been mistaken about the date, which was really August 8. He realized the untrustworthiness of his memory, for he often deplored his failure to keep a diary in his younger days.

From the "History of the First Locomotives in America," by W. H. Brown.

THE "STOURBRIDGE LION."

The first locomotive that ever turned a wheel on American soil.

33

commencement of the railroad connecting the canal of the Delaware and Hudson Canal Company with the coal mines, and he who addresses you was the only person on that locomotive. The circumstances which led to my being alone on the engine were these:

" The road had been built in the summer; the structure was of hemlock timber with rails of large dimensions notched on caps placed far apart. The timber had cracked and warped from exposure to the sun.

" After about three hundred feet of straight line the road crossed Lackawaxen Creek on trestlework about thirty feet high, and with a curve of about three hundred and fifty to four hundred feet radius. The impression was very general that the iron monster would break down the road, or that it would leave the track at the curve and plunge into the creek. My reply to such apprehensions was that it was too late to consider the probability of such occurrences; that there was no other course but to have a trial made of the strange animal which had been brought there at great expense; but that it was not necessary that more than one should be involved in its fate; that I would like the first ride alone, and the time would come when I should look back to the incident with great interest.

" As I placed my hand on the throttle valve handle I was undecided whether I should move slowly or with a fair degree of speed, but holding that the road would prove safe, and preferring, if we did go down, to go handsomely, and without any evidence of timidity, I started with considerable velocity, passed the curves over the creek safely, and was soon out of hearing of the cheers of the vast assemblage present. At the end of two or three miles I reversed the valve and returned without accident to the place of starting, having made the first locomotive trip on the western hemisphere."

Allen played a conspicuous part in the development of the railroad, first as chief engineer of the Charleston and Hamburg, and afterwards as constructing engineer and president of the Erie; but in all the eighty-seven years of his busy life he never again officiated as a locomotive engineer.

This trial convinced Allen and the directors that the road was not suitable for locomotives, so the Stourbridge Lion was run off the rails near the canal dock, where it was permitted to stand, an object of dread to all the children in the neighborhood, who made long detours to avoid passing near the monster. When winter came a rough board shed was built over it, but curious hands soon tore down planks enough to give an unobstructed view. There the Stourbridge Lion stood for fourteen years. By that time so many parts had been broken off and carried away that it was useless as a locomotive. Then the boiler was taken to the Carbondale shops of the company to supply steam for a stationary engine until it was worn out, when it was consigned to the ignominious oblivion of the scrap heap.

The wheels of the other three locomotives of that first consignment were destined never to rest on a rail. They were stored for some time in the warehouse of Abeel & Dunscombe, on the East Side in New York. Their ultimate fate is one of the mysteries which will never be solved.

Soon after this trip on the Stourbridge Lion, Allen went to Charleston to take up the duties of chief engineer of the Charleston and Hamburg Railroad, chartered by the South Carolina legislature May 12, 1828, a little more than a year after the Baltimore and Ohio was organized, to build from Charleston to the Savannah River, one hundred and thirty-six miles away.

One of his first acts in his official capacity was to attend a meeting of the board of directors on January 14, 1830, five days after his appointment, at which he recommended that the locomotive be adopted as the sole motive power, saying " there was no reason to expect any material improvement in the breed of horses, but the man was not living who knew what the breed of locomotives was to place at command." The directors were in a position to appreciate the force of the argument, for they had experimented with sailing cars and found them wanting.

It is curious how remarkably persistent has been the attempt to utilize the sail as a motive power on land. It was first tried in Holland in 1620, where cars containing twenty-eight passengers covered forty-two miles on the smooth, hard beach in two hours. As late as 1878 a Western genius went through the threadbare process of discovering that sailing cars could not be operated successfully.

Having convinced themselves that the wind was unsatisfactory for the movement of trains, the directors of the Charleston and Hamburg Railroad had offered a prize of five hundred dollars for the best horse-power motor. The prize was won by C. E. Detmold with an endless chain platform mounted on the car, by means of which one horse was able to propel a car carrying twelve passengers at the rate of twelve miles an hour.

Without leaving their seats the directors unanimously voted to adopt the recommendations of their chief engineer, thus earning the distinction of being the first railroad company in the world to declare for steam. Allen also recommended that a gauge of five feet be adopted. He afterwards tried to get the Erie to adopt that gauge. Probably there are few railroad officials to-day who do not regret that Allen's recommendations were not followed. The addition of three and a half inches to the width of the track would be a material advantage now. On one occasion James J. Hill gave out a statement for publication, in which he deplored the error of judgment that prevented the adoption of a broader gauge for the railroads. The enormous cost would render a change at this late day impossible.

Having determined to use steam, the directors of the Charleston and Hamburg Railroad lost no time in authorizing the construction of the first locomotive ever built in America for regular service. It was a fearful and wonderful contrivance, designed by E. L. Miller, of Charleston. The vertical boiler looked something like an overgrown porter bottle of the old style. The fire-box had " teats " radiating from its outer wall to afford additional heating surface. The smoke escaped through openings in the sides into an outer jacket encasing the boiler. The four wheels had iron hubs and tires and wooden spokes and felloes. The two cylinders, six inches in diameter by sixteen inches stroke, placed in front of the boiler, worked cranks inside the frame. The engine, which was christened the " Best Friend of Charleston," was built at the West Point Foundry in New York.

Upon arriving in Charleston it was set up by Julius D. Petsch, foreman of Dotterer & Easton's machine shop, assisted by Nicholas W. Darrell. On November 2, 1830, the trial trip was made with Darrell as engi-

From the "History of the First Locomotives in America," by W. H. Brown.

THE "BEST FRIEND" OF CHARLESTON

The first locomotive built in America, with its train. From an old woodcut. It is evident that this cut was made up in sections, since the last car of this train is identical, with its passengers, with the last car of the train drawn by the "West Point." (See page 26.)

neer. The wheels proved to be so weak that one of them sprung out of shape and threw the engine into the ditch on the return trip. A second trip was made on December 14, and a third on the following day, when the Best Friend proved to possess power double the contract requirements. It was able to make sixteen to twenty-one miles an hour with forty or fifty passengers in four or five cars, and to attain a speed of thirty-five miles an hour without cars.

Darrell was so delighted with his experience that he gave up his job as machinist to become the first regular locomotive engineer in America. The Best Friend came very near killing him a few months later. Not liking the noise of steam escaping from the safety valve, the negro fireman fastened it shut. Some accounts say that he " sat " on the valve. If true this statement would seem to indicate that the fireman must have been a combination of a salamander and a remarkably gifted acrobat. Be that as it may, the boiler exploded, scalding Darrell severely and injuring the fireman so that he died two days later. After that exhibition of its untrustworthiness and destructive powers the locomotive was regarded with suspicion. For a long time a " barrier car " piled high with cotton bales was interposed between the locomotive and the train to protect passengers from possible explosions.

Meanwhile, on January 15, 1831, with the aid of the Best Friend, the first regular passenger service on an American railroad was instituted. On that first trip was a passenger who was to exert a unique influence in shaping the destinies of the Erie, as will appear later.

Studying the performances of this first American-built locomotive, Allen came to the conclusion that a radical change would have to be made in the design if results were to be obtained. This conclusion led the young engineer to take another first step in the history of the railroad which was to be of far-reaching importance. Like other early railroads, the Charleston and Hamburg had wooden rails, in this instance six by twelve inches, on which was spiked strap iron half an inch thick by two and a half inches wide. On account of the weakness of the structure, Allen, in a report dated May 16, 1831, recommended that the load on each wheel be limited to a ton and a half. To allow locomotives of effective size to be built, he recommended engines with six or eight wheels.

Receiving the sanction of the directors, Allen accordingly designed a locomotive with a single pair of drivers and with a four-wheeled truck under the front end. The merits of the four-wheeled truck were so obvious that it was universally adopted. Without it the railroad could not have been developed.

This first locomotive with a four-wheeled truck and the second to be built in America, called the " West Point," was also built at the West Point Foundry, and put in service March 5, 1831, when it proved its efficiency by drawing four cars containing one hundred and seventeen passengers, of whom fifty were ladies, a distance of two and three-fourths miles in eleven minutes.

On October 1, 1834, a patent on the four-wheeled truck was granted to Ross Winans, of Baltimore, one of the very earliest mechanical geniuses of the railroad, who had shown that the flange of a car wheel

From the "History of the First Locomotives in America," by W. H. Brown.

THE "WEST POINT"

The second locomotive built in America, drawing a train. The bales of cotton were placed in the train to protect passengers from possible explosions.

43

should be placed on the inside instead of the outside, as was the practice at first, and that the journal should be placed outside. Winans was one of the most successful of the early locomotive builders. He made a great fortune in constructing the first railroad in Russia. It cost twenty years of litigation and two hundred thousand dollars to establish the fact that he was not the first to invent and use the four-wheeled truck. The testimony of Allen and his assistant was the deciding factor that turned the verdict against Winans.

While South Carolina was busy with her first railroad, Massachusetts was also laying the foundations of a transportation system. In 1829, when the population of Boston was sixty thousand and of Lowell six thousand, fifteen thousand tons of freight and thirty-seven thousand passengers were transported annually between these two points. One might take a boat on the Middlesex Canal, which covered the most of the distance of twenty-three and a half miles in seven hours at a cost of seventy-five cents. The traveler could walk the rest of the way into Boston, or, if he was extravagant, could ride uptown in an omnibus for another shilling. If he was in a great hurry, and money was no object, he could cover the distance in a stage coach in three hours for a fare of a dollar and a quarter. Some one proposed a railroad as an improvement even on the swift stage coach. Thereupon the State appropriated two hundred and fifty dollars to make a survey, as the result of which the engineers reported that the road would cost one hundred and sixty-eight thousand dollars.

The canal company was by no means disposed to

give up its traffic without a fight. It set up the claim that its charter gave it a monopoly of the transportation business between Boston and Lowell. The legislature eventually refused to recognize the claim, but the canal people, aided by a considerable faction which disapproved of such perilous innovations as railroads, fought off the charter for two sessions.

Construction was finally begun November 2, 1831, and the road was opened for traffic June 26, 1835. It had cost many times the original estimate, but the directors consoled themselves with the reflection that it was so well built that it would last forever. As a matter of fact it was too well built. It had monster granite ties embedded in broken stone, which simply served as anvils on which even the light equipment of those early days quickly pounded the flimsy wooden rails and thin iron straps to pieces, so that it soon had to be rebuilt. However, even with all this heavy expenditure the road was one of the most profitable of its length in the United States. For a quarter of a century it paid dividends at the rate of six and three-quarters per cent per annum.

The year the road was opened the directors indulged in the luxury of two locomotives imported from England. In common with several other boards of directors the Massachusetts men made the mistake of thinking that locomotives could only be built in the land of their origin, and that only an Englishman could run them. The first locomotive arrived some weeks before its engineer; and the directors, being somewhat eager to try their purchase, had it set up by native talent, none of whom had ever seen a locomotive, or even a picture of one. They had to rely solely upon their own common sense in putting the parts together. When the belated engineer arrived he was alone. He was quite sure a mere Yankee could not run the other engine, but he was willing to send to England for a friend to take the position. But the directors were too impatient. They thought the Englishman might coach an American so he could worry along somehow.

The American proved an exceedingly dull pupil. At least his engine was continually out of order. The English engineer would tinker it up again, always taking care to bring out his own superior skill and the Yankee's lack of it, until the latter became suspicious. He hid himself in the engine house and watched one night. The next night one of the directors kept the vigil with the Yankee engineer. The English engineer was caught red-handed in the act of disabling the locomotive in order to discredit the American. No more imported engineers were ever employed on the Boston and Lowell.

The Boston and Providence Railroad, construction on which was begun in December, 1832, was opened a few days after the Boston and Lowell, and the Boston and Worcester, forty-two miles long, in the following month. In 1839 this road was extended to the Connecticut River, sixty-two miles from Boston.

One of the early railroads that was little heard of because the builders chanced to have the money to carry out their project, and chose to keep the stock in their own possession, was the Paterson and Hudson River, incorporated January 21, 1831, to build from Paterson to Weehawken, now a part of the Erie. In the *American Railroad Journal* of June

23, 1832, is a description of a trip which the editor, D. K. Minor, made on this road, which is of peculiar interest for the light it sheds on the popular idea of what constituted a satisfactory railroad in 1832. Said the editor:

" Seeing a communication a day or two since in the New York *American* from which we learned that a portion of the Paterson and Hudson River Railroad was completed, and that elegant cars were provided for the accommodation of passengers, we determined at once to avail ourselves of the first leisure day to have a ride on the railroad.

" We left Wall Street at 7:30 and crossed to Hoboken at 8 A.M., where we took a seat in an excellent coach with good horses belonging to Kinnely, Rodgers & Roy, whose coaches leave regularly four times, viz.: 8 and 10 and 2 and 4, for Aquackanonk, where the line of the railroad is intersected and the passengers are relieved from the inconvenient small coaches and dusty roads by taking seats in splendid and convenient cars which will with ease accommodate twenty persons inside and from six to twelve on the top, to each of which is attached a fleet horse managed by a careful driver.

" The distance from the Aquackanonk terminus of the railroad to the brick meeting house at Paterson is four and three-fourths miles, and consists of one level and two inclined planes. From Aquackanonk the ascent is gradual for about three miles, passing over one or two embankments and through cuts of rock from ten to twenty feet deep and about one hundred and fifty yards in length. On passing the summit level the descent is at an average of about twenty-one feet to the mile until reaching the depot at Paterson.

" The time required to perform the distance of four and three-fourths miles varies from twenty to twenty-five minutes according to circumstances. We were in going out twenty-three and in returning twenty minutes, and it is scarcely possible for those who have not had an opportunity to participate in the pleasure of an excursion upon a railroad to imagine the delightful sensation which it produces.

" The passenger is scarcely aware of movement except by the rapidity with which he passes objects. He feels in perfect safety, although at times his elevation above surrounding fields may be fifteen or twenty feet. There is not the least danger to be apprehended from a deviation from the rails as the depth of the flange on the wheels and the weight of the cars render it impossible for one or two horses to move it sideways, whilst the guard—an apparatus for removing obstructions—prevents anything over half an inch in diameter from interfering with the wheels. For persons fond of inhaling the cool breezes or enjoying the green fields and the beautiful flowers of the country we cannot imagine a more delightful excursion at so little cost, both in time and money, than a trip to Paterson; which may be performed out and home again in one day with ample time to visit the curiosities of that interesting and growing town."

But American railroad builders progressed so rapidly beyond the stage at which " fleet horses " guided by " careful drivers " hauling " splendid and convenient cars " containing a score of passengers over pine rails at the rate of twelve miles an hour, satisfied their conceptions of what a first-class transportation system should be, that in 1840, or a dozen years after the first crude experiment was tried, they led the world, as they have done ever since. M. Thiers, the great historian and statesman, then prime minister of France, recognized American supremacy in railroad building in that year by sending Michel Chevalier, a distinguished engineer, to study our methods, for the benefit of French roads.

The circumstances under which the evolution of

the great trunk lines was accomplished varied greatly. Each set of conditions produced a distinct type of development. To present the story of the early struggles of representative systems having the strongest individuality will be the aim of the ensuing chapters.

CHAPTER II

AMERICA'S PIONEER RAILROAD

WHEN the rising tide of trade and emigration, which had been held back by the Alleghanies as by a great dam, burst around their flanks in 1825 by way of the Erie Canal and the Lakes, the little stream of traffic which had trickled over their summits along the national turnpike from Baltimore to Cincinnati subsided. In this phenomenon the shrewder business men of Baltimore saw foreshadowed the doom of their city's prosperity.

With such a tremendous advantage as a water route to the heart of the growing West, New York would monopolize the commerce of the country, while Baltimore and Philadelphia would be dwarfed to the proportions of mere local trading centers.

Something must be done promptly to counteract New York's advantage. The era of furious and losing canal speculation which raged from 1810 to 1840 was then at its height. Under such circumstances, the logical thing to do appeared to be to hasten the building of the Chesapeake and Ohio Canal, which had been one of Washington's dreams.

But when a board of government engineers, headed by the renowned General Simon Bernard, who had been aide-de-camp to Napoleon, and who, as a brigadier-general in the United States Engineer Corps, had planned an elaborate system of sea-coast defenses, and had built Fortress Monroe, reported in 1826 that the proposed canal, 241 miles long, would have ascents and descents aggregating 3,185 feet; that to make these 398 locks would be required; that the total cost would be $22,375,427, and that when it was built the water supply, which would have to come from mountain streams, would be uncertain, the majority realized at last that Baltimore's imperiled commercial prestige could never be retained by a canal. Yet no one had an alternative to offer.

One morning, when Philip E. Thomas, a Quaker merchant and philanthropist, and one of the most highly esteemed citizens of Baltimore, reached his desk in the Mechanics' Bank, of which he was president, he found a letter from his brother Evan, who was then in London on business.

He read the letter through twice, mused a while over it, read it a third time, then, calling a messenger, sent for his friend George Brown, one of the directors of the bank.

"George," said the banker when his friend appeared, "I have a letter from brother Evan which, I think, will interest thee. It tells of a plan to build a road from Liverpool to Manchester over which carriages will be drawn upon iron rails. Some say this will afford a cheaper and quicker way of hauling goods than even a canal."

"Why, I have a letter from my brother Tom telling about the same thing."

"I have been thinking, George, that perhaps one of these railroads across the mountains to the West might be the means of maintaining the prosperity of our city."

" The very thing I have been thinking of all morning."

" Let us get together this evening and talk it over."

" Agreed. Let us ask a few of our friends to meet us."

" Very good. Now, thee has a large house. Suppose we meet at thy house at seven o'clock this evening? "

So it came about that twenty-five of the most influential men in Baltimore, including Charles Carroll, of Carrollton, one of the signers of the Declaration of Independence, met in George Brown's house, Monday evening, February 12, 1827, to discuss the feasibility of a railroad from Baltimore to the West. At that time there was no such thing in existence as a railroad for transporting passengers and merchandise between distant points.

There were a few so-called railroads in England, crude and inadequate affairs for moving coal and the like from the mines to the nearest available water transportation. Stephenson had made his first experiments on the Stockton and Darlington, but they were not regarded as demonstrating conclusively the advantage of the locomotive over other motive power.

The construction of the Manchester and Liverpool Railway had been begun after a fierce contest in Parliament. In America, there was a railway at Quincy, Mass., three miles long, from a granite quarry to the Neponset River, on which horses were used.

The only other railway on this side of the Atlantic was from the coal mines at Mauch Chunk, Pa., to the Lehigh River, nine miles away. Empty cars were hauled up the mountains by mules. The mules were then placed on platforms on the loaded cars, and rode to the bottom of the inclined plane, down which the cars were carried by gravity.

It is recorded that the mules had such a keen appreciation of the superiority of the railroad as a means of transportation that they could not be induced to walk down the mountain.

With such a scarcity of material, it did not take long for Messrs. Thomas and Brown to tell their neighbors all they knew about railroads, but so great was the need of some effective form of communication with the region beyond the mountains, and so convincingly were their views presented, that a committee of nine was appointed to investigate the whole subject and report to the others one week later.

When the meeting was called to order, February 19, the committee had ready a report of thirty-four printed pages, showing a comprehension of the usefulness of a railroad which under the circumstances was amazing. It reads as if it had been penned by a railroad promoter in the palmy days of railroading.

The report called attention to the fact that the district mainly dependent on the proposed route across the mountains for the conveyance of its surplus produce already contained nearly two million inhabitants, or one-fifth of the population of the United States, while the population dependent on the Erie Canal was not more than one million; yet the traffic on the canal had grown from three hundred and forty thousand seven hundred and sixty-one dollars in 1824, the year of its opening, to seven hundred and sixty-five thousand dollars in 1826.

There was a great variety of articles produced in the country which from lack of means of transportation were then of little value, but which would become a source of wealth if a railroad were built.

For example, a barrel of flour was worth five dollars in Baltimore; in Wheeling, a barrel of flour for shipment to Baltimore could be sold for only one dollar, because it would cost four dollars to haul it across the mountains in wagons, whereas if a railroad were built the flour could be transported at a cost of one dollar. Thus the railroad would raise the value of flour in Wheeling from one dollar to four dollars a barrel.

But speaking of prophetic foresight, how is this passage from a report penned at a time when the world had not yet seen a real railroad in operation?

" To convince any one that there is no probability that the trade herein estimated will be likely hereafter to decline, it will only be necessary to observe that the population on which the calculations are founded is rapidly increasing and that it must for several generations continue to increase. The country around Chesapeake Bay was first settled by Europeans in 1632, and in 1800 the white population had barely reached the Ohio River; that is to say, in one hundred and sixty years it had advanced westward about four hundred miles, or at the rate of two and one-half miles a year.

" There is now a dense population extending as far west as the junction of the Osage with the Missouri River, which is about nine hundred miles west of the Ohio River at Wheeling. The white population has within the last thirty years traveled more than thirty miles in each year, and is at this time advancing with as great, if not greater, impetus than at any former period, and according to all probability, if not checked by some unforeseen circumstance, it will within the next thirty years reach the Rocky Mountains, or even the Pacific Ocean.

"We have, therefore, no reason to look for any falling off in this trade, but, on the contrary, for an increase to an extent of which no estimate could now be formed."

This first formal report on a railroad project ever made in America was so alluring and so convincing that the project was unanimously approved, and J. V. L. McMahon, a young lawyer only twenty-seven years old, was appointed to draw up a charter forthwith.

When the pioneer railroad builders reassembled to pass upon the document the young lawyer had not read half through its twenty-three sections when the venerable Robert Oliver, astonishment and disapproval stamped on every feature, arose and exclaimed:

"Stop, man; you're asking for more than the Lord's Prayer!"

"But it's all necessary; and besides, the more we ask for the more we'll get," was the smiling reply.

"Right, man; go ahead," said Oliver, resuming his seat.

That first railroad charter ever drawn in America was so skilfully framed that it has served as a model for every similar document drawn since then.

Events moved swiftly. Sixteen days after that first meeting in George Brown's house, the act of incorporation of the Baltimore and Ohio Railroad, the first organized in America, was passed by the Maryland legislature, and, April 24, 1827, the company was organized, with P. E. Thomas, the man who originated the idea, as president, a post which he filled for ten years, and his old friend and business associate, George Brown, as treasurer.

Everybody in Maryland was full of enthusiasm over the proposed railroad, as was shown when the books were opened to receive subscriptions for stock. The capital was fixed at three million dollars, of which five hundred thousand dollars was to be furnished by the State of Maryland and five hundred thousand dollars by the city of Baltimore. Fifteen thousand shares were allotted to the public.

When the books were closed, at the end of twelve days, it was found that the entire allotment had been subscribed three times over by twenty-two thousand individuals in Baltimore alone. Frederick and Hagerstown, also, showed a proportionate oversubscription.

Parties of engineers were put into the field as soon as they could be organized. Then, having arranged to build a railroad, a committee of directors was sent to try to get some idea of what a railroad was by inspecting the nine miles of gravity road at Mauch Chunk and the three miles of horse road at the granite quarries at Quincy.

Not being much enlightened by their investigation, they recommended that a committee of engineers be sent to England to pick up a few pointers from Stephenson's Manchester and Liverpool project. This was done forthwith.

It was not until the 5th of April, 1828, that the engineers were ready to make their report. On the 4th of July, 1828, there was the most imposing procession Baltimore had ever seen on Independence Day.

A great throng assembled on the outskirts of the city, where, after music, oratory and prayer, Charles Carroll, of Carrollton, then ninety years old, laid the corner-stone of the railroad. When he had relinquished the trowel he turned to President Thomas and said:

" I consider this among the most important acts of my life, second only to the signing of the Declaration of Independence, if even it be second to that."

The venerable man was made much of in Baltimore. He was never permitted to forget that he had signed the Declaration of Independence. Nothing of importance could take place without his presence.

He had been made a member of the board of directors of the Baltimore and Ohio Railroad, and he was always present at the experiments by which the promoters sought to solve the mystery of building and operating a railroad.

Ross Winans, publisher of the Baltimore *Gazette* and a director of the road, built a model of a car, which he placed on a few feet of tiny iron rails in an upper room of the Exchange Building. To show how easy it was to pull a heavy load in a carriage running on iron rails, one end of a cord was attached to the car, while the other, dangling in the rotunda, after being passed over a pulley, had a small weight on it.

The venerable Charles Carroll was invited to get into the car, whereupon the small weight was released and promptly drew him up to the end of the track, to the delight of the board of directors, who stood about as pleased as children with a new toy.

On opening bids for the construction of the first

twelve miles, on the 11th of August, it was found that the first section would cost seventeen thousand dollars a mile. The method of construction that was followed would seem strange now.

After the ground was leveled off, two holes, twenty inches wide, two feet long, and two feet deep, were dug four feet apart. These were filled with broken stone of a size to pass through a ring two and a half inches in diameter.

Then a trench six inches deep from one hole to the other was dug and filled with broken stone, and on this a cedar sleeper seven feet long was adjusted with a spirit-level. Notches were cut in these sleepers, into which, after they had been tested with the spirit-level, yellow pine stringers, or rails, twelve to twenty-four feet long and six inches square, were carefully fitted and fastened with wedges.

The outer edges of these rails were beveled to make room for the flanges of the wheels, for it was intended that the car-wheels should have flanges on the outside. When a thin strap of iron had been nailed to the wooden sleeper with wrought-iron nails four inches long the track was complete.

After several miles had been finished in this way, slabs of granite were substituted for the cedar sleepers.

The railroad project steadily grew in popularity. People gave the necessary right of way, and the privilege of using quarries to get the needed stone free of charge, and two acres for a station-site were donated at Ellicott's Mills, thirteen miles from Baltimore.

So keen was the public interest that when the rails

were laid to Vinegar Hill, seven miles from Baltimore, a couple of rude horse-cars were put on to gratify the intensely curious with a ride on the railroad.

But even with the free right of way and oversubscriptions of stock by an eager public, it didn't take those pioneers long to discover that they had sadly underestimated the cost of building a railroad. Scarcely had ground been broken before arrangements were made to increase the capital stock.

One million five hundred thousand dollars was allotted to the public, while the indefatigable McMahon, first of railroad lawyers and second in ability to none who have come after him, induced the State of Maryland to take five hundred thousand dollars more. An effort to get a donation of one million dollars from the United States Government would have succeeded but for the opposition of the canal lobby.

Twenty-five miles of grading had been finished when work stopped for the season in the fall of 1829. One day in May, 1830, the Baltimore *Gazette* announced that a " brigade of cars " would run three times a day on the new railroad from Baltimore to Ellicott's Mills, thirteen miles away, every week-day, beginning Monday, May 24.

The first " brigade," on that Monday morning, started off at nine o'clock, with all the ceremony befitting so important an event. The brigade was operated by one horse. The mayor of Baltimore, members of the city council, officers of the road, newspaper representatives, and, of course, Charles Carroll, of Carrollton, were passengers in the splendid car " Pioneer."

Next morning the papers declared that this first brigade of cars on the new railroad had at times attained the " extraordinary rate of fifteen miles an hour." Another brigade of three cars, with eighty passengers on board, made the trip at an average speed of eight miles an hour.

At a public demonstration of the prodigies that could be performed by the wonderful new railroad, an exhibition brigade of eight cars was loaded with two hundred barrels, or thirty tons, of flour. One horse drew the brigade a distance of six and one-half miles in forty-six minutes outward bound. On the return from Ellicott's Mills the thirteen miles were covered in fifty-four minutes, and the demonstration was voted a " triumphant success."

In their inmost hearts the officers and directors of the road began to have a pretty clearly defined fear that the demonstration was not a success. The suspicion began to dawn upon them that " brigades " of cars drawn by horses would never make the road profitable.

They were continually experimenting with new forms of motive power. Evan Thomas, brother of the president, who had written the momentous letter from London, out of which grew the idea of the road, placed an overgrown clothes-basket on a platform with four small wheels, rigged a mast with a square sail, and found he had a vehicle which would travel beautifully before the wind.

Baron Krudener, the Russian envoy, came up from Washington and had a ride in the sailing car which sent him into such raptures that he begged a model to send to the Czar. It was given to him, and this model, being duly forwarded to Russia, suggested a train of thought which led to the building of the railroad from St. Petersburg to Moscow, just as the inventor's letter to his brother had inspired the idea of building a great railroad in America.

But as the sailing car could only be used when the wind was abaft the beam, it very soon became clear that sails could not be adopted for motive power on a railway.

Then another inventive genius came forward with a horse-power of the treadmill pattern, such as is used to-day in some places for sawing wood. This looked promising. The directors, as usual, invited some newspaper men to go with them on the trial trip, for they realized the value of publicity.

They got on famously for a few miles, until they came to a cow on the track. The cow declined to yield the road to such an outrageous contrivance as the horse-power motor, and as there were no effective brakes, the train ran into the cow and spilled the outfit into the ditch. No physical injuries were sustained, but the incident was made the subject of such atrocious puns in regard to the " cowing " of the editors that the horse-motor was laughed out of court.

Locomotives such as Stephenson was building for the Liverpool and Manchester Railway in England were suggested, but the word came that Stephenson had said that a locomotive could not run on curves of a radius of less than nine hundred feet, and there would have to be curves of four hundred feet radius or less in order to get around Point of Rocks.

The locomotive idea was abandoned, and the directors were on the point of giving up the project in despair, when aid came from a most unexpected quarter.

Peter Cooper, of New York, afterward famous as a philanthropist, had been induced to buy a tract of three thousand acres of land as a speculation on the outskirts of Baltimore, along the line of the railroad, in company with two other men. Having been called upon for frequent remittances to pay taxes and other charges he became suspicious and went to Baltimore to investigate.

He found that he had been sending money down to support his partners; that, not to put too fine a point upon it, he was being swindled. So he bought the interest of the other two. His speculation was sure to result in a loss unless the railroad were a success; he therefore interested himself in the troubles of the directors.

He told them he thought he could knock together a locomotive that would get around the sharp curves all right. He owned a foundry, was handy with tools, and had a knack at contriving.

Going back to New York, he bought an engine with a cylinder three and one-quarter by fourteen and one-half inches, and returning to Baltimore, got some iron and built a boiler about as large as a good-sized wash-boiler. He wanted some iron pipes for boiler-flues, but none were obtainable, so he used old musket barrels for the purpose.

The first American locomotive was built in a carriage maker's shop. However, as it was not intended for actual service, but only as a working model to show the directors what could be done, first honors properly belong to the Best Friend of Charleston,

which was built for regular daily operation, although
it did not make its initial trip until sixty-six days after
Cooper's locomotive appeared, as recounted in the
preceding chapter. Cooper's working model was so
insignificant in appearance that he christened it the
" Tom Thumb."

Steam was raised for the first time one Saturday
night. Everything seemed to be in order, so the
directors were invited to take their first ride on the
following Monday morning. When Monday morning came Mr. Cooper found, to his great chagrin, that
a thief had hacked off all the copper parts to be sold
for junk. It took a week to repair the damage.

On Saturday, August 28, 1830, with six men on
the engine, which was no bigger than a hand-car of
to-day, and thirty-six men on a car attached, the first
trip by an American-built locomotive was made. The
run to Ellicott's Mills, thirteen miles, up an average
grade of eighteen feet to the mile, required one hour
and twelve minutes; the return was made in fifty-
seven minutes. In some places a speed of eighteen
miles an hour was reached.

Some members of the party took out their note-
books and wrote sentences therein, just to prove that
it was possible to do so while traveling at such tremendous speed. Ross Winans, one of the directors,
estimated the weight of the passengers and the
amount of coal and water used. The showing made
by the Tom Thumb was unequaled by any English
locomotive for four years thereafter.

It may not be amiss at this point to emphasize the
fact that American railways were developed entirely
independent of the English by calling attention to

From the "History of the First Locomotives in America," by W. H. Brown.

The exciting race between Peter Cooper's "Tom Thumb" and a horse which proved a triumph for both contestants.

the prior invention by Cooper of two fundamental features of all locomotives—the multitubular boiler and the artificial draft.

Cooper's boiler tubes made of musket barrels have already been mentioned. The air-blast by which a forced draft was secured was obtained by a bellows worked by a belt from the axle of the engine. Stephenson hit upon the correct principle by accident.

The exhaust from his first locomotives frightened horses. When he was building the " Rocket " he was notified by the police that if he kept on frightening horses with his noisy engines he would be arrested. He turned the exhaust into the smoke-stack to muffle the noise, and found, to his joy, that he had thereby provided a forced draft.

Cooper, however, eclipsed Stephenson on every other point. At the famous October trials, in which Stephenson won the prize of five hundred pounds offered for the best locomotive, his Rocket, which had two cylinders, eight by fifteen inches, developing a trifle less than six horse-power, pulled seventeen tons on a level track twelve and one-half miles an hour.

Cooper's Tom Thumb, with only one cylinder, three and one-fourth by fourteen and one-half inches, developing 1.43 horse-power, pulled four and one-half tons up an eighteen-foot grade at twelve miles an hour. In other words, Cooper's locomotive developed more than *three* times as much power as Stephenson's in proportion to the cylinder capacity.

Yet the Tom Thumb was destined to suffer humiliation in the very hour of its triumph. On the return from Ellicott's Mills the locomotive was met at the Relay House, half-way to Baltimore, by a car to

which was hitched the finest horse that Stockton &
Stokes, the stage-line owners, possessed. It was a
fine, clean-limbed young gray.

The stage proprietors had come out to race with
the locomotive. Engine and horse got away with an
even start, with steam hissing from every joint of the
roughly built locomotive. Soon the locomotive began
to pull away from the gray. The passengers yelled
and the driver plied his whip, but the horse lost
steadily.

Just as the driver was about to pull up and
acknowledge himself beaten, the belt which worked
the blower on the Tom Thumb slipped. Without a
forced draft, the steam began to go down at once.
Mr. Cooper lacerated his hands in an effort to work
the blower, but he couldn't do it.

The horse soon forged ahead, and won the race by a
considerable margin. This historic race was run just
seventeen days before the opening of the Manchester
and Liverpool Railway, in England.

In spite of this defeat, the locomotive test was such
an unqualified success that the drooping spirits of the
directors were revived and the confidence of the public
was restored. Railroad stock was once more salable,
and Peter Cooper was assured of an ultimate profit
on his land speculation.

Convinced by the performances of the Tom Thumb
that steam would solve the problem of the railroad,
the directors of the Baltimore and Ohio offered a prize
of four thousand dollars for the most approved locomotive delivered to them before June 1, 1831, and
three thousand five hundred dollars for the next best.

It was specified that the locomotives must burn

THE "YORK."

Built by Phineas Davis. It won the prize of $4,000 offered by the Baltimore and Ohio Railroad in 1831 for the best locomotive.

coal, carry not more than one hundred pounds of steam, weigh not more than three and a half tons, be able to haul fifteen tons fifteen miles an hour on the level, and do all this for thirty days on trial before acceptance.

The only locomotive delivered which met these requirements was the " York," built by Phineas Davis. The York was mounted on springs, the first locomotive ever so equipped.

This at once suggested an idea to the observant Ross Winans. Cars up to that time had been built without springs. He had one provided with springs, and found that the capacity of the car was increased, while it was easier to haul.

Winans also soon afterward invented an antifriction journal and conical wheel, with the flange inside, which reduced the friction from one-two-hundred-and-fortieth part of the weight to one-four-hundredth.

After a controversy which nearly rent Baltimore asunder the railroad was granted the right to lay tracks through the streets to the water's edge, and on to Jones's Falls, where the city donated two squares for terminals.

In this year the company had its first experience with dishonest contractors. One of them ran away without paying his men. They testified to their resentment of this sort of treatment by a determined attempt to destroy the road. Not until the militia had been called out and some sixty of the leaders in the disturbance had been placed in jail was the riot quelled. A swindler took advantage of the notoriety this episode created by advertising in Boston for laborers for the Baltimore and Ohio. After collecting money to pay passage to Baltimore for several scores of men he disappeared.

When on April 1, 1832, the track was completed to Point of Rocks, on the Potomac, seventy-two miles from Baltimore, the traffic on the railroad experienced its first real boom.

Farmers found that they could make money by shipping every species of agricultural products over the railroad to Baltimore, while such articles as lime, paving-stone, timber, and the like, hitherto valueless, began to be worth money when transportation became available. Plaster of Paris, coal, brick, and many other articles were shipped into the interior, where they had been unknown until the advent of the railroad.

The operation of the first seventy-two miles of the Baltimore and Ohio settled for all time the question of the suitability of the railroad as a mode of transportation.

In the first two and a half years that the road was open to traffic three hundred thousand passengers were carried without a single accident to life or limb.

Up to that time the railroad had been regarded as an improved form of toll-road, as was indicated by an act of the legislature by which the Baltimore and Ohio was permitted to charge tolls not to exceed one cent per ton per mile and three cents per ton per mile for transportation on west-bound freight, and not more than three cents per ton per mile in tolls and three cents transportation on east-bound freight.

Perhaps it may be worthy of record that the first drunken man in history to go to sleep on a railroad track was run over and killed near Ellicott's Mills in November, 1832.

Just when prospects for the road began to look really bright the Court of Appeals dealt the enterprise a severe blow in the form of a decision in favor of the Chesapeake and Ohio Canal, which disputed the right to occupy the narrow valley of the Potomac.

The canal company graciously offered to let the railroad devote its resources to the completion of the canal if all idea of extending the road were abandoned. This generous compromise was refused, and work on the road came to a standstill until the legislature interfered and compelled a compromise by which the railroad was to take two thousand five hundred shares of canal stock.

Joint construction of canal and railroad was to begin after May 10, 1833. The railroad had to build a fence between road and canal, to prevent the towhorses from being frightened by the trains. As a further concession to the delicate sensibilities of the canal horses, the railroad was directed to haul its trains by horses through the passes where canal and road lay side by side.

But the fence acted as a dam which caught the floods sweeping down the mountainsides, and the Baltimore and Ohio management had begun to realize that a railroad could not be operated with horses. So there was still further delay until the repeal of the obnoxious law could be secured.

Meanwhile the stockholders began to clamor for dividends. The reply of the board of directors was a demand for more money to extend the road to Harper's Ferry, where connection could be made with the

Winchester and Potomac, a road thirty miles long. The payment of subscriptions by the State of Maryland and the city of Baltimore provided funds for this purpose, and the extension was completed December 1, 1834. The business of the road received an immediate stimulus, notwithstanding an era of hard times had caused a decline in business throughout the country.

While the extension was being built the indefatigable Winans had constructed a car mounted on four-wheeled trucks to carry sixty passengers. This was the progenitor of the modern passenger-coach. Soon afterward special cars were provided for baggage, which hitherto had been carried in racks on the top of the coaches.

The evolution of the car was comparatively more rapid than the development of the locomotive. The first cars on the Baltimore and Ohio were like market carts on flanged wheels. The next were like a stage coach with the old-time leathern braces and C springs, with a capacity of nine passengers inside and outside. For some time these were the fashion. They were gaudily painted and decorated and in winter were lined with green baize curtains, while the seats were arranged around the sides instead of crosswise. Whenever Richard Imlay, the leading coach builder of Baltimore, achieved a new triumph in railroad cars, it was exhibited in Monument Square for the admiration of the public.

Winans' first eight-wheeled car was named the "Columbus." It was merely a large box with seats on top, as well as inside, reached by a ladder at one corner. The Columbus was followed by some extraordinary freaks which were nicknamed the "Sea Serpent," the "Dromedary," and the like. Still, each had some redeeming feature which was preserved in its successor. Then came the "Winchester," and finally the "Washington," which approximated the passenger coach of to-day. When the designs for the eight-wheeled cars were submitted to the board of directors there was a long discussion before they could decide whether to have an aisle down the center of the car or to have a narrow ledge on the outside, in the English style, for the conductor. The advocates of the center aisle finally carried the day, and the American type of car, which has only recently been discovered by the English railroads, was given to the world.

John Elgar had meanwhile invented switches, turntables, chilled-steel bearings, and other devices. Up to July, 1834, the company had but three locomotives, and many cars, especially freight, were still drawn by horses. By the time Harper's Ferry was reached five more locomotives had been received and eight more were under contract.

While the main line was creeping slowly and painfully westward, a branch line under the name of the Baltimore and Washington Railroad was under construction to the National Capital. Like the parent company, the Baltimore and Washington Railroad was the idea of Philip E. Thomas. It was his personal energy and perseverance that led the fierce fight through three sessions of the Maryland legislature, which finally ended in the rout of a strong lobby led by the Philadelphia, Washington, and Baltimore Turnpike Company. The advent of the railroad meant the death of the turnpike. It was a struggle for survival which was won, as generally happens, by the fittest. The act incorporating the railroad became a law March 9, 1833. The struggle for aid from the National Government was less successful, for the canal lobby at Washington was powerful enough to defeat in the House the bill which had already passed the Senate appropriating three hundred and fifty thousand dollars to help the railroad out.

Work was begun at once on the Patapsco Bridge, plans for which had already been prepared by the chief engineer, B. H. Latrobe. This bridge of eight arches of fifty-eight feet span each was the largest in the United States in its day, and was regarded as a very remarkable engineering feat.

On this Washington branch even more than the average amount of trouble was encountered. One of the most annoying difficulties was that of obtaining sober, law-abiding labor. By attempting to enforce reasonable discipline, the deputy superintendents of construction incurred the hatred of the more turbulent spirits.

The principal cause of the trouble was whisky, then cheap and abundant. Caspar Wever, the first superintendent of construction, in his annual reports urged, and so far as lay in his power compelled, total abstinence by all employees of the company. Still, riot and disorder as the result of drunkenness increased so much that after 1829 Wever, with the knowledge and approval of President Thomas, refused to sign any contracts for masonry or " graduation," as grading was called for many years, that did not contain a clause prohibiting the use of intoxicat-

TYPE OF PASSENGER CAR USED ON THE BALTIMORE AND
OHIO IN 1829

TYPE OF "BURDEN" OR FREIGHT CAR USED ON THE BALTIMORE
AND OHIO IN 1832

ing liquors on the work. Thus it may be seen that the fight of the railroad against intemperance, which attracted so much attention a few years ago, is as old as the railroad itself. But the company found itself unable to enforce the prohibition clause in its contracts.

On November 12, 1834, Contractor John Gorman, John Watson, his superintendent, and several others were attacked in a shanty by a number of laborers and beaten into insensibility. The following night the shanty door was battered down and Watson and William Mercer were dragged out and shot to death. John Callon was also shot and left for dead, but ultimately recovered, and several others of the office force and foremen were badly hurt.

A general riot followed this outrage, in which a great many heads were broken. All the stores in the vicinity were looted. Next day the militia, under Lieutenant Colonel Campbell, was rushed to the scene. Four hundred men were placed under arrest. At the preliminary examination, December 9, all but ten were discharged from custody. Of the ten one was found guilty of murder in the first degree; the others were convicted of manslaughter and sentenced to the penitentiary for various terms.

Next March the trouble broke out anew in a general strike. Men were readily secured to take the places of the strikers, but the attempt to set them to work was the signal for a general riot. Once more the militia came to the rescue and drove away the rioters.

The branch was completed and thrown open to traffic with an excursion to Washington, August 25,

1835. Seventeen cars, each containing fifty invited guests, drawn by the locomotives " George Washington," " John Adams," " Thomas Jefferson," and " James Madison," left Baltimore at 9 o'clock in the morning. At Bladensburg a trainload of public functionaries and other invited guests from Washington was met. All hands alighted while the mayor of Washington and the president of the company exchanged felicitations. Proceeding to Washington, the visitors were received with salvos of artillery and cheers from what seemed to be the entire population of the Capital and the surrounding country. After listening to some long speeches the guests were taken to some of the principal points of interest. The return trip to Baltimore was accomplished in two hours and twenty minutes.

It was this branch of the Baltimore and Ohio which achieved the distinction of initiating the modern system of mail transportation. Under a contract signed in January, 1838, the Baltimore and Washington and the Philadelphia, Wilmington and Baltimore began carrying the mails between Washington and Philadelphia.

An epoch-making feat in fast news carrying was accomplished on the Baltimore and Washington branch in 1838, which attracted a great deal of attention. In December of that year Conductor Wilde, the oldest and most reliable man on the road, was commissioned by the board of directors to secure copies of the President's message at the earliest possible moment and deliver them in Baltimore as quickly as possible. Careful preparations had been made long in advance for the exploit, which was expected to do much to advertise the railroad as a means of quick communication.

On reaching the station Wilde found the locomotive " William Cooke " waiting for him, with steam roaring from her safety valve.   The instant his foot touched the step the engineer opened the throttle, and at 1:18 P.M. the William Cooke started out to make a famous record.   One hour and thirteen minutes later the locomotive came to a halt at the Baltimore station.   Wilde sprang to the platform and handed a packet to a waiting messenger from the Philadelphia, Wilmington and Baltimore, and another to a representative of the Baltimore and Susquehanna.   Both locomotives pulled out simultaneously, the one for Philadelphia reaching that point at 6:07 P.M.   The message was delivered in New York at 11:15 P.M., or ten hours for a run of 225 miles.   Limited trains now cover that route in five hours; but this is no such feat as covering the crazy track by the crude locomotives of that early day in ten hours.   The steamer *John W. Richmond* was waiting at New York, chartered by the Boston *Globe,* to take copies of the message to that city.   The copies sent over the Baltimore and Susquehanna reached York, Pa., from which point they were rushed forward to Harrisburg, Pa., by pony express in two hours and twenty-eight minutes from the time of leaving Baltimore.

Reconnaissances by the engineers showed that the mountains could be passed by locomotives to Wheeling and Pittsburg, so the board of directors in 1837 recommended the extension of the line to Cumberland, at a cost of four million six hundred thousand dollars. The State came to the rescue with a subscription of three million dollars, and Baltimore took a like amount. But the money was not available.

Trouble now began to thicken for the enterprise which had started out so brilliantly a decade before. The directors were destined to learn from bitter experience what so many boards have learned over again since—that building a railroad on paper is a vastly different matter from its construction on the ground.

When Louis McLane succeeded P. E. Thomas as president, in April, 1837, he found that the cost of construction had exceeded the capital paid in by the tidy sum of two hundred and three thousand dollars, which had been raised by notes. There was not a dollar in the treasury to meet these notes.

Money was urgently needed to rebuild the crude and inadequate experimental road that had been constructed in the beginning to meet the necessities of the growing traffic. There was no school but experience in which to learn the science of railroad-building.

There had been many mistaken economies in construction, and many inadequate estimates of cost of building through unfavorable territory. New rolling-stock was also needed. Moreover, the time limit on their franchises for the extension was about to expire.

The company's credit was not good, and the State bonds, with which the State's subscription of three million dollars had been paid, could not be sold in Europe because of the glut of American securities, and also because of certain repudiation acts by several States, including Maryland.

Confronted with the necessity of extending the road in the face of these overwhelming difficulties, the expedient was adopted of paying bills for right of way, labor, and so on in certificates for from one dollar to one hundred dollars, redeemable in Baltimore city six per cent stock at par, to the amount of three million dollars, which the city had subscribed toward the extension. But Baltimore city stock was unsalable, so the working men into whose hands these certificates found their way lost heavily, but the road was put through to Cumberland, one hundred and seventy-eight miles from Baltimore, on the 5th of November, 1842.

The effect of the extension was manifested in an increase of earnings from three hundred and ninety-one thousand and seventy dollars the year before reaching Cumberland to five hundred and seventy-five thousand two hundred and thirty-five dollars the year afterward, and to six hundred and fifty-eight thousand six hundred and nineteen dollars in 1844, notwithstanding a reduction in passenger rates enforced by the completion of the Pennsylvania lines.

President McLane went to Europe in 1844 to try to raise the money for extending the road to the Ohio River. He failed in this, but he brought home many valuable ideas on improved methods of organization, division of labor, more adequate accountability, better forms of tickets, and checks on conductors and agents, which he at once put into use.

In 1846 it became absolutely necessary to reconstruct the entire eighty-one miles of road from Baltimore to Harper's Ferry and lay the new edge-rail in place of the antiquated plate-rail, money or no money. This was accomplished by selling bonds at ten per cent discount.

Construction to the Ohio River was delayed for seven years. In 1848, Thomas Swann, a brilliant financier and an administrator of rare executive ability and indefatigable energy, was elected president. In his first speech he wrought the board of directors up to such a pitch that George Brown jumped up in great excitement and said:

" Mr. President, I move that the chief engineer be instructed to put the entire line to the Ohio River under contract as speedily as possible."

Swann's first coup was to dispose of one million dollars of the unsalable State bonds to Baring Brothers, the great London bankers. This at once provided both funds and prestige, which made possible the building of the remaining two hundred miles through the mountains to Wheeling, on the Ohio.

The line was located through the roughest region yet traversed by any internal improvement in America. Even engineers were astonished. Between Cumberland and Wheeling there were eleven tunnels with a total length of 11,156 feet, and 113 bridges with a total length of 7,003 feet, including the Monongahela viaduct, 650 feet long, then the longest iron bridge in America.

President Swann declared after the road was opened that " if the people of Baltimore had known at the commencement of the work west of Cumberland what the difficulties to be encountered really were we would have been locked up as lunatics." Even Swann himself must have had his misgivings, for he once confessed in a speech that when the opening of the section from Cumberland to Piedmont was celebrated in 1851 with a formidable excursion

THE FIRST "CAMEL" BUILT BY ROSS WINANS,

A type of locomotives that played a conspicuous part in the early success
of the Baltimore and Ohio.

to which all the dignitaries of Baltimore and the State of Maryland were invited, he took care to stand near an open car door, where escape to the woods would be easy, while Chief Engineer Latrobe rode on the engine, where the smoke would hide his mortification in case the locomotive should prove to be incapable of climbing the grade of one hundred and sixteen feet to the mile.

Fortunately the precautions of the president and chief engineer proved to be unnecessary, for locomotive No. 71, built by Ross Winans, the indefatigable inventor and locomotive builder, took four heavily laden coaches and five cars of rails to the top of the hill without difficulty, a feat which was acknowledged by the enthusiastic cheers of the party. Without Winans the Baltimore and Ohio Railroad could hardly have been built; for it was his fertility in resource which supplied the motive power to meet peculiarly difficult conditions. As the head of the great shops at Mount Clare, near Baltimore, he introduced many details that helped to make the early locomotive efficient, and finally evolved an entirely new type that enabled the heavy mountain grades to be overcome. This was the " Camel," so-called because the cab was perched upon the top of the boiler like the ungainly hump on the animal after which it was named. The entire weight of the Camel was carried on four pairs of drivers, so that every pound of weight was available for tractive force. The Camel was inconceivably ugly, but it did wonderful service on the sharp curves and steep grades of the Alleghanies. For years it was the favorite type of engine on the Baltimore and Ohio, one hundred and nineteen being built, and its performances were not surpassed by the locomotives of any other builder.

The most remarkable performance credited to the Camel was achieved on the temporary track over the mountain while the Kingwood tunnel was building. This temporary track had a grade of five hundred and thirty feet to the mile. It was so steep that sometimes when the rails were slippery with frost the Camel, after getting part way up, would slip, and then, with locked wheels, would slide all the way down to the bottom of the grade. Only one car could be taken up at a time, yet by this laborious method material was conveyed over the mountain for the extension of the line without waiting for the tunnel to be completed, in order to get the road into Wheeling on schedule time.

Chief Engineer B. H. Latrobe had promised in 1851 to have trains running into Wheeling by January 1, 1853. The last rail was laid on December 24, 1852, and on January 1, 1853, the first train rolled into Wheeling. The veteran chief engineer declared that he was prouder of this than he was of his triumphs over the difficulties in the mountains.

Of course the completion of the road to the Ohio had to be celebrated with something more than the customary splendor. Accordingly the legislatures of Maryland and Virginia, led by their respective Governors and supported by the city officials of Baltimore, the directors of the road, and all the citizens sufficiently distinguished to secure invitations, making a grand total of something more than four hundred persons, left Baltimore Monday, January 10, 1853, for Wheeling in two trains. Dinner was served by a Baltimore caterer en route in two new cars, in which temporary board tables had been laid lengthwise of the cars. This, the first appearance of the dining car on any road, was duly appreciated by the dignitaries in whose honor it was devised.

The party arrived at Fairmount, seventy-seven miles east of Wheeling, at 9 o'clock Tuesday morning. Near this point a broken axle delayed the special trains so long that Board Tree Tunnel, near Wheeling, was not reached until dusk. As the tunnel was not completed, trains were run over the summit on a switchback railroad two miles and a quarter long and having grades of 293 to 340 feet to the mile. Ten extra engines were waiting at the eastern end of the switchback, for one engine could take but two cars over the mountain. The darkness, the noise of so many snorting locomotives, and the frail looking railroad clinging to the steep mountainside and spanning awe-inspiring gorges, was too much for the nerves of men unused to railroad travel. A large portion of the guests got out and stumbled on foot through the darkness over the mountain rather than trust their lives in such unfamiliar conveyances.

Just how the "appalling enterprise of transporting five hundred human beings fastened up in railroad cars right over the summits of Old Alleghany" impressed those pioneer passengers is vividly set forth in the following account penned by a newspaper correspondent accompanying the party:

"It was a day—and especially a night—of great excitement and interest, more particularly as connected with the passing of Pettibone Mountain. Here the great tunnel is being cut through the deep bowels of one of the most romantic of mountains. It will be, inclusive of cuts, from seven-eighths to a mile long. The tunnel not being finished the mountain is scaled to the very summit in despite of its rugged frowning sides, by means of a track laid over it. This feature of the road is stupendous in its conception and wonderful in its execution. The summit is gained by a series of counter Y movements. Of course the grades are steep and require great locomotive power, one of the largest class of engines ever yet operated on any railroad being required to carry up two cars.

" But the scene was grand. We were composed of ten caravans, each attached to one of the most powerful engines. I was in the third; and night was settling down on the broad landscape as we began the ascent. Before us were two parties slowly climbing their zigzag way far above us upon different elevations and their panting iron horses, as if angry with their loads, spit out volumes of black smoke and sparks against the blackened sky as from the crater of a deep volcano.

" The summit gained we halted a short time, which gave us an opportunity to survey the picture. What a magnificent scene! Around and beneath us were the stupendous hills, far as the lurid shadows of evening could be pierced, while far down the mountainside from terrace upon terrace the upheaving locomotives glowed; and then away in the deep valleys hundreds of torches gleamed from the hands of workmen leaving their allotted task in the depths of the tunnel below. We now descended the western slope, which is more precipitous than the eastern. Below us gleamed the serpentine way and in our turn we looked up to those behind us. It seemed as if the children of Babel were winding down from the huge mountain pile. The locomotive screamed, to us an unmeaning sound, while the deep dells below threw it back in echoing mockery. But skilful were our pilots, as we seemed to swim along the mountainside, and in a few hours we were landed without a scratch on a solid rail below.

" Many of our party were in an ecstasy of delight and enjoyment; but others, more fearful, walked the crooked way, while some who remained on the cars trembled like the aspen leaf."

As it was midnight and rain was falling in torrents when the jaded excursionists, with nerves shaken by their terrifying passage of the mountain, arrived at the end of their journey, the triumphal march, banquet, and oratory which the citizens of Wheeling had planned for their guests had all to be postponed until next day.

Regular train service between Chesapeake Bay and the Ohio River was established at last. The railroad that had been begun and operated with horses less than a quarter of a century before by men who had no conception of what a railroad should be now owned 139 locomotives, 96 passenger cars, and 2,567 freight cars.

But if the originators of the Baltimore and Ohio Railroad had no idea of what a railroad should be, events abundantly confirmed their estimate of its value in developing traffic, as a few samples will show.

Before 1842 the rich coal deposits of western Maryland were worked only at Frostburg, a hamlet where a few hundred bushels of coal were dug and floated down the Potomac to Alexandria in flatboats. Boat and cargo were sold, and the crew walked home.

In 1843, the first year after the railroad reached Cumberland, 4,964 tons of coal were shipped by rail. In 1850 the amount had increased to 132,534 tons. Three hundred and fifty-three tons of grain were shipped over the road in 1832; in 1852, 5,000 tons were transported.

But Wheeling was not a satisfactory terminus. In order to get the benefit of Western traffic, it was necessary to strike the Ohio River farther down. The Northwestern Virginia Railroad was chartered in 1851, to build from Grafton, on the Baltimore and Ohio Railroad, to Parkersburg, on the Ohio River.

Mr. Swann was president of the company, and its bonds were guaranteed by the Baltimore and Ohio and the city of Baltimore. May 1, 1857, the line was completed, and the Baltimore and Ohio assumed management of one hundred and three miles of the best-constructed railroad in the country up to that time.

The maximum grades were fifty-two feet to the mile, and the sharpest curves were of one thousand feet radius. There were twenty-three tunnels on the line, the longest being two thousand seven hundred feet.

The simultaneous opening, on June 1, of this line from Baltimore to the Ohio at Parkersburg, of the Marietta and Cincinnati Railroad from a point nearly opposite Parkersburg to Cincinnati, and of the Ohio and Mississippi from Cincinnati to St. Louis, completed a through line by which a passenger could go from New York to St. Louis by changing cars not more than five times and making two short steamboat voyages and two ferry trips.

To continue his westward journey from Parkersburg the traveler on the Baltimore and Ohio embarked on a steamboat which struggled twelve miles up the yellow current of the Ohio to Marietta. From this point the Marietta and Cincinnati, organized August

18, 1847, at Chillicothe, the original capital of Ohio, and built by donations from towns and counties aggregating two million and fifty thousand dollars, extended one hundred and ninety-six miles to Cincinnati.

The first road projected between Cincinnati and St. Louis was chartered in 1832. Though some subscriptions were paid in, no work was done. The country was so new and so poor that so great an undertaking was absurdly impracticable. Sixteen years later the project was revived by a new company under the name of the Ohio and Mississippi Railroad. Preliminary surveys were begun November 1, 1848. The first section of twenty-six miles from Cincinnati to Cochran was opened April 2, 1854. A connection with the Cincinnati and Indianapolis Railroad at the latter point gave the road a considerable traffic at once. Before the end of the year the rails had been extended to Seymour, Ind., eighty-seven miles from Cincinnati.

Ground was broken on the western end of the road February 9, 1852. Page & Bacon, of St. Louis, the contractors, found themselves unable to sell the securities of the road as they had anticipated, so they were obliged to carry on the work solely on their own resources. In 1854 the contractors on the eastern end failed, and Page & Bacon assumed the contract. The burden of building the entire road swamped the plucky contractors and forced them to suspend in January, 1855. The Ohio and Mississippi became a jest and a by-word.

But with a courage and energy that have not been surpassed in the history of the railroad, H. D. Bacon contrived to raise a half-million dollars and completed the western division to Vincennes. Then the road was sold under foreclosure proceedings and bought in by Page & Bacon, who held $2,700,000 of its securities. Then a syndicate of New York capitalists, headed by W. H. Aspinwall, bought out the plucky contractors, and finished the road. When the last spike was driven it was found that the road had cost twenty million dollars instead of six millions, the original estimate. This was not due to high finance or faulty construction that had to be replaced; but was simply the result of inexperience in railroad building. The Ohio and Mississippi, like the Erie, was of six feet gauge.

Such an event as the completion of a through route from New York and Baltimore to St. Louis was considered worthy of a great National celebration, which was accordingly carried out with a pomp and circumstance that are recorded in history as " The Great Railway Celebrations of 1857." With the exception of that on the completion of the first transcontinental railroad, the celebrations of 1857 constitute the greatest event of the kind in the history of the Nation.

The initiative was taken by the Ohio and Mississippi in an invitation dated April 8, 1857, which was sent to President Buchanan, the members of his cabinet, foreign ministers, and a large number of other prominent men East and West.

An interesting side light on the great number and small size of railroads in the '50's is found in the fact that to afford guests a choice of routes between New York and St. Louis the passes accompanying the invitations were indorsed by forty-two railroads.

The forthcoming celebration at once became the talk of the country. Every one who had any real or imaginary influence brought it to bear on the railroad officials to elicit one of the coveted invitations.

The Ohio and Mississippi Railroad Company invited seven hundred guests from the East and nine hundred from the West. Among them were George Bancroft, W. W. Corcoran, Stephen A. Douglas, Henry Ward Beecher, and Nathaniel P. Willis. Washington Irving was cheated out of the trip by some perverse fate which sent his invitation astray and delayed it until the festivities were over. The Baltimore and Ohio invited four hundred and fifty guests, including State officers and the judiciary of Maryland and Virginia, members of the diplomatic corps, and newspaper correspondents.

Most of the Eastern guests made their way West at their own convenience. The only regular party from the East was organized by the Baltimore and Ohio. Leaving Baltimore at 6 o'clock on the morning of Monday, June 1, 1857, by special train, the run of two hundred and seventy-nine miles to Grafton was made in fifteen hours. Here the party spent the night. At Parkersburg, which was reached in the forenoon of the next day, the party, now increased to six hundred souls, embarked on the steamboats *Albemarle* and *John Buck,* which were lashed together, for the voyage of twelve miles against the turbulent yellow current of the Ohio.

Booming cannon, cheering crowds, and braying bands greeted the guests at Marietta. Governor Salmon P. Chase, of Ohio, and a dozen others made speeches. Then everybody was ferried across the

Muskingum River to reach the trains of the Marietta
and Cincinnati Railroad.

The second night was spent at Chillicothe. By the
time the old Ohio capital was reached the host of visitors had been swelled to a thousand persons. As the
hotel accommodations were totally inadequate, most
of the visitors had to be billeted at the homes of private citizens.

Upon reaching Cincinnati the steadily growing
party of excursionists found that they formed a part
of a host of twenty thousand people, a tremendous
crowd for a new country so sparsely populated, which
had gathered to take part in a program of oratory,
feasting, and noise such as the West had never known
before. As at Chillicothe the guests had to be entertained at private homes.

The city was fairly hidden under a lavish display
of flags, banners, and mottoes, of which the following
is a sample:

A LOCOMOTIVE IS THE ONLY GOOD MOTIVE

FOR

RIDING A MAN ON A RAIL.

The day, which was observed as a universal holiday
such as Cincinnati had never known before, and such
as she probably has never seen since, was brought to
a close by an exhibition of the new steam fire engines,
an innovation of which the young city was justifiably
proud.

Some fifteen hundred guests, as many as could be

crowded on the special trains, continued the triumphal progress to St. Louis, Thursday, June 4. Precautions as elaborate as usually attend the travels of royalty in Europe had been taken to insure the safety and promote the comfort of the guests. Flagmen were posted on every mile of the track, and extra locomotives with steam up were disposed at strategic points to take the place of those drawing the special trains if they broke down.

But in spite of all precautions the locomotives obstinately refused to break down where they could be replaced conveniently, but took particular pains to get into as many difficulties as possible between stations. Consequently there were several long waits in the woods, necessitated by a pump that persisted in going wrong at the most inopportune times, a hot driving box, or something of that sort. These unforeseen delays troubled the excursionists not at all, for there were plenty of aspiring orators on board fairly bursting with burning rhetoric. The average American of half a century ago doted on oratory. Whenever the trains came to a stop the passengers ranged themselves around the nearest stump, upon which long-winded speakers would hold forth until the whistle choked them off in the middle of a period as it summoned them to the train again.

The pumps, the hot boxes, and the orators combined delayed the special trains so much that the eastern bank of the Mississippi was not reached until after midnight.

The visitors alighted in the glare of hundreds of pine torches to an accompaniment of booming cannon, and hurried to four brilliantly illuminated steamboats that had been moored to the Illinois shore for their sleeping quarters.

Next morning there was a procession several miles long to the St. Louis Fair Grounds, where the entire day was devoted to speechmaking, with the exception of a brief respite for dinner. An evening of fireworks and serenades brought the first of the great railway celebrations to a close.

The second celebration was held to give the East an opportunity to repay the hospitality of the West. The guests left St. Louis Wednesday, July 15, and after the usual program of feasting and oratory and fireworks, arrived at Baltimore Saturday, July 18. After being photographed at the "Daguerrean Establishment" of Henry Pollock, the procession of one hundred and ten carriages proceeded to Maryland Institute, where they found the chief feature of the second railroad celebration a banquet at which a thousand men sat down. As a gauge of pioneer appetites and a memento of the disastrous results of the first desultory struggles with bill-of-fare French in America, the menu of this famous dinner deserves recording. Here it is exactly as printed:

SOUPS.

Green turtle   Soup a la Julienne

FISH.

Boiled Salmon, Lobster sauce   Boiled Sheepshead, White sauce
Striped Bass, baked, Genoise sauce
                    Chesapeake Bay Mackerel, a la Maitre d'Hotel

RELISHES.

Worcestershire sauce   French Mustard   Assorted pickles
Apple sauce   Currant Jelly   Cucumbers
Olives   Anchovies

BOILED

Ham   Lamb   Spring Chicken

ENTREES.

Filets de Boeuf, Madeira wine sauce   Petits Pates a la Reine
Mountain Oysters, Sauce Royale   Sweetbreads larded, Gardinere sauce
Filets of veal Perageaux   Galantine de Poulets
Vol au Vent a la Financier   Young Chickens Maryland style
Lamb Chops, Soubaise sauce   Timbale de maraconi, Milanaise

MARYLAND COURSE

Roast Saddle of Mountain Mutton, Currant Jelly
Soft Crabs fried, Butter and parsley sauce
Soft Crabs Broiled   Hard Crabs Deviled
Summer Ducks with olives   Green Goose, apple sauce
Roast Ham, Champagne sauce

VEGETABLES.

Stewed tomatoes   Green corn   Boiled beets
Baked Tomatoes   String beans   Cymlings
Green Peas   Boiled Potatoes

COLD DISHES

Ham on a Pedestal, decorated with Jelly   Boeuf Sale en Presse
Boned Turkey on a Socle, French Style   Pate of Liver Jelly
Salade de poulets Historee   Lobster Salad, Mayonnaise
Buffalo Tongues garnished with jelly   Aspic d'Huitres
Crab Salad, Baltimore fashion

DESSERT

Nougat Basket   Madeira Wine   Bisquit Glacee au Cream Caisse
Punch Cakes   Vanilla Ice Cream   Almond Ice Cream
Strawberry Ice Cream   Orange Ice Cream   Raspberry Ice Cream
Pineapple Ice Cream   Charlotte Russe   Maraschino
Plombiere   Charlotte Russe (Lemon)   Fancy Cakes
Bisquit Glacee au Chorolade

FRUITS

Watermelons   Apples   Oranges   Pears
Pineapples   Bananas   Apricots   Raspberries

Responses to ten set toasts and to five volunteer
toasts and two extra speeches furnished an intellectual

feast that rivaled in quantity the prodigal dinner that had preceded it. A trip to Washington, where President Buchanan made a speech, and an excursion to Norfolk, during which less distinguished orators held forth on the boat throughout the voyage, ended the second celebration, and established trade relations between Baltimore and the West that put new life into the through rail route of which the Baltimore and Ohio was the first and the most important link.

CHAPTER III

EARLY DAYS ON THE ERIE

THE first bride who ever made a honeymoon trip on a railroad in America did more by that act to expedite the building of the world's first trunk line than the ablest statesmen, engineers, and financiers of the Empire State had been able to accomplish by their united efforts in half a dozen years.

Indeed, it is within bounds to go much further than this and say that the inspiration drawn from this bride's delight over her novel ride pushed the hands of progress ahead ten years on the dial of history.

The bride who achieved so much was Mrs. Henry L. Pierson, of Ramapo, N. Y. Mr. and Mrs. Pierson were in Charleston, S. C., early in January, 1831, on their wedding tour. When Mrs. Pierson heard that a steam locomotive was to make its first trip with a trainload of passengers over the South Carolina Railroad from Charleston to Hamburg, six miles away, on January 15, she was eager to take the ride; and her husband, like a dutiful bridegroom, agreed.

That was the first regular train that ever carried passengers in the United States. It was then less than eighteen months from the time when the first successful locomotive had made its trial trip.

The locomotive which drew the first regular passenger train in America and the first bridal couple to take a railroad journey was the Best Friend of Charleston, which has been described in a previous chapter.

The two cars were crazy contraptions on four wheels, resembling stagecoach bodies as much as they did anything else. The train contrived to get over the entire system of six miles and back again at a fairly satisfactory speed.

All the passengers were highly pleased with their strange experience. The bride was in a transport of delight. She could talk of nothing else. When she returned to Ramapo she gave her brother-in-law, Eleazer Lord, and her father-in-law, Jeremiah Pierson, such glowing accounts of her railroad trip that they were fired with enthusiasm. The bridegroom had already become almost as ardent an advocate of railroads as his bride.

Jeremiah Pierson, the father of the bridegroom, was one of the nation's first captains of industry. He owned several thousand acres of land around Ramapo, on which he conducted tanneries, a cotton-mill, iron-works, and a nail factory. His son-in-law, Eleazer Lord, was one of the leading merchants, financiers, and public men of New York City.

For half a dozen years the two had been deeply interested in Governor De Witt Clinton's ideas for the development of southern New York by means of a State highway or canal or other method of communication, but politicians in central New York, where the Erie Canal had been in operation from 1825, by methods not unknown even among politicians of to-day, turned all the efforts of the Governor and his public-spirited supporters into a farce.

Later, Mr. Lord and his father-in-law had been greatly interested in the possibilities of a railroad as the best form for Governor Clinton's proposed highway to take. But their original idea of a railroad was an affair of inclined planes and horse-power.

Of course, they had heard all about the experiments with locomotives and the building of the South Carolina Railroad, the first in the world projected from the outset to be operated by steam locomotives, and they had been deeply interested in William C. Redfield's famous pamphlet, so widely circulated in 1829, proposing a steam railroad from the ocean to the Mississippi; but the idea of a steam road through southern New York was not clearly developed in their minds until the bride's glowing accounts of her experience fired their imaginations.

Young Mrs. Pierson gave it as her opinion that if a steam railroad were built it would be possible to go from New York to Buffalo in twenty-four hours. At first, the men folks were inclined to smile at this, but they were thoroughly impressed with the value of the locomotive as described by this ardent advocate.

Mrs. Pierson's girlish enthusiasm was the determining factor which crystallized the ideas of those men and led them to take the steps which finally resulted in the building of what is now known as the Erie Railway, which, by uniting the ocean with the Great Lakes, became the world's first trunk line.

No railroad has had a more romantic history than this one, which had its inception in so romantic an incident. It required twenty years of toil and anxiety, sacrifice and discouragement, to get the line through, but it was accomplished at last, and the bridegroom and bride who had made the memorable first wedding journey by rail were again passengers on a trip which will live in history as long as railroads exist.

This time the bride was a handsome woman of middle age, but she was just as proud of her husband as she was on that first trip, for he was vice-president of the road, the longest continuous line in the world, and the trains did move at a speed that would have carried them from New York to Buffalo in twenty-four hours, just as she had prophesied two decades before that they would.

Mr. Lord at once began corresponding with the most influential citizens of southern New York on the subject of building a steam railroad from the ocean to the Lakes. The idea was well received everywhere; so well, in fact, that a public meeting in furtherance of Mr. Lord's railroad scheme was held at Monticello, July 29, 1831; another at Jamestown, September 20, and a third at Angelica, October 25. Finally, a great central convention was called to meet at Oswego, December 20, 1831.

People were inclined to believe that so vast an enterprise as the building of five hundred miles of railroad was too much for one company to undertake. It was pretty generally believed that two companies would be required—one to build from New York to Oswego, the other from Oswego to Lake Erie.

A convention at Binghamton, December 15, had formally approved the two-company plan, and public opinion had pretty definitely decided that two companies were necessary.

But while the Oswego convention was in session a

citizen rushed breathlessly in, interrupting a delegate who was delivering an address, and in the most orthodox style known to melodrama handed the president a letter. It was from Eleazer Lord, briefly but emphatically declaring that the undertaking could be carried to success only by a single corporation.

His reasoning was so cogent that the convention without much ado decided in favor of one corporation, and nothing further was heard of the two-company proposition.

Public opinion was so pronounced in favor of the railroad that the politicians from the canal counties could make no headway against it. A charter drafted by John Duer, of New York, was granted the New York and Erie Railroad, April 24, 1832.

But the fine Italian hand of the politicians who could not prevent the granting of the charter was clearly to be seen in the document itself. That instrument provided that the entire capital stock of ten million dollars must be subscribed and five per cent of the amount paid in before the company could incorporate.

The canal counties had served public notice that the projectors of this great public work would have to combat all the pettifogging intrigues of which small politicians were capable before they could even begin their titanic contest with nature.

The little band of enthusiasts led by Eleazer Lord were undertaking the most stupendous task that had been set before the nation up to that time. The country was poor in resources; the region through which the road was to run was a wilderness except for a few scattering villages.

Missouri was the only State west of the Mississippi. Chicago was a village clustered around Fort Dearborn. Railroad building was a science unknown to promoters or engineers. The building of five hundred miles of road then was a far more stupendous task than the building of ten thousand miles would be to-day.

Seeing the hopelessness of complying with the terms of the charter, the incorporators contrived to bring enough pressure to bear on the legislature to have the amount of subscription required before organization reduced to one million dollars.

Finally, on August 9, 1833, the New York and Erie Railroad Company was organized, with Mr. Lord as president. The next month the board of directors issued an address asking for donations of right of way and additional donations of land.

As no survey had been made, and no one had any idea where the road would be located, this address failed to bring out either donations or subscriptions of stock, but there was a great deal of harsh talk about land-speculation schemes.

In desperation, a convention was held, November 20, 1833, in New York City, to ask for State aid. The aid was not forthcoming. Next year the company took the little money received for stock from the incorporators and started the surveys. The eastern end of the line began in a marsh on the banks of the Hudson, twenty-four miles north of New York City.

Considering that the fundamental purpose of the road was to secure the trade of the interior to New York, this did not make any new friends for the road.

The western end of the road was to be Dunkirk, a village of four hundred inhabitants, on the shores of Lake Erie.

The talk about land speculation and the failure to make satisfactory progress created such strong opposition to his policy that Mr. Lord resigned as president at the January meeting in 1835, and J. G. King was elected to succeed him. King, by superhuman exertions, was able to make an actual beginning.

He went to Deposit, some one hundred and seventy-seven miles from New York, where at sunrise on a clear, frosty morning, November 7, 1835, on the eastern bank of the Delaware River, he made a little speech to a party of thirty men, in which he expressed the conviction that the railroad for which he was about to break ground might in a few years earn as much as two hundred thousand dollars a year from freight.

This roseate prophecy being received with incredulity, Mr. King hastened to modify it by saying the earnings might amount to so vast a sum " at least eventually." Then he shoveled a wheelbarrow-load of dirt, which another member of the party wheeled away and dumped, and the great work was begun.

But it was only begun. No progress was made that year, nor did it look as if any further progress ever would be made. The great fire in New York, December 16, 1835, ruined many of the stockholders, and the panic of 1836-1837 bankrupted many more.

Once more the company resolved to appeal to the legislature for aid as a last desperate expedient. The sum required was fixed at three million dollars.

Although the request was supported by huge petitions from New York, Brooklyn, and every county in the southern tier, the opposition was bitter. However, public opinion was too strong to be ignored, so the opposition went through the form of yielding to popular clamor by presenting a bill to advance two million dollars when the company had expended four million six hundred and seventy-four thousand five hundred and eighteen dollars.

This was a safe move, because the company had not a dollar in the treasury, and no means of getting one. Subsequently the conditions were modified and the credit of the State to the amount of three million dollars was loaned. Ultimately the amount was given outright.

In December, 1836, the board issued a call for a payment of two dollars and a half a share. Less than half the stockholders responded. Then a public meeting was held, at which a committee of thirty-nine was appointed to receive subscriptions. The committee opened its books and sat down to wait for the public to step up and subscribe. The public didn't step.

By 1838 President King had had enough of the effort to materialize a railroad out of the circumambient atmosphere, and the board of directors again turned to Eleazer Lord, who had a new plan to offer. It was to let contracts for the first ten miles from Piermont, the terminus of the road on the Hudson, twenty-four miles above New York, and solicit subscriptions in the city to pay for that amount of work, and to solicit subscriptions from Rockland and Orange counties to pay for the next thirty-six miles, to Goshen. Middletown was to be asked to pay for nine miles between that point and Goshen.

Before this plan could be put in operation, the company had a very narrow escape from an untimely end. People were getting so impatient to see some progress made that the legislature of 1838-1839 was swamped with petitions for the immediate construction of the road by the State.

February 14, 1839, a bill authorizing the surrender by the New York and Erie Railroad Company of all its rights, titles, franchises, and property to the State was defeated in the Senate by the narrow margin of one vote.

The Assembly succeeded in passing a similar bill, but it was defeated in the Senate, seventeen to twenty-four. The Governor stood ready to sign the bill if it had been adopted by the legislature.

In the spring of 1839 grading was begun under Lord's newest plan. October 4, 1839, Lord was again made president, and H. L. Pierson, who with his bride had taken that historic ride on the first passenger train, was made a director. Mr. Lord continued to keep things moving in his second administration so effectively that on Wednesday, June 30, 1841, the first trainload of passengers that ever traveled over the Erie Railroad was taken to Ramapo, where the party was entertained by the venerable Jeremiah Pierson, the father-in-law of the bride who made the memorable trip ten years before, who was one of the directors of the road. Three months later the line was opened for traffic to Goshen, forty-six miles from Piermont.

Slowly, very slowly, the rails crept westward. Not until December 27, 1848, more than seven years after reaching Goshen, did the first train enter Binghamton, one hundred and fifty-six miles beyond. In all those seven years the Erie Company was experiencing a continuous succession of perplexities, annoyances, difficulties, and dangers that in number and variety have probably never been equaled in the history of any other commercial enterprise in this country.

The financing of the work was one prolonged vexation. Times innumerable it seemed as if the whole enterprise must fail for want of funds, but at the last minute of the eleventh hour some way out would be found.

Then, too, the company had to learn the science of railroading as it went along. There was no telegraph in those days to facilitate the movement of trains. The only reliance was a time card and a set of rules.

Locomotives and rolling stock were small and crude. Officials and employees had everything to learn, since railroads were new, and every point learned was paid for in experience at a good round figure. The living instrumentalities through which the evolution of the railroad was achieved were very much in earnest, as they had need to be. They were too busy with the problems of each day as they arose to glut their vanity with profitless reflections upon the magnificence of the task upon which they were engaged, or to enjoy the humor of the expedients which led to their solution. Posterity gets all the laughs as well as the benefits.

An interesting example of the quaint devices by which important ends were attained is afforded by the origin of the bell cord, the forerunner of the air whistle, now in universal use on American roads for signaling the engineer from the train. A means of communication between the engine and the train has always been considered indispensable in America. In Europe the lack of such means of communication has been the fruitful source of accidents and crimes.

The bell cord was the invention of Conductor Henry Ayers, of the Erie Railroad. In the spring of 1842, soon after the line had been opened to Goshen, forty-six miles from the Hudson River, there were no cabs on the engines, no caboose for the trainmen, no way of getting over the cars, and no means of communicating with the engineer. There were no such things as telegraphic train orders, no block signals, no printed time cards, no anything but a few vague rules for the movement of trains. The engineer was an autocrat, who ran the train to suit himself. The conductor was merely a humble collector of fares.

Conductor Ayers, who afterwards for many years was one of the most popular men of his calling in the country, was assigned to a train whose destinies were ruled by Engineer Jacob Hamel, a German of a very grave turn of mind, fully alive to the dignity of his position, who looked upon the genial conductor with dark suspicion. When Ayers suggested that there should be some means of signaling the engineer so he could notify him when to stop to let off passengers, suspicion became a certainty that the conductor was seeking to usurp the prerogatives of the engineer. Hamel decided to teach the impertinent collector of small change his place.

One day Ayers procured a stout cord, which he ran from the rear car of the train to the framework of the cabless engine. He tied a stick of wood on the end of the cord, and told Hamel that when he saw the stick jerk up and down he was to stop. Hamel listened in contemptuous silence, and as soon as the conductor's back was turned threw away the stick and tied the cord to the frame of the engine. Next day the performance was repeated.

On the third day Ayers rigged up his cord and his stick of wood before starting from Piermont, the eastern terminus, and told Jacob that if he threw that stick away he would thrash him until he would be glad to leave it alone.

When they reached Goshen the stick was gone, as usual, and the end of the cord was trailing in the dirt. Ayers walked up to the engine, and without saying a word yanked Hamel off the engine and sailed in to thrash him. This proved to be no easy task, for Hamel had all the dogged tenacity of his race. But one represented Prerogative, while the other championed Progress, and Progress won at last, as it usually does.

That hard-won victory settled for all time the question of who should run a train. Also it showed the way to a most useful improvement. Once the idea was hit upon it did not take long to replace the stick of wood with a gong. In a very short time the bell cord was in universal use on passenger trains.

To Conductor Ayers is also due the credit of introducing another new idea, which, if not so useful in the operation of trains, was at least gratefully appreciated by a numerous and influential class of patrons: the custom of allowing ministers of the Gospel half rates.

Early in the spring of 1843 the Rev. Dr. Robert

McCartee, pastor of the Presbyterian Church at Goshen, was a passenger on Conductor Ayers's train. On account of a very heavy rain the track was in such bad condition that the train was delayed for hours. The passengers, following a custom that has been preserved in all the vigor of its early days, heaped maledictions upon the management. Some of the more spirited ones drew up a set of resolutions denouncing the company for the high-handed invasion of their rights, as manifested in the delay, in scathing terms. These resolutions were passed along to be signed by all the passengers. When Dr. McCartee was asked for his signature, he said he would be happy to give it if the phraseology was changed slightly. Upon being requested to name the changes he wished, he wrote the following:

" *Whereas*, the recent rain has fallen at a time ill-suited to our pleasure and convenience and without consultation with us; and

" *Whereas*, Jack Frost who has been imprisoned in the ground some months, having become tired of his bondage, is trying to break loose; therefore be it

" Resolved, that we would be glad to have it otherwise."

When the good Dr. McCartee arose and in his best parliamentary voice read his proposed amendment, there was a hearty laugh, and nothing more was heard about censuring the management.

Conductor Ayers was so delighted with this turn of affairs that thereafter he would never accept a fare from Dr. McCartee. Not being selfish, the Doctor suggested a few weeks later that the courtesy be extended to all ministers. The company thought the

idea a good one, and for a few months no minister
paid for riding over the Erie. Then an order was
issued that ministers were to be charged half fare.
That order established a precedent which was universally followed until railway legislation put an end
to the practice.

The modest but invaluable ticket punch was also
evolved on the Erie. When the first section of the
road was opened in 1841 there were no ticket agents.
Each conductor was given a tin box when he started
out for the day, which contained a supply of tickets
and ten dollars in change. The passenger on paying
the conductor his fare received a ticket, which he surrendered on the boat during his voyage of twenty-
four miles down the Hudson from Piermont to New
York. These tickets were heavy cards bearing the
signature of the general ticket agent. These were
taken up and used over and over again until they
became soiled.

Travelers soon found a way to beat the company.
They would buy a through ticket which they would
show according to custom. At the last station before
reaching their destination they would purchase a
ticket from that station to destination. This latter
ticket would be surrendered and the through ticket
kept to be used over again. The process would be
repeated on the return trip. The passenger would
then be in possession of through transportation, which
enabled him to ride as often as he liked by merely
paying for a few miles at each end of his trip.

It was some time before this fraud was discovered.
Then a system of lead pencil marks was instituted,
but pencil marks were easy to erase. The only sort

of mark that could not be erased was one that mutilated the ticket. This led to the development of the punch.

Another interesting innovation which originated on the Erie was intended for the laudable purpose of protecting passengers from the dust which has always been one of the afflictions associated with railroad travel. A funnel with its mouth pointed in the direction the train was moving was placed on the roof of the car, through which, when the train was in motion, a current of air was forced into a chamber where sprays of water operated by a pump driven from an axle washed the dust out and delivered the air sweetened and purified to the occupants of the car. A small stove was provided to heat the wash water in winter. Several cars were so equipped, and they seem to have satisfied the demands of the day, for David Stevenson, F.R.S.E., of England, who made a tour of inspection of American railroads in 1857, recommended their adoption by English railroads. But the combined ventilator and washery did not stand the test of time; and in later years passengers on the Erie, in common with the patrons of other roads, were obliged to be content with unlaundered air.

While it was learning the rudiments of railroading the company acquired some interesting side-lights on human nature, also at war prices. People of a certain type were eager to have the railroad built, but they never permitted this eagerness to blind them to the immediate interests of their own pockets.

One of the natives near Goshen had bought a tract of land along the right-of-way, expecting to make a fortune out of it when the road was in operation. The fortune manifested no indications of appearing until the native observed that the railroad had established a water-tank opposite his land, which was supplied by a wooden pump which required a man to operate.

Thereupon the native scooped out a big hole on top of a hill near by, lined it with clay to make it waterproof, and dug some shallow trenches from higher ground to the basin, which was soon filled by the rains.

Then the native went to New York and told the officers of the road that he had a valuable spring which would afford a much more satisfactory supply of water than the pump. He would sell this spring for two thousand five hundred dollars if the bargain was closed at once.

Commissioners were sent to examine the spring and close the deal. The two thousand five hundred dollars were paid over, and the company spent two thousand five hundred dollars more laying pipes from the " spring " to the track. Of course, the water all ran out in a short time, and no more took its place. Then the railroad company found that the land was mortgaged, and that if they did not get their pipe up in a hurry it would be lost, too.

A neighbor of this same native had a mill run by water-power, which had been standing idle for a couple of years. The railroad skirted the edge of the mill-pond. One day a train got tired of pounding along over the rough track and plunged off into the mill-pond.

The company asked the owner to let the water off,

so that it could recover its rolling stock. But the mill man suddenly became very busy, started up his mill, and declared he couldn't think of shutting down unless he was paid six hundred dollars to compensate him for lost time. Not seeing any other solution of the difficulty, the railroad company paid the six hundred dollars.

Going down the Shawangunk Mountains into the Neversink Valley there was a rocky ledge through which a way had to be blasted. The German owner of the rocks, when approached by the right-of-way agents, gave some sort of non-committal reply which was interpreted as consent. But when the workmen began operations on the rocks the owner stopped them and would not let them do a stroke until he had been paid a hundred dollars an acre for two acres of rock that was not worth ten cents a square mile. All along the line owners suddenly appeared for land that had been regarded as utterly worthless who had to be paid extravagant sums for right-of-way through their property. Fancy prices were also extorted for ties, fuel, and bridge timbers for the railroad.

Retribution overtook the greedy ones at last. The Irish laborers employed on the grade overran the country, digging potatoes, robbing hen-roosts and orchards, and helping themselves to whatever else took their fancy.

The company had its full share of trouble with these same Irishmen. Some were from Cork, some were from Tipperary, some from the north of Ireland, called the " Far-downers," while all were pugnacious to the last degree. There were frequent factional riots, in one of which three men were killed.

According to popular report, a good many others were killed and their bodies buried in the fills as the easiest way to dispose of them and the chance of troublesome official investigations. On several occasions the militia had to be called out to suppress disturbances. Prevention by a general disarmament and the confiscation of whisky was ultimately found to be the most effective way of dealing with the turbulent ones.

Still, there were a few incidents of a more agreeable nature. In 1841, G. W. Scranton, of Oxford, N. J., attracted by the rich deposits of iron and coal in the Luzerne Valley, Pennsylvania, bought a tract of land there and established iron-works, where he was joined later by S. T. Scranton. They had a hard struggle to keep going for five years.

Then W. E. Dodge, a director in the Erie, who knew the Scrantons, conceived the idea of having the Scrantons make rails for the road. The company was having great difficulty in getting rails from England, and the cost was excessive.

A contract was made with the Scrantons to furnish twelve thousand tons of rails at forty-six dollars a ton, which was about half the cost of the English rails. Dodge and others advanced the money to purchase the necessary machinery, and the rails were ready for delivery in the spring of 1847. This Erie contract laid the foundations of the city of Scranton.

To get the rails where they were needed it was necessary to haul them by team through the wilderness to the Delaware and Hudson Canal, at Archbold, thence by canal-boat to Carbondale, thence by a gravity railroad to Honesdale, thence by canal-boat, again, to Cuddebackville, and finally by team once more over the Shawangunk Mountains on the western extension, a distance of sixty miles.

By the time the road had reached Binghamton, two hundred and sixteen miles from New York, the Erie company seemed to be at its last gasp. Every dollar of the three million that by superhuman exertion had been raised for construction was gone, and there seemed no way to raise more.

At the last moment Alexander S. Diven, of Elmira, came to the rescue with a device which has since become the standard method of railroad-building. This was a construction syndicate, the first ever organized. An agreement was made by which the Diven syndicate was to do the grading, furnish all material except the rails, and lay the track from Binghamton to Corning, a distance of seventy-six miles, taking in payment four million dollars in second-mortgage bonds.

This saved the situation and aroused new interest in the road. It made fortunes for the members of the syndicate, but it increased the heavy burden of debt on the company and helped to make trouble for the future.

In 1849 the company tried the interesting experiment of building iron bridges. Three of them, the first structures of the kind ever built for a railroad, were erected during that year. An eastbound stock train was crossing one of the iron bridges near Mast Hope July 31, 1849, when the engineer heard a loud cracking. Instantly divining the reason, he jerked the throttle wide open and succeeded in getting the engine across in safety. So narrow was his escape that even the tender of the locomotive followed the train into the creek along with the wrecked bridge. A brakeman and two stockmen lost their lives.

This accident caused the company to lose faith in iron bridges. Thereafter all bridges were built of wood, including the famous structure over the chasm of the Genesee River at Portage. This chasm was two hundred and fifty feet deep and nine hundred feet wide. A congress of engineers being assembled to devise means of crossing it, a wooden bridge in spans of fifty feet was decided upon.

It required two years' time and an outlay of one hundred and seventy-five thousand dollars to build. When it was opened August 9, 1852, sixteen million feet of timber, the product of three hundred acres of pine forest, had gone into the structure. The science of iron bridge building was making progress; and when the great wooden structure burned in 1875 it was replaced in forty-seven days with a modern steel bridge.

The road was completed to Corning on December 31, 1849. By this time business throughout the country was improving, and the prospects of the Erie looked brighter.

There now remained a gap of one hundred and sixty-nine miles from Corning to Dunkirk, on Lake Erie, the western terminus, to be filled in. But the company having learned how to issue bonds, the rest seemed easy. An issue of three million five hundred thousand dollars of income bonds, bearing seven per cent interest, floated at a heavy discount, followed later on by a second issue of the same amount, paid for the completion of the work, in the spring of 1851.

The driving of the last spike, which completed the

road that linked the ocean with the Lakes, marked an epoch in the history of railroads. The first great trunk line was now ready for traffic. The Pennsylvania was then only a local line from Philadelphia to Hollidaysburg, in the foothills of the Alleghanies.

New York was connected with Buffalo by an aggregation of ramshackle roads of assorted gauges. The only other road of importance in the world was the line from St. Petersburg to Moscow, which was opened also in 1851.

So notable an event called for something unusual in the way of a celebration. Whatever may have been its shortcomings in financial acumen or constructive genius, and it had many such to answer for, the Erie management was a past master in the art of celebrating. Beginning with the opening of the first section of the line to Ramapo, away back in 1841, every achievement in construction had been celebrated with great éclat. The completion of the line to Goshen, to Port Jervis, to Binghamton, to Elmira, the completion of the Starucca viaduct and of the wooden bridge over the chasm of the Genesee at Portage, had all been celebrated with prodigal pomp.

When the time came that the world's first long-distance railroad excursion could be made the celebration arranged eclipsed anything of the kind that had been done. The guests included President Fillmore, Secretary of State Daniel Webster, Attorney-General John J. Crittenden, Secretary of the Navy W. C. Graham, Postmaster-General W. K. Hall, and some three hundred other distinguished guests, including six candidates for the Presidency, twelve candidates for the Vice-Presidency, United States Senators, governors, mayors, capitalists, merchants, and President Benjamin Loder and the other officers and directors of the company.

When President Fillmore, the members of his cabinet, and other distinguished guests came up from Amboy on the steamer *Erie* in mid-afternoon on May 13, 1851, all the shipping in the Harbor was dressed in bunting. Batteries at Forts Hamilton and Diamond and on Governor's Island and Bedloe's Island boomed forth National salutes. Cheers from fifty thousand throats and a salute from pieces used in 1776, fired by veterans of the Revolution, greeted the President and his suite as they disembarked at the Battery. Nine thousand militia were on hand to escort the President to the Irving Hotel at Broadway and Twelfth Street. Webster, who was already showing marked indications of his approaching end, went to the Astor House, where he always stopped. An elaborate dinner was the event of the evening.

According to the program, the boat carrying the guests was to leave for Piermont at 6 A.M. on Wednesday, May 14, 1851. There was a pouring rain that morning, but, despite the unearthly hour and the rain, the streets were packed with people to cheer the departing guests. A blundering porter was slow with Webster's baggage, and the boat did not get away until 6.10.

The famous Dodsworth's Band, which had been engaged to accompany the party to Dunkirk, rendered an elaborate program on the way up the river. Another very important member of the party was George Downing, the most famous caterer of his day, who had with him a picked corps of waiters, whose duty it was to see that no one lacked refreshment—liquid or solid.

On arriving at Piermont, at 7.45 A.M., the party was received with the ringing of bells, the booming of cannon, and the cheers of a multitude. The two trains which were to carry the invited guests were decorated with bunting, and there were flags and banners everywhere.

At eight o'clock the first through train that ever carried passengers from the ocean to the Lakes pulled out of Piermont, and was followed seven minutes later by the second section. President Fillmore was on the first section, and Webster was on the second, seated in a comfortable rocker on a flat car, for the rain had ceased and he wanted to enjoy the scenery to the utmost.

The only man on either train who was not happy was Gad Lyman, the engineer of the first section. Gad had not got many miles out of Piermont before his engine, a Rogers, No. 100, manifested unmistakable symptoms of " laying down." Under any conditions, this would have been mortifying, but the peculiar circumstances in this case made the conduct of No. 100 doubly humiliating.

In those days there was a fierce rivalry between the different makers of locomotives, and engineers were not infrequently zealous partisans of the various manufacturers. Some months previous Gad had been given a new Swinburne engine, No. 71, just out of the shop.

Being partial to Rogers machines, Gad could do nothing with the new Swinburne. On the strength of his reports the 71 was condemned as worthless, and

Gad was given the new Rogers, with which he declared he could pull the Hudson River up by the roots if he wanted to.

Josh Martin, another engineer, was a warm personal friend of Swinburne, the maker of the 71. Josh asked for the 71 after it had been condemned, and after much solicitation was given profane permission to take the old thing and go to blazes with it.

On this memorable day, after Gad's vaunted No. 100 had laid down on a little hill, a messenger was sent to a siding near by for a plebeian gravel-train engine to help him into Port Jervis, where he arrived an hour late and inexpressibly crestfallen to find Josh Martin waiting with the 71 to take his train.

Swinburne, the locomotive-builder, who was on the train, hurried forward and climbed on the 71. Josh slapped him on the back and exclaimed:

"Swinburne, I am going to make you to-day or break my neck!"

Josh didn't break his neck, but every one on board the train was fully persuaded his own neck would be broken, for Josh covered the thirty-four miles from Port Jervis to Narrowsburg with the heavy train in thirty-five minutes. Such a record as that had never been approached in the history of railroading.

Swinburne was in raptures, the officers of the road were astounded, and some of the distinguished passengers were so nervous that they insisted on getting off and walking. By the time they had covered the eighty-eight miles from Port Jervis to Deposit, Josh had made up the hour Gad had lost.

At every station along the route there were cheering crowds, booming cannon, waving banners, and oratory. Wherever the trains stopped long enough, some of the distinguished guests would make brief speeches. As the observation platform, since found so convenient in National campaigns, had not then been thought of, the orators held forth from flat cars attached to the rear of the trains for the purpose. One of these flat cars was also occupied by the railroad official who had been designated to receive flags. By a singular coincidence the ladies at every one of the more than sixty stations between Piermont and Dunkirk had conceived the idea that it would be as original as it was appropriate to present a flag wrought by their own fair hands to the railroad company when the first train passed through to Lake Erie. As it would have consumed altogether too much time to make a stop for each of these flag presentations, the engineer merely slowed down at three-fourths of the stations enough to allow the flag officer to scoop up the banner in his arms much like the hands on the old-fashioned Marsh Harvesters gathered up armfuls of grain for binding. At the end of the journey the Erie Railroad had a collection of flags that would have done credit to a victorious army.

The party reached Elmira, two hundred and seventy-four miles from New York, where the night was to be passed, at 7 P.M. As the President alighted a national salute was fired. There was an imposing procession to escort the President to one hotel and Webster to another; two banquets were served, with Downing, the caterer, and his staff helping the hotel men.

All night long the streets were filled with enthusiastic crowds. Hospitality was unbounded, and many citizens on all other occasions staid and sober men grew hilarious as the night wore on. Elmira has never had another such night as that which marked the opening of the Erie from the ocean to the Lakes.

At 6.30 A.M., on Thursday, May 15, the special trains left Elmira for Dunkirk, where they arrived at 4.30 P.M.

The scenes of the day before were repeated at every station along the way. H. G. Brooks, an engineer, ran his locomotive out several miles to meet the trains, which had been consolidated for entering Dunkirk, and escorted them to the station under a canopy made of the intertwined flags of the United States, England, and France.

There was a procession, led by Dodsworth's Band, to the scene of a barbecue for which the whole country had been preparing for weeks.

There were two oxen barbecued, ten sheep, and a hundred fowls; bread in loaves ten feet long and two feet wide, barrels of cider, tanks of coffee, unlimited quantities of ham, corned beef, tongue and sausage, pork and beans in vessels holding fifty gallons each, and vast quantities of clam chowder.

President Fillmore manifested deep interest in the pork and beans, while Webster was attracted by the clam chowder. He was something of a specialist in making clam chowder himself, he said. He strongly recommended the addition of a little port wine to give the chowder the proper bouquet. After several dinners in as many different places, accompanied by much speech-making, the celebration was at an end.

The first trunk line, an unbroken road five hundred miles long, from tide-water to the inland seas, was now open for traffic, but that was about all that could be said. It began nowhere, ended nowhere, had no connections, and could have none. The track was un-ballasted, and the rolling-stock was in such bad condition that the insecurity of travel over the road was notorious. In two months there were sixteen serious accidents on one division alone.

Part of these anomalous conditions was due to peculiar ideas of what a railroad should be that seem strange enough now but were not considered peculiar in those early days. The road was built to secure for New York City the trade of the southern part of the State. To make sure that none of this trade should go to Boston or Philadelphia or any other places which were casting covetous eyes in that direction, the Erie was prohibited, under penalty of forfeiture of its charter, from making any connections with any other road.

Even if connections had been desired, there could have been no direct interchange of traffic, because the Erie was built on a six-foot gauge, while all the other roads were adopting the standard English gauge of four feet eight and one-half inches.

When the railroad had reached Middletown, the chief engineer at that time, Major T. S. Brown, after a trip to Europe to study the best railroad practice there, urged a change of gauge to four feet eight and one-half inches. He said the gauge of the fifty-four miles of track then in operation could be changed then at a cost of two hundred and fifty thousand dollars, but his recommendations were not approved.

When the Erie was confronted, forty years later, with the alternative of changing its gauge or going out of business, the change was made at a cost of twenty-five million dollars.

In this connection it is interesting to note that the problem of gauge was not finally settled by the railroads of the United States until 1886. Between May 22 and June 2 of that year upwards of twelve thousand miles of railroad in the South were changed from wide to standard gauge. The Louisville and Nashville, by using a force of 8,763 men, was able to change the gauge of 1,806 miles of main-line and sidings in a single day.

Notwithstanding the road was built to benefit New York, its terminus was twenty-four miles away from the city, and the company had refused an opportunity to gain an entrance over the Harlem Railroad. It didn't take long for some shrewd Jerseymen who were not in the Erie directorate to see that the natural terminus of the road was at a point in Jersey City opposite New York, and but a very little longer for them to preëmpt the only practicable route by which the Erie could reach that point. This was from Suffern through the Paramus Valley to Jersey City *via* Paterson.

The Paterson and Hudson Railroad, from Jersey City to Paterson, and the Ramapo and Paterson Railroad, from Paterson to Suffern, were duly chartered. The former was opened in 1836, the latter in 1848. The Erie might refuse to connect with other roads. But no legislative fiat could prevent a passenger on the Erie from leaving it for another road that stood ready to save him twenty miles of travel and an hour and a half of time. The Erie tried every device of discrimination in rates and increased speed of its boats and trains, but utterly failed to convince the traveling public that the longest way round was the shortest road home. On February 10, 1851, the Erie capitulated on terms dictated by the shrewd Jerseymen, taking a perpetual lease of the short cut to the Metropolis.

This alarmed the people of Piermont, who petitioned the legislature to come to the rescue of their town with a law compelling the Erie to continue to run its trains to that out-of-the-way terminus. But the legislature, like the railroad, gave up the attempt to prescribe routes of travel by statute and left Piermont to oblivion.

An event of far greater historical importance in the same year was the discovery that trains could be moved by telegraph. Although seven years had elapsed since Morse had sent his first telegraph message from Washington to Baltimore, capitalists were still scornfully skeptical of the investment value of his wonderful invention, and other folk were more or less incredulous of its practical utility. Such occasional messages as were sent began with " Dear Sir," and closed with " Yours respectfully."

No one dreamed of using the telegraph to regulate the movements of trains. The time card was the sole reliance of railroad men for getting over the road. The custom, still in vogue, of giving east- and north-bound trains the right of way over trains of the same class moving in the opposite direction had been established. If an east-bound train did not reach its meeting point on time the west-bound train, according to the rules, had to wait one hour and then proceed under a flag until the opposing train was met. A flagman would be sent ahead on foot. Twenty minutes later the train would follow, moving about as fast as a man could walk. Under this interesting arrangement, when a train which had the right of way was several hours late, the opposing train had to flag over the entire division at a snail's pace.

On September 22, 1851, Superintendent Charles Minot was on Conductor Stewart's train west bound. They were to meet the east-bound express at Turner's. As the express did not show up Minot told the operator to ask if it had arrived at Goshen fourteen miles west. On receiving a negative answer he wrote the first telegraphic train order ever penned. It read as follows:

" *To Operator at Goshen:*
    " Hold east-bound train till further orders.
                    " CHARLES MINOT, *Superintendent.*"

Then he wrote an order which he handed to Conductor Stewart, reading as follows:

" *To Conductor Stewart:*
    " Run to Goshen regardless of opposing train.
                    " CHARLES MINOT, *Superintendent.*"

When Conductor Stewart showed this order to Engineer Isaac Lewis that worthy read it twice with rising amazement and indignation. Then he handed it back to the conductor with lip curved with scorn.

"Do I look like a d—— fool? " snorted Lewis. " I'll run this train according to time card rules, and no other way."

Upon hearing of this Superintendent Minot used all his powers of persuasion to induce Lewis to pull out; but the engineer refused in most emphatic terms. He wasn't prepared to cross the Jordan that morning, so he proposed to abide by the rules in such cases made and provided. No other course being open Minot ordered the obstinate engineer down and took charge of the engine himself. Lewis took refuge in the last seat of the rear car, where he would have some show for his life when the inevitable collision occurred, while the superintendent ran the train to Goshen. Finding by further use of the telegraph that the opposing train had not reached Middletown he ran to that point by repeating his orders and kept on in the same way until he reached Port Jervis, saving two hours' time for the west-bound train.

The account of the superintendent's reprehensible conduct when related by Engineer Lewis caused a great commotion among the other engineers. In solemn conclave they agreed that they would not run trains on any such crazy system. But Minot issued an order that the movements of trains on the Erie Railroad would thenceforth be controlled by telegraph, and they were.

When the Erie was at last in operation from Jersey City to Dunkirk it had cost $43,333 a mile exclusive of equipment, or six times the original estimate made in 1834, yet it was a railroad more in name than in fact. Motive power and rolling stock were insufficient and dilapidated, while the track demanded an expenditure of large sums before traffic could be handled with profit.

But in spite of all its drawbacks this first trunk line justified the enthusiasm of the bride which expedited its building, and even justified the reckless language of President King, who thought " Eventually it might earn two hundred thousand dollars a year on freight"; for the receipts on through business in the first six months after the line was opened to Dunkirk were $1,755,285, and the first dividend, 4 per cent, was declared for the last six months of 1851.

The opening of the Erie to Dunkirk and the completion of a through route from New York by way of Albany to Buffalo a few months later, upon the opening of the Hudson River Railroad, completely revolutionized travel between the East and the West. People congratulated one another on the comfort, safety, and cheapness of travel with which, in that progressive age, the great distance between the Mississippi and the Atlantic could be " traversed in an almost incredibly short space of time." Before these roads were opened for traffic the journey from St. Louis to New York was a formidable enterprise which nothing but the most urgent necessity could induce any one to undertake. The usual route was by steamboat to Wheeling or Pittsburg, thence by stage through a nightmare of rough roads, sleepless nights, stiffened limbs, and aching heads to Baltimore or Philadelphia, thence to New York.

But the opening of the Eastern roads and of a road from Cincinnati to Lake Erie reversed the current of travel. Instead of going by way of Baltimore or Philadelphia to New York, nearly all the traffic moved to Cincinnati by boat, from whence New York could be reached by rail by way of Dunkirk or Buffalo in less than forty-eight hours, and Washington in about fifteen hours more. This was less time than was required to go from Cincinnati to Pittsburg by steamboat. The routes by Wheeling and Pittsburg were practically abandoned, while travel by the new railroads, according to the newspapers of the day, became " almost incredibly great."

Under the circumstances, then, such superlatives as these from the *American Railroad Journal* anent the formal opening of the Erie Railroad to Dunkirk seem quite pardonable:

" The occasion was an era in the history of locomotion. Its influence will at once be felt in every part of the United States. The Erie Railroad is the grand artery between the Atlantic and our inland seas. Its branches compared with other trunk lines would be great works. . . . The New York and Erie Railroad lays high claims to being one of the greatest achievements of human skill and enterprise. In magnitude of undertaking and cost of construction it far exceeds the hitherto greatest work of internal improvement in the United States, the Erie Canal. When we consider its length, which exceeds that of the great railway building by the Russian Government from Moscow to St. Petersburg; when we reflect upon the extensive tracts of country teeming with rich products it has opened up, it is doubtful whether any similar work exists on the earth to compare with it."

Yet Dunkirk was scarcely more satisfactory as a western terminus than Piermont as the eastern. The struggle to create a railroad, instead of being at an end, was only begun.

Although the first public meeting to create the sentiment which ultimately led to the building of the Erie was held at Jamestown in 1831, when the road was finally opened twenty years later, that town was left thirty-four miles from the line. Being determined to have a railroad the people of Jamestown in

May, 1851, organized the Erie and New York City Railroad to build from Salamanca, named after the Duke of Salamanca, financial adviser to Queen Isabella, of Spain, who was instrumental in placing a quantity of bonds in Spain, through Jamestown to the Pennsylvania State line.

About the same time it occurred to Marvin Kent, a manufacturer of Franklin, Ohio, that the real terminus of the Erie should be at St. Louis through a connection with the struggling Ohio and Mississippi, which was also of six feet gauge. Acting on this idea he procured a charter from the Ohio legislature for the Franklin and Warren Railroad to build from Franklin east to the Pennsylvania State line and south to Dayton. A formidable obstacle to the execution of this project for a through route from New York to St. Louis and the west was the State of Pennsylvania, which interposed between the Franklin and Warren and the Erie and New York City. There was no railroad connection across the State of Pennsylvania between New York and Ohio, and there was no prospect that there ever would be any if the selfish jealousy of Erie, Pittsburg, and Philadelphia could prevent it. These cities had resolved that all the traffic between the East and the West through Pennsylvania should pay tribute to them.

A combined lobby from these cities controlled the legislature and so effectually prevented all the numerous attempts to charter any railroad that threatened their commercial supremacy. But a way out was found even from this hopeless situation. When it was made an object to the Pittsburg and Erie Railroad that company stretched its privileges to cover the construction of a " branch " across Pennsylvania that would make a connecting link between the New York and Ohio roads then projected. Following the devious ways necessary to legalize its operations, and hindered by the delays required to capitalize it, this " branch " in the course of seven years became first the Meadville Railroad and then the Atlantic and Great Western. The Erie made the surveys for this connection, which would have been so helpful, and promised to finance it; but for several years was too desperately hard up to fulfil that promise.

Not until the assistance of James McHenry, an Irishman, who after being brought up in America went to Liverpool and made an immense fortune by creating the first trade in America dairy products, had been secured were the funds to build the Atlantic and Great Western forthcoming. McHenry's indorsement was enough to give the road good standing with English investors. Their capital was lavished on the project as foreign money had never before been lavished on anything American. Agents were kept in Canada and Ireland to recruit labor, which was sent over by the shipload during the Civil War.

By virtue of achievements in railroad building then unparalleled the first broad-gauge train from the East was able to enter Cleveland November 3, 1863. On June 20, 1864, a special broad-gauge train arrived at Dayton from New York. From Dayton connection was made by the Cincinnati, Hamilton and Dayton by way of Cincinnati, and the Ohio and Mississippi with St. Louis, thus opening a broad-gauge route from the ocean to the Mississippi. The Atlantic and Great Western was leased by the Erie January

1, 1869, and thus became a link in the present main line.

Before this the Erie had become great enough to rouse the cupidity of rival manipulators, who in their struggle for possession nearly ruined the property. High finance was then a new art and its methods were crude.

But the Erie survived it all, and half a century after it was ushered into Dunkirk with such elaborate ceremony it had developed into a system of nearly two thousand five hundred miles with annual earnings of more than forty million dollars.

CHAPTER IV

PENNSYLVANIA AND THE PENNSYLVANIA RAILROAD

PENNSYLVANIA had a hard struggle to become reconciled to the railroad. Perhaps it was arrogance born of prosperity, for in early days Philadelphia was the foremost city of the nation, and the country population was thriving; perhaps it was something deserving a less charitable characterization which inspired the desperate resistance to innovation.

The fact remains that the opposition to the railroad in the Keystone State was more bitter and prolonged than elsewhere. As a result Pennsylvania paid a higher price than any other commonwealth for having the blessing of rail transportation thrust upon her.

The plain truth is that the good people of Pennsylvania were strenuously opposed to anything that smacked of progress. They were entirely content with pack trains winding single-file over the mountains between Philadelphia and Pittsburg in charge of men who carried a bag of parched corn and venison for food and slept under trees. When turnpikes were proposed a vigorous protest was raised on the ground that the packers and horse breeders would be ruined. General Alexander Ogle, member of Congress, started a campaign of education which was notable for plain speaking. General Ogle was wont to tell his constituents that one wagon would carry as much salt, iron and brandy as a whole caravan of half-starved mountain ponies and that " of all people in the world fools have the least sense," a remark which was open to disagreeable inferences.

At last the advocates of the turnpike had their way and Conestoga wagons supplanted the pack horse. In 1786 a fortnightly stage coach made the rounds between Philadelphia and Pittsburgh. In 1804 this was increased to a daily service and the wagons began to grow numerous. Taverns sprang up every few miles along the way. Thus a strong vested interest soon grew up which was able to bring a powerful opposition to bear when a few radicals proposed canals as superior to turnpikes.

The clamor of opposition to progress reached a climax when the extremists attempted to maintain that railroads would be superior even to canals. The popular view was succinctly expressed by an old Pennsylvania Dutchman who was listening to General Simon Cameron, who was making a speech at Elizabethtown in favor of the proposed railroad from Philadelphia to Lancaster. The General said he hoped to see the day when he could take breakfast at Harrisburg, go to Philadelphia, transact business, and return to Harrisburg in time for a good night's rest. This was too much for the Dutchman, who called over his shoulder as he turned away in disgust:

" Simon, I always knew you were half cracked, but I never suspected you were such an ass as to talk that way."

Another vested interest now joined the alliance against the railroad—the truck farmers in the outskirts of Philadelphia. They said if a railroad were built the Lancaster truck farmers could ship their potatoes and cabbages to Philadelphia and thus set up a ruinous competition with the local farmers. In justice to the Philadelphia farmers it must be said that their forebodings proved to be only too well founded. The road to Lancaster was built and the Philadelphia truck business was destroyed so utterly that the farmers had to cut up their truck patches into town lots, any one of which sold for more money than the whole farm could earn in a lifetime.

John Thomson, who up to that time had always been one of the most respected citizens of Delaware County, built a quarter of a mile of crude wooden railroad in 1809 and called upon his neighbors to witness that one horse could pull with ease a heavier load on the wooden rails than two horses could drag along the muddy road.

But the neighbors told John Thomson in plain terms that he was a fool; whereupon, in extreme disgust, he chopped Pennsylvania's first railroad up for firewood and said no more about it. That is, not until his son John Edgar, then a year old, was big enough to talk to.

Instead of sending the boy to school and giving him a chance to get on in the world, John Thomson kept him at home and filled his young head with fool notions about railroads until he left at the age of nineteen to accept a position as engineer, to assist in laying out and constructing the first important railroad ever operated in the State of Pennsylvania.

He stuck to the job until as chief engineer and

president he had extended that apology for a railroad across the Alleghanies and then to the Mississippi and the Great Lakes, developed and expanded it into one of the greatest transportation companies in existence, and, dying, left behind him immortal fame as one of the foremost constructive geniuses in the history of the railroad.

While young Thomson was at home preparing for his life-work, Pennsylvania was learning things, too. Summed up, the lesson was that no community can prosper without adequate facilities for trade. The opening of the Erie Canal and the building of the Baltimore and Ohio Railroad demonstrated in a rather pointed way that transportation was foremost of those facilities.

Colonel John Stevens, of Hoboken, who wore out his life trying to induce people to build railroads, had applied for a charter to build a railroad from Philadelphia to Columbia in 1823. Just to humor an old man it was granted, but not a dollar could be raised to build even an experimental mile of road, even though Horace Binney and Stephen Girard, two of the foremost conservative business men of Philadelphia, permitted their names to appear as incorporators. They were willing to lend dignity to the scheme, but lending money was quite a different matter. Other charters were granted in the next few years, but nothing came of them until the Philadelphia, Germantown and Norristown Railroad was authorized by an act of the legislature approved by Governor Wolf February 17, 1831.

With commendable prudence the legislature took care that the incorporators should not get rich too quickly by expressly providing that the dividends should not exceed twelve per cent per annum. In order to keep the profits down to this liberal figure the fare was limited to one cent a mile. All this legislative caution proved to be unnecessary, for it was many years before the road paid any dividends at all, even after the tariff was raised to two cents a mile. The road was opened for traffic June 6, 1832, with " nine splendid cars " according to contemporaneous accounts, which were greatly admired by some thousands of spectators.

The " splendid cars," as a matter of fact, were old Concord stages, provided with flanged wheels to enable them to stay on the rails and footboards along which the conductors walked to collect fares. Horses furnished the motive power.

This road is chiefly interesting from the fact that the building of " Old Ironsides," its first locomotive, laid the foundation of the great Baldwin Locomotive Works. Matthew Baldwin, the builder, was a watchmaker by trade. For some unexplained reason a curious affinity existed between watchmakers and locomotives in early days. Phineas Davis, who built the prize locomotive for the Baltimore and Ohio, was a watchmaker. So were Stacy Costell, who organized the Pennsylvania Locomotive Works in 1831, and Ezekiel Childs, who also tried his hand at the business. But neither made a success of it.

Baldwin made himself so famous by building a stationary engine to run his factory for the manufacture of calico printing rolls, for the sufficient reason that he had to have an engine and could not get a satisfactory one in any other way, that his friend

Franklin Peale, the manager of the Philadelphia Museum, asked him to build a working model of a locomotive, which he wanted as a star attraction for his museum. Being finished and placed on exhibition on a circular track April 28, 1831, this model caused a great sensation.

Among those whose interest was aroused were the directors of the Germantown Railroad, which had then been extended to a point six miles from Philadelphia.

They asked Baldwin to build a full-sized locomotive for them. Although he had no patterns, no machine tools, and no experience, and there were but five mechanics in the city competent to do any part of the work on a locomotive, Baldwin took the job. The cylinders were bored out with a chisel fixed in a stick of wood turned by a crank worked by hand. Six months of hard work were required to finish " Old Ironsides." On November 23, 1832, the engine was placed in service.

There were no brakes on cars or engine. The only means of stopping was by reversing the engine, a process as laborious as it was uncertain. The rock shaft was placed under the footboard. It was operated by treadles worked by the feet of the engineer which actuated a loose eccentric for each cylinder. To reverse required two distinct operations: first to shut off and then throw the engine out of gear in one direction; next, to throw it into gear in the other direction—that is, provided it could be done. But those loose eccentrics were the most nerve-racking devices that ever tried the patience of a long-suffering engineer. They responded to the efforts of the

"OLD IRONSIDES."

The famous first locomotive built by M. W. Baldwin, founder of the greatest locomotive works in the world.

treadles when so disposed; when they took a notion they balked, so the engine could be moved neither forward nor backward. They caused the poor builder a great deal of anxiety.

To make matters worse the engine weighed seven tons instead of the five tons prescribed in the contract. This so displeased the purchasers that they would have rejected the locomotive but for the strenuous efforts of Henry R. Campbell, the chief engineer, a friend of Baldwin, and James Moore, the consulting engineer. The directors finally accepted Old Ironsides, but would only pay three thousand five hundred dollars for it instead of the four thousand dollars they had agreed to pay. This so disgusted Baldwin that he vowed he would never build another locomotive. But the Fates had decreed otherwise: he never did anything else but build locomotives for the rest of his life.

When the opening of the Erie Canal had suddenly diverted Philadelphia's trade with the West to New York, the State government undertook what private enterprise would not by creating a Board of Canal Commissioners to construct improved avenues of communication with the western part of the State. It was agreed that canals were the best system of transportation, but, owing to the mountainous character of the State, railroads might have to be built to fill in the gaps between canals.

The Board of Canal Commissioners were careful to have it understood, however, that they favored railroads only as a last resort. In their annual report published in December, 1831, they stated their position thus clearly:

" While the Board avow themselves favorable to railroads where it is impracticable to construct canals, or under some peculiar circumstances, yet they cannot forbear to explain their opinion that the advocates of railroads generally have greatly overrated their commercial value. To counteract the wild speculations of visionary men and to allay the honest fears and prejudices of many of our best citizens who have been induced to believe that railroads are better than canals and consequently, that for the last six years the efforts of our state to achieve a mighty improvement have been misdirected, the canal commissioners deem it to be their duty to state a few facts which will exhibit the comparative value of the two modes of improvement for the purpose of carrying heavy articles cheaply to market in a distinct point of view."

After giving estimates of both methods of transportation, in which the canal appeared to much greater advantage than the railroad, the report proceeds:

" The introduction of locomotives and Winans cars upon railroads where they can be used to advantage will diminish the difference between canals and railroads in the expense of transportation. But the Board believe that notwithstanding all improvements which have been made in railroads and locomotives it will be found that canals are from two to two and a half times better than railroads for the purposes required of them by Pennsylvania.

" The Board have been thus explicit with a view to vindicating the sound policy of the Commonwealth in the construction of canals; yet they again repeat that their remarks flow from no hostility to railroads, for next to canals they are the best means that have been devised to cheapen transportation."

The Philadelphia and Columbia Railroad, eighty-two miles long, was the eastern link in the chain of

State works. It was here that the boy Thomson began his railroad career as engineer.

Work was begun on a twenty-mile section at each end of the line in April, 1829. By the end of the succeeding year these sections were ready for operation with horses as the motive power. April 16, 1834, the locomotive Black Hawk made a trip from end to end of the road, a single track having been completed by that time.

This was merely an inspection trip, and was not regarded as the opening of the road. The little party which made that long journey of eighty-two miles can hardly be said to have enjoyed it, for the Black Hawk was as capricious as a coquette. When it felt disposed to go, it went; and when it felt the need of a little rest it stopped until the passengers got tired, when they would get out and push the sulky machine along.

They found consolation in the fact that the management had taken the precaution to send a horse-car with relays of horses to follow them. Although the Black Hawk did get over the road, the trip was not regarded as a triumph for steam.

The formal opening of the road was on October 7, 1834, after the double track had been completed. Governor Wolf and staff left Harrisburg early Monday morning by an express packet on the canal, which whirled them down to Columbia at the rate of four miles an hour. Next morning the journey to Philadelphia was continued by rail.

Governor Wolf was idolized by the people because of his advanced stand on the questions of public schools and public improvements, and he may have divided honors with the new railroads on that memorable day. At all events, there was a holiday all along the line.

Men left shop and field and office; women their household duties, and children their schools to cheer the train, and there were speeches from the rear platform at every stop, just as if it were a twentieth century political campaign.

There were two trains into Philadelphia that day, run by rival companies: the Union Line, operated by Peters & Co., and the People's Line, operated by Osborne, Davis, Kirke & Schofield. The private car-line is by no means a modern innovation; it was originated at the very beginning of railroads in Pennsylvania.

The great bugbear of the people three-quarters of a century ago was monopoly, just as it is to-day. It was considered to smack too much of monopoly to have a railroad on which cars and track were both controlled by the State or by a corporation.

The original idea of a railroad in Pennsylvania was a sort of improved turnpike, to be kept up by the State, upon which any one who owned a car and could pay the toll was free to come and go at his own sweet will.

The results of this method of operation were more amusing to spectators than they were to the man who wanted to get his car over the road. They were still more unsatisfactory when the Board of Canal Commissioners proposed to introduce locomotives which could be used to haul trains for a fee.

This revolutionary step roused a new storm of opposition. Town meetings were held at which peti-

tions to the legislature for and against steam were prepared. Thaddeus Stevens was the leader of the opposition to steam.

Stevens held that if authority to purchase locomotives and thus place the motive power of the railroad
in the hands of the State were granted the Board of
Canal Commissioners, its patronage and power would
be largely increased and the results would be detri-
mental to the interests of the people.

Under pressure from the prominent men of his
party, fortified with a promise that he should have a
chance at the patronage and power, Stevens dropped
his opposition and an act was passed authorizing the
Board of Canal Commissioners to purchase locomotives. Under this authority the superintendent was
instructed in April to purchase twenty locomotives,
to be ready for use for the spring trade of 1835.

E. F. Gay, the principal engineer, corresponding
to a later day superintendent of motive power, reported on November 7, 1834, that two locomotives had
been received and had been in daily use for some
weeks. These were the " Lancaster " and the " Columbia," both built by M. W. Baldwin.

Each weighed eight tons, and had a four-wheeled
truck and a single pair of drivers, which was believed
to be the only arrangement that would take the sharp
curves. They were capable of hauling forty-eight
tons gross, or thirty tons of freight. The running
time for seventy-seven miles was eight hours. Fuel,
oil, and wages of the engineer and attendants cost
$14.60 a trip.

The Lancaster's performance was so satisfactory
that it was regarded as the standard by which to

gauge other locomotives. It was in continuous service for sixteen years, when it became too badly worn out to be worth repairing and was consigned to the ignominious oblivion of the scrap-heap. The Columbia had met the same fate two years before.

The Board's experience with English locomotives wasn't so satisfactory. Five of the English locomotives were purchased under the act of April, 1834. They couldn't pull their trains, and were forever breaking down.

Finally, they were sold for scrap-iron, the superintendent declaring in his disgust that the State would have saved money by giving the English machines away as soon as they were received.

When the locomotives were put in service the fun began in earnest. There were several companies, called transporters, engaged in business on the road, each with its own cars. Some made a specialty of passengers, others of freight.

But the farmer who had a load of potatoes to take to Philadelphia was still as free to come and go on the railroad as the winds, so long as he paid the wheel tolls. There were no turnouts by which one train or car could pass another.

The first man out at one end of the road was, therefore, the first to reach the other end. The speed of all users of the road at any given time was, therefore, regulated by the slowest car.

Any one who has lived in a city where the police have too high a regard for the tender susceptibilities of truck-drivers to enforce the ordinances regarding the use of the streets, and who has been compelled to make a street-car journey at the rate of speed adopted by the coal wagons and drays which hold the track, can fully appreciate the joys of travel on the Philadelphia and Columbia Railroad in the early days.

It was the particular delight of a farmer with a pair of crowbaits attached to a dilapidated four-wheeled car, on which a hatful of potatoes bobbed about, to stop every few miles to water his horses with extreme deliberation, get a drink himself, light his pipe, inquire of a neighbor returning on the other track the price of potatoes in Philadelphia, look his car over and whittle a wooden pin to stick in somewhere to keep the crazy thing from falling to pieces, while a trainload of passengers, drawn by a locomotive following him, fretted and fumed and swore, and then grew apoplectic with impotent rage.

Still, railroad travel even under such conditions had its compensations. There were no stations in those early days. The roadside inns sprinkled all over the country at intervals of a few miles, in response to the requirements of stage-coach travel, took their place. Coaching customs were still kept up.

As the stage always stopped at every inn, so the trains would come to a halt whenever they passed in sight of one. All hands—engineer, firemen, trainmen, and passengers—would alight and trudge across the field, leaving the train deserted on the main line until the thirst and appetites of all were satisfied.

Each inn carried the fundamental necessity of life in the thirties, to wit, whisky, of course; but in addition each had its own particular specialty by which its fame was spread among travelers.

At one place it would be coffee and big, fat doughnuts; at another, apple-pie with milk; at another, waffles and fish; at still another, chicken fricassee or beer and gingerbread, and so on. To any one not dyspeptic nor in haste, therefore, a trip over the Philadelphia and Columbia Railroad was one prolonged delight.

This happy-go-lucky method of operating the road at last grew intolerable. The Board of Canal Commissioners then took the advanced step of prescribing hours when locomotives might use the road. The order was that locomotives might leave the top of the Belmont Plane, which was at the Philadelphia end, only between the hours of 4 and 10 A.M. and 5 and 8 P.M., the last to leave carrying a signal to indicate that fact.

This left a period of seven hours during the day and eight hours at night free for the use of horses. Beyond this, rules for running were conspicuous by their absence.

There was a continual conflict between individual transporters who wished to use horses and the Board of Canal Commissioners, who wished to use steam and control the movement of trains. Finally the Board took the bull by the horns and prohibited the use of horses on the railroad after April 1, 1844.

Meanwhile improvements were being made in methods of railroad operations. A great advance in carrying mail and baggage was made when " Possum Belly " cars were introduced. The " Possum Belly " car had a huge box or cellar beneath the floor of the car into which mail-bags, portmanteaus, and bundles could be thrust.

Sam Jones, known to the traveling public as " Grubey Sam," a deformed negro, the first of his race to be employed on a railroad in the State, had charge of the " Possum Bellies," and he was fully aware of the dignity and importance of his position. But he was bright, faithful, and alert, so he made more friends than enemies.

Locomotives necessitate shops; so as soon as the first batch of twenty engines had been ordered a site was chosen for the first railroad shops in Pennsylvania. The location chosen was in a field midway between Philadelphia and Columbia. One reason for this was that John G. Parke, a wealthy and influential man, was aggrieved because he was unable to collect a claim of $3,273 for damages sustained by reason of the road passing between his house and his barn.

For political reasons the Board could not afford to incur his enmity, so they accepted his offer of a site, laid out a town, and called it Parkesburg. Work on the first shop was begun December 4, 1833.

But another important reason for locating the shops in the country was to spare the shopmen the corrupting influence of the engineers. In those days enginemen were hard to get, and the Board had to wink at peccadilloes that would not be passed over so lightly now.

At these shops safety chains were first put on between engine and tender, because an engine while on the road broke away from its tender, spilling the fireman and engineer to the ground between the rails, where both were torn to pieces.

The " Grasshopper level," four miles from Lancaster, was responsible for another important improvement in locomotives. The place was so called because one summer the grasshoppers were so thick in the vicinity that they wore the fence rails smooth passing from field to field in search of food. Also, they were so thick on the rails that the locomotive wheels slipped on their crushed bodies and the trains were stalled.

Edwin Jeffries, the manager of the Parkesburg shops, sent out men to pour sand on the rails so the locomotives' driving-wheels could take hold. This suggested putting a box of sand on the front end of the locomotive for the convenience of the men. Then the box was placed on top of the boiler, with pipes running from the box to the rails in front of the drivers, and a valve in the pipes which could be operated by the engineer. Thus was evolved the sand-box of to-day, and also that favorite story, ever on its travels, about the grasshoppers stopping the train.

Jeffries also conceived the idea of putting cabs on the engines, but the men at first refused to ride in them. They were afraid of being trapped in case of an upset, and the fear was not groundless.

The rails were laid in chairs on stone blocks, and held in place by wedges. Of course, the wedges were forever working loose and permitting the rails to spread. Derailments were of frequent occurrence, particularly in bucking snow.

In spring when the frost was coming out of the ground, heaving the tracks in all sorts of kinks, several trains a day would be off the rails.

There were no telegraph, no telephone, no block-signals, nor even any headlights on the engines. The first intimation of a wreck would be the arrival of a messenger on a farmer's horse. A wrecking-crew was kept constantly in readiness at each end of the line and at Parkesburg.

Experience taught in due time that it wasn't always necessary to wait for the arrival of a messenger with news of disaster. If a train didn't show up when it should the wrecking-crew would start out in search of the derelict, with two men riding on the front end of the locomotive, who would take turns in sprinting ahead with a red light around curves as a precaution against an additional wreck.

While the Philadelphia and Columbia Railroad was being built, good progress was being made on the Alleghany Portage Railroad. One track of this remarkable road was opened November 21, 1833, and early in the spring of 1834 a double track was completed and the road was ready for traffic.

When the engineers in laying out a railroad came to a hill they could not go around they laid a line of rails straight up the slope, called it an inclined plane, and placed a stationary hoisting engine at the top to haul the cars up. Even the Philadelphia and Columbia Railroad had an inclined plane at the Philadelphia terminus on the banks of the Schuylkill, with a length of 2,800 feet and a rise of 196 feet, and another at Columbia 1,800 feet long, with a rise of 90 feet. The heaviest grade on the road was forty-four feet to the mile.

Engineers took it for granted that locomotives could only travel on practically level track, just as they had previously taken it for granted that the driving wheels of a locomotive or a steam road carriage would revolve impotently on the rail or on the ground without moving forward.

But William Norris, a brilliant and energetic young locomotive builder of Philadelphia, Baldwin's most formidable rival, built a locomotive in 1836 which he named the " Washington " of the remarkable weight of fourteen thousand four hundred pounds. It had cylinders ten by eighteen inches and a single pair of drivers forty-eight inches in diameter. The boiler carried the heavy pressure of ninety pounds of steam.

This prodigy performed so well on its trial trip that Norris, who always was regarded as a reckless person, decided to see what it would do on the inclined plane at Philadelphia, on a grade of three hundred and sixty-nine feet to the mile. To his unbounded delight the Washington puffed its way steadily to the top of the plane. No one would believe Norris when he told what the new locomotive had done. They said his tale was a fabrication on the face of it, since it was perfectly obvious that a locomotive simply could not ascend an inclined plane solely by its own power. Even after the feat had been repeated in the presence of many witnesses it could scarcely be credited. Eight months after Norris had demonstrated that a locomotive could not only climb an ascending grade by its own power, but could also haul a train up, A. G. Steere, of the Erie Railway, in a long communication to the *Railroad Journal* of March 11, 1837, proved by elaborate algebraic formulæ that the Washington did not climb the hill, because it could not; and that no other locomotive ever could climb an ascending grade by its own power. Mr. Steere was very nice about his exposure of Mr. Norris' alleged " deeds done in flagrant and open

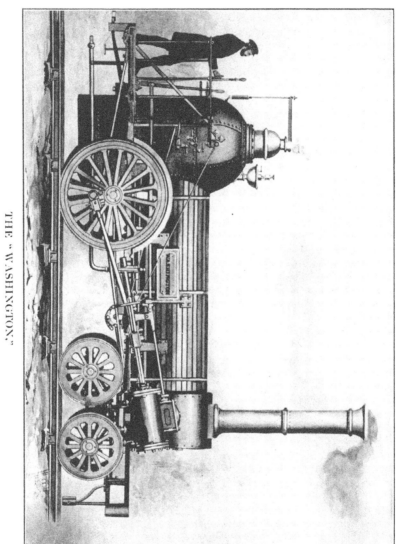

THE "WASHINGTON."

Norris' famous engine which, in 1836, created a tremendous sensation by showing that locomotives could run up grade.

violation of the laws of gravitation." He explained the motives which led him to show up the preposterous claims as follows:

" Accounts of the very wonderful feats said to have been performed by Mr. Norris' engines on the Columbia Railroad have not been noticed by scientific men from the fact, I suppose, that the errors in them were so enormous and apparent that they supposed they would be detected by all and were, therefore, not worth exposing. But the mass of those who read these accounts, now again put forth as facts, and who are interested in railroad improvements are not scientific men; and it is to prevent such from daily quoting and swallowing absurdity with such grave astonishment that I send you the following exposition. I have not the least desire to prejudice the community against Mr. Norris' engines, which, I have no doubt, are really very superior ones, but I do not wish capitalists to mistake steep roads for cheap ones or to suppose engines are going to draw loads which are really impossible for Mr. Norris' engines or any others."

This was the opening gun in a long and earnest discussion in the columns of the *Railroad Journal* concerning the possibility or the impossibility of an engine climbing a hill. It was rather difficult, however, to maintain that a thing could not be done when it was being done daily, and the controversy finally died out.

As the real development of the railroad dates from the astounding discovery that locomotives could haul trains uphill, the following contemporary account from the *Railroad Journal* of July 30, 1836, of a trial trip made by Norris with his locomotive Washington at the request of D. K. Minor, the editor of the *Journal,* may be of interest:

WHEN RAILROADS WERE NEW

" In pursuance of our request Mr. Norris made arrangements with the Commissioners of the Columbia Railroad for the use of his locomotive. Tuesday, July 19 [the first trial had been made on July 9 when the Washington ascended the plane with a trainload of 19,200 pounds in 2 minutes and one second], was the day appointed for the trial.

" We left New York Monday afternoon at 4 o'clock, accompanied by Mr. George N. Miner, of New York; Theo. Schwartz, of Paris, and Messrs. Elliot and Betts, of Alabama. Mr. Schwartz, who was to sail to Europe next day, gladly made the trip with a view to carrying home his testimony as an eye witness. Our journey over the Camden and Amboy and Trenton and Philadelphia Railroads was highly interesting and the conversation of the evening will long be remembered with pleasure. We arrived at Philadelphia about midnight, and after sundry mistakes and mischances succeeded in obtaining some repose.

" On Tuesday morning two cars drawn by horses set out with a party of upwards of forty. We arrived at the foot of the inclined plane before 6 o'clock while the rails were yet quite wet with the dew. On our arrival it was found that by accident or design, while the fire was burning the water had been blown out of the boiler so as to endanger the tubes. The result was a leakage of some consequence during the day.

" The engine started at the foot of the plane and on the plane. After proceeding a few feet the wheels were found to slip and the engine returned. It was said that the rails were found to have been oiled at this place; but a small quantity of sand was strewn on the spot and the engine proceeded. She regularly and steadily gained speed as she advanced to the very top, passing over the plane in 2 minutes and 24 seconds.

" The enthusiasm of feeling manifested cannot be described. So complete a triumph had never been obtained. The doubts that had been entertained by some and the fears of others were dispelled in an instant. The eager look that settled upon every one's face gave way to that of confident success while all present expressed their gratification in loud and repeated cheers.

"The length of the plane is 2,800 feet; the grade 369 feet to the mile, or 1 foot rise in 14.3 feet, which is a much steeper grade than the planes on the Mohawk and Hudson Railroad, those being 1 foot in 18, making an ascent of 196 feet in 2,800. The weight of the engine with water was 14,930 pounds; the load drawn up the plane, including the tender with coal and water, two passenger cars with 53 passengers, was 31,270 pounds; steam pressure less than eighty pounds to the square inch; time of run 2 minutes, 24 seconds. It is to be remembered that the rails were wet with dew. As to the oil, it was afterwards mentioned that bets were made with the workmen to a considerable amount and those having been lost by the successful performance of the engine on a former day were quadrupled, and to save themselves it is not unlikely that this means was provided to accelerate the descent rather than the ascent of the engine.

"The party again embarked after examining the workshops and proceeded to Paoli for breakfast and thence to Lancaster, the engine conveying at the same time a number of freight cars. The unfortunate location of this road is very evident; frequent and short curves are introduced so uniformly that it would be supposed that such a location was to be preferred to a direct one.

"We arrived at Lancaster and partook of an excellent dinner. After dinner the company were presented to Governor Ritner, who was then in town. He afterwards accompanied the party some few miles from Lancaster when he left us much gratified with his rapid journey. We returned in an eight-wheeled car, a form that we much admired. The whole weight attached to the engine, tender and so forth included, must have been over fourteen tons. The time of the run, exclusive of stoppage, from Lancaster to the head of the Schuylkill inclined plane, was 3 hours, 11 minutes, being a distance of 76 miles. This, it is to be remembered, was over a road having curvatures of less than six hundred feet radius, up ascents of sometimes 45 feet to the mile. On level and straight portions of the road a velocity of forty-seven miles an hour was attained. As the trip had already been protracted this engine was obliged to leave on her return to Lancaster the same evening and we descended by the rope. We returned to the city about 8 o'clock in the evening convinced of the success of our host, Mr. Norris, and having in the language of one of our party ' lived six days in one.'

" The following are the dimensions of the George Washington engine of William Norris: diameter of cylinders, 10 1-4 inches; length of stroke, 17 5-8 inches; number of tubes, 78; outside diameter of tubes, 2 inches; length of tubes, 7 feet; diameter of driving wheels, 4 feet; diameter of truck wheels, 30 inches; whole weight of engine, 14,930 pounds; actual weight on drivers, 8,700 pounds. It must be remembered that there is no contrivance, as in some engines, for increasing the adhesion by throwing the weight of the tender upon the engines, the axle being in front of the firebox, preventing any such arrangement. This engine, we are informed, is making the regular trips, though a full load has not yet been obtained on account of a scarcity of cars. The greatest load as yet drawn by it over the road was one hundred and nineteen tons gross weight in twenty-two cars."

This account was accompanied by a certificate signed by fifty-three passengers attesting the fact that they had actually been drawn up the inclined plane as described. Soon afterward Norris built the " Washington County Farmer," weighing 18,170 pounds, for the Commonwealth of Pennsylvania, which was tested on the same plane, according to the

National Gazette of October 19, 1836, " to the complete satisfaction of numerous scientific gentlemen invited expressly for the occasion." The time required for the ascent was 3 minutes and 15 seconds. In descending, the engineer, according to the same authority, repeatedly " came to a dead stand from a great speed, and for some minutes played up and down the grade, thus proving most satisfactorily the great power of the engine and the perfect safety in its performance. The engine is a masterpiece of machinery and of beautiful exterior. The result here obtained has never been equaled by the best engines in this country or Europe, excepting only similar performances of the George Washington engine by the same maker. The advantage of this great improvement in locomotives is self-evident. Railroads can be constructed at much less cost than heretofore now that engines can be procured to perform on grades of seventy feet or even a hundred feet rise in the mile."

So little did the general public understand what a locomotive could do or should be that a genius named French actually induced the legislature of Virginia to appropriate a sum of money as late as 1850 to make a practical test of his locomotive for wooden railroads. French had observed that wooden rails would not answer the purpose because the weight of the locomotives broke and splintered them. As he was convinced that wooden rails were much better than iron, and as he had found that beech and maple rails would last five years or more under favorable conditions, the problem was to adapt the locomotive to the rails and not the rails to the locomotive. He did this by means of horizontal driving wheels, which, by means of a lever, were made to grip a wooden third rail in the middle of the track. As these horizontal driving wheels held the locomotive on the track, the necessity for flanges on the wheels was thus done away with and another source of destruction to wooden rails avoided. George E. Sellers, of Cincinnati, also invented a "gripping" locomotive that found many advocates.

An equally brilliant design for cars that could not upset was evolved by one Lawrence Meyers, of Pottsville, Pa., a year later. It was alleged that the Meyers car won the approval of President John Tucker, of the Reading Railroad. Meyers' car consisted of a cylinder of wrought iron 42 inches in diameter, on each end of which a wheel 52 inches was riveted so that it would roll along the track. The cylinder was to be filled with coal, of which it would hold two tons. Several of these cylinders being connected by means of a wooden frame were to constitute a "Revolver train."

When it came to passing the Alleghanies, the engineer laid out a succession of ten inclined planes with "levels" between, on which the grades were not heavy enough to require the employment of a hoisting engine and cable. The total length of the Portage road was thirty-six miles.

The summit was 1,398 feet above the eastern canal basin, and 1,171 feet above the western, and 2,326 above sea-level. The longest of these planes was 3,116 feet, and the rise was 307 feet. The most conspicuous features of the road were the Conemaugh Viaduct, eight miles east of Johnstown, which was destroyed by the great flood of May 31, 1889, and the Staple Bend tunnel, nine hundred feet long, four miles east of Johnstown. This was the first tunnel built in America.

The engines for operating these planes had two cylinders fourteen inches in diameter by sixty inches stroke, made fourteen revolutions a minute, and at a steam pressure of seventy pounds developed about thirty-five horse-power. They hauled cars up the planes at the rate of four miles an hour, by means of ropes eight inches in diameter and from 3,316 feet to 6,662 feet long. These ropes were the cause of considerable outlay, since they cost on an average three thousand dollars and lasted only about sixteen months.

Toward the last John A. Roebling, the great bridge builder, induced the Board of Canal Commissioners to experiment with wire cable. The first trials were not satisfactory, but a little investigation showed how to overcome all difficulties, and then wire displaced hemp.

To run each of these planes required an engineer at $2.00 a day, a fireman at $1.12½, and a man at top and bottom at $1.00 per day to attach and detach the cars. On reaching a level, horses or a locomotive would be attached and the cars hauled to the next level on a road laid with malleable iron rails imported from Wales.

The use of horses was found wasteful, expensive, slow, and unsatisfactory, so before the second track was finished the Board had ordered a first instalment of a couple of locomotives. But the use of horses by individual transporters continued until 1850, with the same results as on the Philadelphia and Columbia Railroad.

No two teamsters wanted to start at the same time, and no two were willing to stop at the same place to feed. These teamsters were an exceedingly difficult lot of men to handle. They were rough, quarrelsome, stubborn, and unmanageable, fearing neither man nor fiend. It was impossible to get them to regulate their movements by a time table. The officers of the road had no power to discharge them or keep them off the road, so they worked their own sweet will, for was not the railroad a public highway provided by the State, and were they not as good citizens as any other man, if not better?

It sometimes happened that a teamster would get stalled so that he could not go forward. Being too stubborn to go back, he would stay where he was, blocking the entire road, perhaps for hours, until a better man came along and thrashed him into a reasonable frame of mind. Theoretically an unruly teamster could be arrested for obstructing the railroad and taken before a magistrate, who might fine him. But as the magistrates were miles away, and an arrest meant a fight first, such extreme measures were not often resorted to.

When the road was first opened it had but a single track. In order to keep it in operation at all it was necessary to set up center posts half-way between turnouts and make a rule that the man who passed the center post had the right to proceed in case of meeting a team going in the opposite direction, which would have to go back to a turnout. This caused the drivers, who were always reluctant to turn back, and never did so if they could bully the other fellow who had the right of way into doing so, to start slowly in leaving a turnout so they might not have to return so far. As they proceeded they would increase their speed until by the time they reached the center post the horses would be going at a wild gallop, with drivers plying the lash, shouting, and swearing. Sometimes cars collided near a center post while going at high speed, wrecking both cars and tying up traffic until the wreckage could be cleared away. In one of these collisions a man was killed.

Even after the road was double-tracked the situation became so intolerable that S. W. Roberts, the chief engineer, determined to have conditions changed if possible. A change could only be brought about by legislation, which was not easy to obtain. The State was Democratic, and the methods then in use of allowing every man to do as he pleased were considered to be the popular way to operate a railroad. The proposal to exclude private transporters from the Portage Railroad and operate it by the State met with the most vehement opposition, both from the public and the legislature. Roberts finally had his way when he won Thaddeus Stevens, who bossed the Pennsylvania legislature as he afterwards did Congress, to his view of the way a railroad should be operated. The average load on the cars was six thousand pounds, and the cost of moving freight over the Portage road averaged ninety-six cents a ton. Five minutes were consumed in going up or down the longest plane, and three minutes more were required to attach and detach the cars.

The limit of capacity was five hundred and seventy-six cars one way in twenty-four hours. In the six months ending October 31, 1836, 19,171 passengers and 37,087 tons of freight passed over the Portage road.

Charles Dickens made a trip over the Portage road in 1842, and was delighted with the experience, which he describes in his " American Notes." But, then, Dickens was not accustomed to Pullmans. If he had been, he would hardly have been enraptured with a journey that consumed seven hours in traversing thirty-six miles.

With the Portage road open it was possible to make the journey of 395 miles from Philadelphia to Pittsburg, on public works, 118 miles being by rail and 277 on canals, in 91 hours, or an average of 4.34 miles an hour. The fare was fifteen dollars. In both time and expense even this was a decided advance on the stage coach, which required seven days to make the trip, and cost the passenger twenty dollars for fare and eight dollars and twenty-one cents for meals en route. For twenty years the Pennsylvania Public Improvements were an important trade route.

Some time after the Portage road was opened an emigrant, who had loaded his family and all his earthly possessions on a boat on the Susquehanna, arrived at Hollidaysburg on his way to Missouri. He was going to sell his boat and continue his journey as best he could; but the accommodating superintendent of the Portage Railroad told him to wait a minute, and he'd see what he could do.

In a couple of hours he had rigged up a sort of cradle on a couple of cars, which were run into the water under the boat. The latter was fastened to the cars, which were attached to the cable, and away went boat, emigrant, and all over the mountains. In due time the boat was deposited in the canal at Johnstown.

This incident led to the building of canal boats in sections and of trucks to transport the sections over the mountains, thus avoiding the expense and delay of breaking bulk on each side of the mountains. To move one of these sectional boats over the mountains required the services of twelve stationary engines, twelve different teams of horses, nine locomotives—thirty-three changes of power in thirty-six miles—and fifty-four men.

While this line from Philadelphia to Pittsburgh was being constructed, the link which was to extend the line to New York was being evolved out of a chaos of conflicting interests and financial difficulties. New Jersey was just as much wrought up over the relative merits of canals and railroads as any other commonwealth.

In fact, it reached a point in the winter of 1829-1830 at Trenton when partisans of either side were afraid to venture out after dark unarmed. The legislature poured oil on the stormy waters by chartering simultaneously the Camden and Amboy Railroad and the Delaware and Raritan Canal to open communication between Philadelphia and New York.

In order that the companies might be able to offer inducements to capital the legislature granted each a monopoly in its own line of construction.

Grading on the railroad was begun at Bordentown, December 1, 1830. That made the canal people jealous, and in spite of all pledges to keep to their own specialty they insisted on building a railroad also. There was another battle of the lobby at the legislative session of 1830-1831, which was so virulent as to endanger the existence of both companies.

This contest also ended in a compromise by which the two companies were merged under the famous " marriage act " of February 15, 1831.

Enough track was laid to enable the company to give an exhibition trip November 12, 1831, behind one of the many John Bull locomotives,* which were almost as numerous as Washington's headquarters. The first woman who ever rode on a railroad on New Jersey soil was a guest on this occasion. She was Mme. Murat, wife of Prince Murat, Napoleon's nephew.

* Of the numerous " John Bull " locomotives, this one, the oldest complete locomotive in America, has at last come to be known as *the* John Bull. It is not a model nor a reproduction but the original engine. The picture on the opposite page is from a photograph made at the World's Columbian Exposition in 1893.

Originally the John Bull was locomotive No. 1 built by Stephenson & Co. in 1830-1 for the Camden and Amboy Railroad, now a part of the Pennsylvania system. It was shipped from Liverpool July 14, 1831, and made its first trip in regular service November 12, 1831.

The John Bull and its train was exhibited at the Centennial Exposition in Philadelphia in 1876. On April 17, 1893, the engine with train, as shown in the picture, left New York City under its own steam and made the run of 912 miles over the Pennsylvania Railroad to Chicago, meeting with a continuous ovation throughout the trip, and arriving April 22. It was one of the greatest attractions at the World's Fair, carrying thousands of passengers over the exhibition tracks in the Terminal Station yard. The locomotive left Chicago under its own steam again December 6, 1893, going over the Pennsylvania system by way of Harrisburg and Baltimore to Washington. Having made its last trip under steam it was returned to the United States National Museum to remain there permanently.

The two Camden and Amboy coaches shown are of the model of 1836. One is the original car, the body of which was used as a chicken coop at South Amboy, N. J., for many years.

By courtesy of the Pennsylvania Railroad.

THE "JOHN BULL," BUILT IN 1831, AND COACHES, BUILT IN 1836.

Mme. Murat was the daughter of Colonel Frazier, a Scotch officer who, while serving in the British army in the Revolution, fell madly in love with a beautiful Virginia girl, and returned and married her as soon as he could give up his commission.

The directors of the New Jersey Railroad and Transportation Company issued an address on January 1, 1839, in which they congratulated themselves and the public on the opening of an all-rail line from Camden to Jersey City, by which it was possible to go from Philadelphia to New York in six or seven hours with almost as much comfort as the traveler could have at his own fireside, whereas the journey had formerly required eleven to twenty hours, and had been made at the expense of great discomfort and even hazard to life.

Another important link in the State system of railroads, destined later to become a part of the great Pennsylvania system, was the Cumberland Valley Railroad, which was formally opened from Harrisburg to Chambersburg, Thursday, November 16, 1837. A double-header was run over the road to accommodate the great number of guests.

Shouts of welcome greeted the train at every revolution of the wheels. The people were wild with delight. Here is the way the Carlisle *Republican* described the trip of that first train:

" Dogs dropped their tails between their legs and ran like frightened fiends, howling and trembling, to the far-off mountains. Men there were who cleared ditches and fences at a single bound as the hissing engines approached. Others rolled on the ground and cracked their heels together to express in a new way a new delight.

" Old men and women leaned on their staffs and gazed in visible awe as if doomsday were at hand. Blooming maidens capered and danced and looked with more delight on the grim and besooted countenance of the steam demon than ever they did on clean-washed lovers dressed in Sunday clothes."

While the Board of Canal Commissioners was publishing assurances that the system of canals and railroads built under its direction, at an expenditure of nearly twenty million dollars, placed Pennsylvania on an eminence where there could be no apprehension of rivalry from sister States, the people were growing more and more dissatisfied.

The management of the State railroads and canals had become a public scandal. The paymaster openly counted out ten per cent of the wages of the employees, which he tossed into a bag at his side labeled " political assessments." Gravel trains loaded with men were run over the road on election day, the men getting off at every town and voting.

The public service was fairly swamped with employees whose chief duties were to draw their salaries and vote. Transporters who refused to do the bidding of the party in power were ruined, while the more complaisant received rebates equal to the amount of the tolls they had paid.

The pass system originated in Pennsylvania under State ownership of the railroads. At first the State officials claimed the right to travel over the State highways free of charge. Then county officials claimed the same right, then politicians were unable to see why they should pay, and so it went on until more deadheads than paying passengers were being carried.

THE PENNSYLVANIA RAILROAD

Thaddeus Stevens, who had been so apprehensive of the dangers of putting locomotives on the State railroads on account of the patronage they would place in control of the party in power, on being made chairman of the Board of Canal Commissioners at once proceeded to demonstrate that his fears were well founded.

He owned some iron lands in the southern part of the State to which he undertook to build a railroad, which was so wildly impracticable and so devious that it is known in history as " Stevens's tapeworm." He spent three-quarters of a million dollars of State money on it before he was deposed, not one dollar of which was ever of any earthly benefit to the State.

But the worst of it all was that the State was not reaping the commercial benefits expected. In addition to mismanagement the canals were frozen over and useless in winter. Philadelphia, as well as other parts of the State, was steadily falling behind.

A mass-meeting was held in the Chinese Museum building, Philadelphia, December 10, 1845, at which a memorial was prepared asking the legislature to charter a private railroad corporation to build a railroad system that would be up with the times.

There was a savage fight in the legislature that winter, for the Baltimore and Ohio wanted to build to Pittsburgh, and the people of the southern and western parts of the State, who felt that they had been badly treated by the State Board, favored the Baltimore and Ohio project.

The outcome was a charter for both roads, but the Governor was authorized to give preference to the Pennsylvania Company if it should have one million dollars in the treasury and thirty miles under contract by July 30, 1847, by annulling the charter of the Baltimore and Ohio.

The Pennsylvania Railroad Company was organized March 31, 1847, and J. Edgar Thomson, son of the man who had built the little wooden railroad thirty-eight years before, was made chief engineer and general manager. Ground was broken for the Pennsylvania Railroad at Harrisburg, its eastern terminus, July 7, 1847. Connection was made with the Portage Railroad, November 1, 1850.

Trains were run from Philadelphia to Pittsburgh, December 10, 1852, by the Philadelphia and Columbia Railroad and the Alleghany Portage Railroad. A line through the mountains, to cut out the Portage road, was not completed till February 2, 1854.

As soon as the engineering difficulties were solved and the construction department was running smoothly, Thomson was called to the president's chair to create an effective working organization.

Mr. Thomson was a man of splendid physique and a tireless worker. He talked little, but was a good listener. Above all, he had the gift of selecting the right man to do a given task.

A remarkable example of this is shown in his choice of a man to establish that discipline and *esprit de corps* for which the Pennsylvania System is so famous that to this day it is held up by many as the apotheosis of all that is desirable in a railroad staff.

This work fell upon General A. L. Roumfort, who was born in Paris, educated at West Point, had conducted a military school in which some of the most prominent men of their time were educated, had been a member of the legislature for several terms, and finally had filled the position of superintendent of the Philadelphia and Columbia Railroad. He was six feet tall and built in proportion. He had a military bearing and dignified manner.

His first task was to create an orderly baggage system out of the chaos at Aqueduct and Harrisburg. During the spring freshets swarms of raftsmen passed over the road, leaving at Aqueduct to proceed up the Susquehanna. They were rough, boisterous, and lawless. Their baggage consisted of stoves, pots, pans, rope, carpet-bags, bundles of clothing, and provisions and chests.

General Roumfort's appearance commanded respect and obedience. He established order at Aqueduct and he created system where confusion had reigned in the baggage department. He attempted to uniform the trainmen. Passenger conductors were required to appear in blue cutaway coats with brass buttons, buff vests, and black trousers, and passengers brakemen in gray sack suits; but the plan was not popular and when the first suits wore out they were not replaced until the Civil War had earned respect for uniforms.

General Roumfort's favorite seat in fair weather was on a corner of the second-story porch of the old station at Harrisburg, where he could hear the whistle of the approaching trains.

There was a bell in a little tower on the top of the depot, which was rung to announce the arrival and departure of trains. As soon as the whistle was heard General Roumfort's sonorous voice would wake the echoes.

" Billie! O Bil-lie! Ring that bell."

When the " tub," the first through train between Harrisburg and Philadelphia, was put on, the general sent for William Wolf and Benjamin Kennedy, the engineers who were to take the run. Both men were undersized. The general thus addressed them:

" Now, boys, you are going to run through to Philadelphia over a strange road. When you leave Columbia you will have a steep grade to Mountsville. See that you have a good supply of water in the boiler. Also instruct your firemen to have in a good fire for the Gap grade.

" When you reach Downingtown instruct your firemen to have a good fire for the Byers hill, thirteen miles to Paoli. Now, you two little engineers, run along to your two little engines and see that you make time."

The choice of Thomas A. Scott as superintendent of the western division was equally felicitous. The road was not finished to Pittsburg when Scott took up his duties there. Pittsburg had wanted the Baltimore and Ohio Railroad, and the city had waxed extremely hostile when that road's charter had been annulled.

But Scott handled the situation with such consummate diplomacy that he not only allayed all animosity but actually secured one million dollars for the Pennsylvania and many valuable franchises and privileges besides.

Diplomacy was quite as much needed as engineering skill in the first stages of the Pennsylvania Railroad. At first the company was not permitted to run its trains over the Philadelphia and Columbia Railroad. When it was granted this boon it could not run its own comfortable cars, because the tracks were too close together, and the roof of the Elizabethtown tunnel was too low.

Individual transporters were still doing business on the State road, and their operations sadly interfered with the development of the transportation business the new road needed. But too radical or too sudden a change would have aroused public opposition which would have been disastrous.

The difficulty was solved by the purchase of the main line of the public works by the Pennsylvania Railroad Company for seven million five hundred thousand dollars, possession being given by the State August 1, 1857. The first through train from Philadelphia to Pittsburg without transfer of passengers was run July 18, 1858. On the same day smoking-cars were first run on through trains and Woodruff's sleeping-cars on the night trains.

The Pennsylvania Railroad was now fully launched. Its development was so rapid that when the Civil War began, three years later, it was in a position to do the nation a great service, not only on its own rails, but also by supplying skilled and disciplined executive and operating men to the Government.

December 1, 1871, it acquired by lease for nine hundred and ninety-nine years the line to Jersey City, and six years later had a double track in operation across the State of Pennsylvania. It had long since acquired lines to Chicago, St. Louis, and the Central West, the westward extension being greatly accelerated through the kind assistance of Jay Gould. It cannot be truthfully said, though, that the Pennsylvania was at all grateful to the great manipulator.

The Pennsylvania had been encouraging by financial assistance and otherwise the development of a chain of little railroads between Pittsburg and Chicago, which was afterwards welded into the Pittsburg, Fort Wayne and Chicago. The Pennsylvania, however, was satisfied with a traffic arrangement and did not attempt actual possession.

When Gould, after establishing himself as the master of the Erie, began reaching out right and left for every railroad property that was lying around loose, other managements were thrown into a panic. Before the Pennsylvania could recover its self-possession sufficiently to profit by the object lesson Gould had given, that astute operator had secured possession of a majority of the stock of the Pittsburgh, Fort Wayne and Chicago. An election for directors was to be held in March, 1869, when he would have established himself securely in the management of a line that was absolutely essential to the continued prosperity of the Pennsylvania, had not that road established a world's legislative record by securing the passage of a bill by both houses of the Pennsylvania legislature and its signature by the Governor in thirty-four minutes by the clock on February 3, 1869. This was the famous " classification bill," which divided the board of directors of the Fort Wayne road into three classes in such a way that it would require three years to elect a majority. This was too slow for Gould, and he withdrew. After such a narrow escape the Pennsylvania lost no time in securing its Western extension against the possibility of any such embarrassing complications in future.

The same zeal was displayed in adopting improvements and in extending the system and perfecting organization. The Pennsylvania Railroad was the first to use steel rails, in 1863; the first to use Bessemer steel rails, in 1865; the first to adopt the airbrake, in 1866; the track tank, in 1872, and the signal block-system, in 1873.

When the semi-centennial of the company was celebrated in Philadelphia, April 13, 1896, President Roberts was able to report as a net result of all these endeavors that the Pennsylvania Railroad comprised 138 separate railroads, representing what were originally 256 separate corporations with 9,000 miles of main line having an aggregate capital of $834,000,-000, an army of 104,000 employees, who received $59,000,000 in wages annually, and that the company, in its existence of fifty years, had paid $166,-000,000 in dividends.

CHAPTER V

GENESIS OF THE VANDERBILT SYSTEM

"TICKETS, please!"

As Master of Transportation John T. Clark uttered this phrase for the first time on the first train on the first railroad in the Empire State, on the morning of August 9, 1831, the spectators, who had been poking their fingers into the mechanism of the first locomotive, abandoned that diversion and pressed toward the speaker to witness the exciting operation of taking up tickets.

That first collection of tickets was made in a distinctly open-and-aboveboard, public style. The train was standing on the crest of a hill on the outskirts of Albany, where it had awaited its first load of passengers, for the excellent reason that it did not dare to venture down for them.

In those days locomotive builders thought they were doing pretty well to evolve a machine that would move on level ground, without attempting to climb hills. So, the passengers were hauled up an inclined plane with a total lift of one hundred and eighty-five feet above the valley of the Hudson, on little platform cars drawn by a cable operated by a twelve-horse-power engine, on exactly the same plan that is used to-day on the Otis Elevating Railway in the Catskills.

The first passengers, having bought their tickets

From a photograph at the World's Columbian Exposition in 1893. By courtesy of the New York Central Railroad.

THE "DE WITT CLINTON" AND TRAIN.

The first train in the State of New York. Operated in 1831 between Albany and Schenectady.

at the hotels the night before, found themselves objects of the admiration and envy of several hundred persons who had assembled to see the start of the first train on the Mohawk and Hudson Railroad. The only contemporaneous pictorial representation extant of that historic first train was cut out of black paper with a pair of scissors by the famous silhouette artist, W. H. Brown.

Because Mr. Brown ran short of paper, his silhouette represents only the engine—the " De Witt Clinton "—and two coaches, but in reality there were five coaches. Those first cars were literally coaches—stage coaches mounted on flanged wheels to enable them to run on rails, and coupled together with three long links between each two coaches.

The foremost two were reserved for the more distinguished passengers, while the others were provided with planks for seats, in order to accommodate as many as possible of those who wished to risk their necks in experimenting with the new mode of travel. Although the coaches were packed like an electric trolley-car in the rush hours, several hundred who wished to make the trip were left behind for lack of accommodation.

The engine had but one occupant—Dave Matthews, the mechanic who had built the machine at the West Point Foundry, in New York City, from plans drawn by John B. Jervis, the chief engineer of the road, and had brought it to Albany and set it up, laboring night and day to induce the thing to run. He had had trouble enough in doing it, too, for about everything went wrong that could do so.

The work of building began April 1, 1831. It

was shipped up the Hudson on June 25, and a week later Matthews had steam up.   The De Witt Clinton was eleven feet six inches long, weighed 6,758 pounds, had two cylinders five and a half by sixteen inches, and four wooden driving wheels with iron tires four feet six inches in diameter.

The boiler held 115 gallons of water and carried a steam pressure of fifty pounds.   The locomotive was expected to develop ten horse-power and to be able to haul fifteen tons on the level at a speed of fifteen miles an hour.   It could be pushed along readily by the pressure of one hand.

When Matthews raised steam for the first time his troubles began.   In the first place, the chimney was too large, and the ends of the exhaust-pipes—they hadn't got around to nozzles yet—were placed so low down that they couldn't get a draft; so, some rebuilding had to be done at once.

When the Clinton was given its second trial the water surged over into the cylinders, threatening to knock them to pieces, as the engine bobbed over the rough track.   A dome was built, and trouble number two was overcome.

The Clinton was planned for anthracite, but the coal packed and wouldn't burn at all until a steam-blower was put on, and then the grates were burned out, so they had to fall back on pitch-pine as the fuel for that first trip with passengers.

Yet, with all its faults, the De Witt Clinton, the third locomotive built on American soil, was a pretty good machine, for it developed a capacity for getting over the road with something more than its rated load and considerably more than its anticipated speed that formed an agreeable contrast to the performances of locomotives imported from England.

Two weeks after the Clinton was placed in service, the Mohawk and Hudson Company received a locomotive called the " Robert Fulton," from George Stephenson, the famous English railroad builder, weighing twelve thousand seven hundred and forty-two pounds, double the weight of the Clinton. Stephenson sent a letter with the Fulton, in which he said:

" As to the power of this engine, it will take twenty tons without difficulty, but with twelve tons it will be much better. The small inclination of 1 in 225 will affect the motion of the engine very little."

As a matter of fact, the Fulton quickly demonstrated its inability to pull twelve tons or any other weight. Being assigned to pull an excursion train to take the Governor, Lieutenant-Governor, State Senators, Congressmen, members of the New York City Council, the mayor of Albany, and other distinguished guests over the road one day in the latter part of August, the Fulton broke down, and the party was hauled to Schenectady and back by the Clinton, with three coaches and in seven other cars, the latter drawn each by a single horse.

Having collected the tickets on this first run of the Clinton by walking from coach to coach and climbing up on the steps, Master of Transportation (long since degenerated into conductor) Clark walked forward to the little platform car which, being laden with a cask of water and a few sticks of wood, fulfilled the function of tender, and seating himself, drew from a pocket a tin horn, on which he blew a long blast.

At this signal Matthews opened the throttle with a suddenness that almost caused the Clinton to jump off the rails. To tell the truth, he had secret misgivings about his ability to start the load, and he meant to take no chances. Besides, there was no superintendent to lecture him on the importance of handling his passengers gently.

The result of those tactics, with so much slack between the coaches, can be imagined. There was a violent jerk on each coach in succession, which almost snapped the passengers' heads off as boys jerk the heads off snakes by swinging them by the tails. Many a beaver rolled into the ditch or on to the coach floor, and not a few of the passengers sprawled after them.

But as the Clinton moved on at an increasing speed the jerks gradually tapered off into a steady pull as the cheers of the admiring spectators died away in the distance. By the time the passengers dared draw a long breath and look about them, they found themselves in the midst of new tribulations.

Matthews had tinkered with the exhaust and the smoke-stack until he had produced a pretty strong draft. The result was that a steady stream of pitch-pine cinders, from the size of a pin-head to that of a man's thumb-nail, poured back upon the passengers, and particularly those on the roofs.

Umbrellas were raised as a protection, but they burned up like so much tinder, and before a mile was passed the ruins of the last umbrella had been pitched overboard. Meanwhile, there was wild confusion as the clothing of one passenger after another burst into a blaze, which his neighbors scrambled frantically to put out.

Five miles from Albany the first stop was made to the accompaniment of a succession of violent bumps and jerks like those which marked the start. Clark and some of the passengers raided a fence near the track to procure rails, which were lashed to the coupling-chains with some of Matthews' supply of packing-yarn to stop the jerking by holding the coaches rigidly apart.

After this improved coupling had been devised the inside passengers and Master of Transportation Clark, who was hugging himself with joy because he was so near the engine that the sparks flew over him, were better able to enjoy the fun.

The flight of that first train had been pretty well advertised, and the whole countryside had turned out to see it. Farmers, with their families and their wives' relations, had driven over to the road in lumber-wagons, light wagons, and all sorts of conveyances, and being naturally desirous of obtaining a good view, had driven up as close to the track as they could get. The track for nearly the entire distance from Albany to Schenectady was lined with farmers' rigs like the infield fence at a race-course.

When the engine came snorting along, the horses, with their noses close enough to the track to touch the monster as it came along, did what any self-respecting horses might be expected to do under such circumstances—that is, they reared, snorted, shied, and ended by running away. The result was a grand stampede all along the line, which strewed the right-of-way with prostrate forms and débris until it looked like a battle-field at the close of a great conflict.

Schenectady, the western terminus of the road, sixteen miles from Albany, was reached in forty-six minutes. The train stopped at the top of a hill, the passengers were lowered down an inclined plane with a lift of one hundred and fifteen feet, and the first railroad trip in New York was at an end. There was a great celebration, with music, cannon salutes, processions, and speech-making, closing with a dinner in the evening, at which C. C. Cambreleng, the general manager of the road, with the title of agent, proposed this toast:

"The Buffalo Railroad: May we soon breakfast at Utica, dine at Rochester, and sup with our friends on Lake Erie."

His wish was granted at an early date.

The passengers on that first train returned to their homes to find themselves almost as great heroes as the veterans of the Revolution. They told the story of their wonderful experiences over and over, and their stories didn't shrink a bit from frequent reiteration, either. Soon the railroad fever was spreading through the State like measles in a boarding-school.

Sixty days after the De Witt Clinton's first trip a single issue of the Albany *Argus* contained notices of intention to file applications for charters for railroad companies with an aggregate capital of twenty-two million dollars. Matters came to such a pass that when a man went away from home he was ashamed to register from his own town unless it had a railroad enterprise mapped out.

The legislature which met in the January succeeding the opening of the Mohawk and Hudson Railroad was confronted with no fewer than forty-nine applications for railroad charters.

At the session of 1836 fifty-eight railroad charters were granted or renewed. The Assemblyman who could not take home at least one railroad charter from Albany need expect no further political favors from his outraged constituents. Up to 1849 one hundred and fifty-one separate railroads had been chartered in New York. Fortunately, but thirty of these lines were ever built. In that year the legislature, in self-defense, delegated its chartering powers to the Secretary of State, and was thus enabled to devote some time to other public business.

As early as 1840 the State had dipped into its treasury to the extent of $3,478,000 to help poor but worthy railroads. No fewer than fifty railroad companies have received cash gifts from the people of New York through the State and local governments. Of these, ten companies received cash aid direct from the State treasury aggregating $10,060,591, while two hundred and ninety-four cities, towns, and villages contributed $29,978,905 more, making a grand total of $40,039,496 as a free gift toward the total value of the $500,000,000 worth of railroad property in the State.

At all events the popular attitude toward railroads now afforded an interesting contrast to the apathy with which the proposal to build the Mohawk and Hudson, the first railroad in New York, was received. The charter for this road was granted February 28, 1826, upon the application of Stephen Van Rensselaer, of Albany, and George W. Featherstonhaugh, of Duanesburgh. There was not a railroad in the country then; but as the petitioners asked no favors from the State, but professed their willingness to pay the cost of the experiment themselves, the legislature saw no harm in granting the desired permission. Stock in the enterprise proving unsalable, the legislature was asked two years later to modify some of the conditions on which the charter was granted.

The messages of Governor Clinton in 1827 and 1828, and of Governor Van Buren in 1829 and 1830, had not a word to say on the subject of railroads. Governor Throop in 1831 referred in his message to the opening of the Liverpool and Manchester Railroad in England, and hazarded the opinion that a railroad across the State might be found useful in winter when the canal was frozen up.

Early in September, 1831, a convention at Buffalo addressed a circular to the State at large urging that immediate steps be taken for the construction of a railroad from Lake Erie to the Hudson River. It was argued that such a road, instead of injuring the Erie Canal, would benefit it by relieving it of passenger and light freight traffic, thus leaving it free to handle exclusively the heavy freight to which it was particularly adapted. Buffalo, Rochester, and Syracuse united in a great convention at the latter place October 12, 1831, in furtherance of the project. At this great mass-meeting a committee was appointed to apply for a charter for a company with a capital of five million dollars to build the road. Four railroad charters were granted by the legislature that winter.

Despite the desire for a through railroad from Albany to Buffalo, experienced most keenly by the towns which had sprung up along the Erie Canal, its construction was not begun as a single undertaking, but in a desultory way as an aggregation of disconnected fragments, the first link being the Mohawk and Hudson from Albany, sixteen miles to Schenectady. The next link bridged the gap of seventy-eight miles from Schenectady to Utica.

As public opinion grew enlightened through discussion, people became ready, and even eager, to back their schemes with their own money. The Syracuse and Utica Railroad is a striking instance in this connection.

The company was chartered May 11, 1836, to build fifty-three miles of road to connect the towns of Syracuse and Utica. The capital stock was eight hundred thousand dollars. Within two weeks after the books were opened subscriptions were recorded totaling two million five hundred thousand dollars.

This Syracuse and Utica Railroad was remarkable in many ways. Interesting features cropped up from the moment the scheme was broached. While every one concerned wanted the road, they could not agree on the route it should take. One faction favored a direct route south of the Erie Canal; another was determined to have it built on a northern route, which was much longer. Utica fought desperately for the longer route because that would necessitate a transfer through the town by omnibus and wagon from the proposed eastern connection, and Utica wanted things arranged so passengers would have to stay over night at its hotels. A formidable lobby descended on Albany. The legislature neatly sidestepped embarrassing alliances by directing that the road should be built " by the most available route."

The lucky ones who obtained stock paid in their money promptly, surveys were made at once, and the line was completed and opened for traffic fourteen months after the contracts were let, at a cost of one hundred thousand dollars less than the capital.

The pile system of construction invented by E. P. Williams, of Utica, was used. This was supposed to be a great improvement on the stone blocks used in the Mohawk and Hudson. Piles first soaked in salt to prevent rotting were driven to a depth of from twenty-five to thirty feet by splicing them.

Most of the way was through marshy ground and heavy timber. On top of the piles longitudinal stringers were laid, tied together at intervals of twenty feet by cross-pieces. On top of the stringers were laid " ribbon pieces."

According to the contract, these ribbon pieces were to be of " white oak, free from wain, sap, and knots, one and one-half by three inches, and ten to fifteen feet long." On top of these ribbon pieces the iron strap-rail was spiked.

The first train from Utica arrived at Rome on Thursday, June 27, 1839, when the editor of the Rome *Sentinel* boasted that he had achieved the re- markable feat of shaking hands in the streets of his own town with men who had left Utica forty-five minutes before.

In the afternoon the train continued its journey to Syracuse. There was great excitement—cheering multitudes, booming cannon, speech-making, and dining.

On the same principle that the inventor of a new breakfast food sends out demonstrators to distribute free samples of his product, the management of the Syracuse and Utica Railroad gave free sample rides for the rest of the week to all who could find room to hang on to its trains.

Business was pretty generally suspended along the road for that week while the population satisfied its craving for railroad travel. The scheme worked like a charm; for when the collection of fares began on Wednesday, July 3, the receipts averaged six hundred dollars a day for many weeks thereafter. Considering that the country was new, and that it wasn't much of a railroad, after all, this was doing pretty well.

On the Fourth of July an excursion was run over the road that they are still talking about in that part of the State. All the available rolling-stock, which wasn't a great deal, was crowded to suffocation by an ecstatic crowd which went into raptures over the swift motion through the great forests, which at that time of year were at their best. The road being elevated on piles, the excursionists were able to fancy they were sailing through the air.

Henry Clay came up from his Kentucky home for a ride on the wonderful pile railroad. He praised it until the people were filled with delight. Even President Van Buren heard so much about it that he had to come up and take a ride, spending the night of September 10, 1839, at Utica.

No wonder that the stock quickly rose to one hundred and ten, or that the company was able to pay dividends of five dollars a share every six months.

The next link westward in the Buffalo Railroad which Mr. Cambreleng toasted at that memorable dinner of August 9, 1831, the Auburn and Syracuse Railroad, was organized some seventeen months before the Syracuse and Utica, but it did not have the smooth and pleasant career of the latter.

In fact, it encountered greater difficulties than any other of the railroads in the Buffalo chain. Surveys were begun in April, 1835, and construction in the following December, but the financial disturbances of 1836 and 1837, and the great advance in the price of provisions, material, and labor, came pretty near wrecking the company.

However, the road was finished, and, with wooden rails and horses for motive power, was opened January 8, 1838. The company raised money enough to buy a locomotive, the " Syracuse," with which H. Perry, the master mechanic, took the officers over the road June 4, 1839. Meanwhile, iron strap-rails had replaced the wooden ones.

The Auburn and Syracuse Railroad enjoyed the unique distinction of having been conceded by the legislature the privilege of carrying freight. All the other early railroads were restricted to the carrying of passengers and their baggage and the mails. One of the first things to do, therefore, was to organize the freight business. W. G. Fargo, the great express man, began life by doing what he could to establish this important branch of the Auburn and Syracuse Railroad's business as freight agent in the old Genesee Street depot at Auburn.

The business of freighting by wagon was pretty well established by this time, and it promised to be none too easy a task to make head against this wagon competition at the outset.

But the company got in a master stroke of diplomacy. Uncle Nat Williams, a well-known character, on the shady side of fifty, with a cheery voice, a beaming face framed in a fringe of white whiskers, and a pleasant word for everybody, had the cream of the freighting business out of Auburn. To Uncle Nat the scheming railroad company proposed that if he would withdraw his teams from the freighting business he should be made freight conductor.

Uncle Nat yielded to this temptation, and thus became the first freight conductor in the State of New York. His cheery voice waked the echoes along the Auburn and Syracuse road, for Uncle Nat continued to give signals with his lungs just as he had done when he was handling horses instead of railroad men, until September 5, 1841, when he retired to enjoy the rest his busy life had earned.

The trains of which Uncle Nat and his fellow conductors had charge were not at all imposing. The box cars were not much bigger than a good-sized packing-case. They had four wheels, and thirty barrels of flour loaded one to the limit of its capacity.

Switching was done with horses. When the cars were loaded they would be hauled down to the main line, where they were coupled to the locomotive. Fourteen loads made a full train.

Passenger cars were more like instruments of torture than vehicles for travel. Like the freight cars, they had four wheels. They were divided into three compartments, on the order of European cars of to-day, only they were not so large.

Each compartment would seat eight persons, provided care was exercised not to select too large persons, four on each seat, face to face. There was no elbow-room, and no room to stand up straight.

Neither were there any stoves to heat the cars in winter. The conductor got around to collect fares by walking from one side door to another along a ledge outside the car barely four inches wide, holding to a hand-rail near the top.

This was anything but a cheerful task in stormy or windy weather. Conductor George Williamson lost his hold one cold, snowy night near Marcellus, and fell to a snow-drift beside the track, from which he rolled under the wheels and was killed.

Stevenson & Co., stage builders, of New York City, built an eight-wheeled passenger car in 1839 which was tried on the Auburn and Syracuse road. It was the only eight-wheeled passenger coach run on any of the railroads between Albany and Auburn for several years.

It was so much larger than the little bandboxes for which the road had been built that it would barely clear obstructions. Soon after this car was put into service Conductor Samuel Wildrick was crushed to death between it and the depot doorway at Syracuse as his train was pulling out in the evening for Auburn.

The space between car and doorway was less than four inches. Wildrick was not missed until the train had run three miles. It was backed up, and the body was found lying where it had fallen.

For a long time the motive power of the Auburn and Syracuse consisted of three locomotives, all of Rogers make, weighing ten and a half tons each. They had a single pair of drivers, and it kept them busy to get over the road with fourteen of the little cars.

At first the company tried to run the locomotives on wooden ribbon pieces, but they would not stay on the track, so it was necessary to lay " snakeheads." These snakeheads, or strap-rails, were in universal use for eight years in New York, up to 1847.

They were nothing in the world but flat bar iron two and one-half inches wide and three-quarters of an inch thick, laid on six-by-six pine string-pieces and held in place by spikes eighteen inches apart. The weight of the train would cause these iron straps to curl up like a hoop with force sufficient to break or pull out the spikes near the ends, which would be left sticking up from the wooden base all the way from a few inches to two feet.

These projecting ends had a playful habit of poking themselves up through the cab of an engine or the floor of a car when a train struck them from the wrong direction. If an engineman or a passenger happened to be in the way he was pretty likely to be hurt.

R. P. Witherspoon, a young lawyer of Syracuse, had occasion to go to Auburn one December evening in 1840. The day being cold and blustery, his wife insisted on turning up his overcoat collar with her own hands and wrapping so many thicknesses of woolen comforter around his neck that he couldn't bend his head to kiss her good-by, but was obliged to have her stand on a chair to receive the salute.

He grumbled about being muffled up like a hired man, but his wife insisted that he would surely catch his death of cold if he didn't submit. Being newly married, he agreed to wear the muffler as his wife had arranged it.

Mr. Witherspoon entered the car next the engine, and selected the right-hand end seat facing forward, in the middle compartment. Two strangers occupied the same seat, while two friends sat opposite. After riding a few miles, Mr. Witherspoon changed to the opposite seat, in order to converse more comfortably with his friends.

He had scarcely made the change when there was a crash. Turning his head quickly, Mr. Witherspoon had barely time to get a glimpse of a snakehead pushing up through the seat he had just vacated when it curled over, and catching him in the throat, pushed him violently back through the thin wooden partition.

He was stunned for an instant. When he recovered his wits he found himself lying with head and shoulders through the broken partition, with both hands clutching the snakehead, the end of which rested against the numerous folds of coat collar and comforter under his chin. That comforter had saved his life. The train was stopped until the snakehead could be spiked back in its place.

Emigrant traffic, which was very heavy in the early days of the Auburn and Syracuse, promptly forsook the canal as soon as there were railroads to travel upon; for, crude as those pioneer roads were, they were a decided improvement on canal boats. This emigrant traffic, which included household goods and farming implements, together with its regular freight traffic, and heavy passenger business the road was poorly equipped to handle. New engines had to be obtained. Two were ordered of Dennis, Wood & Russell, of Auburn. They were built under the direction of William S. Hudson, as superintendent, who afterward became noted as a locomotive builder.

These engines were the first built in America to work steam expansively. One of them, the " Wyoming," was considered the best engine of its capacity ever on the road.

The first engine with six-foot drivers to run west of the Hudson was built for the Auburn and Syracuse in 1848 by Rogers. It was named the " How," after Thomas Y. How, treasurer of the road. This engine was a hoodoo from the beginning of its career. It was always getting off the rails or into some other sort of difficulty.

Its career terminated about a year after it began. William Delano, engineer, with Thomas Hooper, fireman, left Syracuse with four coaches and a baggage car one day. There were two visitors in the cab, who wanted to try the novelty of a ride on an engine—C. C. Dennis, one of the directors of the road, and Howard Delano, brother of the engineer.

While running fifty miles an hour the engine left the rails one mile west of Sennett. The engineer and fireman were instantly killed, Dennis received severe injuries which disfigured him for life, while Howard Delano, by some strange freak of fate, was only slightly hurt. The hoodoo engine was so utterly demolished that no attempt was made to rebuild it.

A telegraph office was opened at Auburn in May, 1846. Soon afterward an attempt was made to use it in sending train orders, with disastrous results. The passenger train due in Auburn from Rochester at 4 A.M. had not arrived at 5:30, and as the engine which was to leave Auburn had to be in Syracuse in order to leave there with a passenger train at 7 A.M., it was ordered to leave without waiting for the Rochester train.

Meanwhile the Rochester train got in and was ordered to run to Syracuse, where the west-bound train was to be held by telegraph. Unfortunately, the operator at Syracuse must have had an extra good breakfast that morning. At any rate, he didn't get to his office until the west-bound train had left.

A fine large heap of kindling-wood marked the spot near Fairmount where the trains attempted to pass on a curve. Fortunately, no one was seriously hurt.

Piece by piece the longed-for Buffalo road was growing. The seventy-eight miles from Schenectady to Utica were finished in 1836; the thirty-three miles from Rochester to Batavia were opened in 1837, and extended twelve miles farther, to Attica, in 1842; the seventy-eight miles from Auburn to Rochester were opened in 1841, and the thirty-one miles from Attica to Buffalo in December, 1842.

By the beginning of 1843 there was a rail route by which it was possible to travel from Albany to Buffalo in thirty hours without changing cars more than six times.

There were no through tickets and no baggage checks. A ride over each of the seven independent roads was a complete transaction in itself. When the passenger got to the end of the road he hunted up his baggage, if he had any, had it chalked to the next stopping place, bargained with expressmen and hackmen for transfer to the station of the next road in line, bought a new ticket, and took a fresh start.

Under such circumstances a pass over these diminutive railroads would hardly seem to be worth the trouble required to get it. Yet applicants for these favors were so persistent, and they had so serious an effect upon the revenues of the road, that early in 1850 the representatives of the roads between Albany and Buffalo were compelled to appoint a committee to find some means to abate the nuisance. The committee recommended that after July 1, 1850, the granting of passes should cease, and that employees should be especially charged not to ask or receive free passage over any other roads.

By 1850 the science of railroading had progressed so far that the traveler could purchase through tickets between Albany and Buffalo for $9.75, though he could not obtain at any price any information upon which he could rely about the movement of trains. Theoretically the express trains covered the distance between Albany and Buffalo in fourteen hours, as the "ticket master," the predecessor of the modern ticket agent, blandly assured all inquirers, and there were five trains a day each way. How faithfully these promises were fulfilled may be gathered from the narrative of a traveler who left Albany at 7 o'clock on a Saturday evening in May, 1850, with the assurance that he would be taken through to Buffalo in fourteen hours.

Arriving at Utica at 11:30 P.M., the train was switched onto a side track and left there. The traveler with his fellow passengers sat in the stuffy little coaches, in which a candle at each end struggled to

make darkness visible, without being able to learn
when they could proceed or whether they ever would
be taken any further. Then, at 2 A.M. a locomotive
bumped down against their train, and after a ride of
three hours they arrived at Syracuse at 5 o'clock
in the morning. Here the passengers were left
without any intimation of what Fate and the railroad company had in store for them. All attempts
to obtain information were fruitless. They could
only hover about the cheerless boxes of cars and wait
for twelve hours and a half. Then, at 5:30 P.M.
they resumed their journey to Rochester, where they
arrived at midnight, only to wait another six hours
for an engine to take them to Buffalo, where they
arrived completely exhausted after a journey of two
hundred and ninety miles, which had lasted thirty-
eight hours and a half.

Nor were maddening delays the only unpleasant
feature of a railroad journey in those early days. In
1845 the *Railroad Journal* complimented the Harlem Railroad on its enterprise in introducing cars
" so high that one can stand erect when he cannot
find a seat." For years after this step in advance
it was all a tall man could do to stand erect in the
average passenger car. The clerestory did not come
into general use until after the Civil War. The
windows were very small and the sashes were so
loose that they rattled a continuous obligato to the
creaking and groaning of the flimsy frame. In fact,
the cars were nicknamed " rattlers," " hyenas," and
" cribs." As travel was too heavy for the facilities
available the cars were generally overcrowded and
the air in the tiny boxes was foul almost beyond en-

durance. Heat was furnished by a stove at each end. Passengers near the stoves were almost roasted alive, while those in the middle of the car shivered with cold.

The sleeping cars, though, were the uttermost extreme of atrocity. Desultory attempts were made to introduce sleeping cars from the time the first ones were tried on the Cumberland Valley in Pennsylvania in 1836. By 1859 several lines, including those in central New York, were using so-called sleeping cars. They were simply " rattlers," crude and rough as they were, fitted up with three tiers of shelves. With three bunks to the section in these low cars the passenger had to spread himself out pretty thin to get into his berth at all. However, there was no superfluous bedding to take up space. The only things in that line furnished by the railroad company were pillows and mattresses, which were piled up in one corner and dragged by the passengers to the scene of torture when required.

Yet one of these wheeled torture chambers was directly responsible for the luxurious limited trains of the twentieth century. One night in 1859 a young man who had just cleared twenty thousand dollars raising houses to grade in Chicago indulged in the luxury of a berth in a sleeping car from Buffalo to his old home at Westport. After a few hours of agony he fled from his berth to a day coach to rub his aching bones and think of cutting remarks he would have made to the builder of that sleeping car if he had had the chance. But George M. Pullman soon forgot his grievance in more practical musings on the curious fact that no one had yet devised a sleeping car in which people could sleep, which led him to wonder why he could not do it himself.

To a man with youth, health, energy, ambition, and twenty thousand dollars, all things are possible. Pullman returned to Chicago, and with Benjamin Field, of New York, arranged to operate sleeping cars on the Chicago and Alton and the Galena and Chicago Union railroads. But for this one time in his career Pullman did a thing first and thought about it afterward. The experiments were so unsatisfactory that he gave them up and went to Colorado, attracted by the Pike's Peak gold excitement. He found no gold, but he found an opportunity to think over the sleeping car idea more fully. He reached the conclusion that if he were to build a car comfortable and complete in accommodations, handsome and suitable for occupancy both by night and by day, night travel would become popular and the business would grow to vast proportions. This time he formulated his plans fully before he made a move.

Once his mind was made up, Pullman returned to Chicago, and again made an arrangement with the Chicago and Alton to run sleeping cars. The Chicago and Alton was then in desperate straits. The sheriff made frequent calls to attach the receipts, and the management was ready to clutch at any straw or enter into any agreement that held out any hope of relief, however shadowy. The management even gave Pullman the use of a shed in which to build his first sleeping car.

Pullman's first sleeping car worried other people more than it did himself while it was building. His friends gave proof of their fidelity by protesting long and earnestly against his folly. Railroad men reasoned with him and explained the many things which made it impossible for him to succeed in his venture. Even the workmen who were hired to build the car felt sorry for their employer's inexperience and lack of business judgment and ignorance of cabinet-making and all the other handicrafts called into requisition. Whenever he wanted a certain thing done in a certain way, there were always innumerable reasons why it couldn't be done in that particular way or any other way.

But Pullman obstinately insisted on having his own way, in spite of well-meaning friends and railroad men who understood the transportation business down to the ground, kindly disposed workmen who knew better than he did himself what he wanted, and the intelligent public that always knows everything. As a crowning act of folly, he employed a famous artist, who had just finished decorating Samuel J. Tilden's house, to come to Chicago and decorate his first car. At last, after several months of toil, the first Pullman palace sleeping car was finished. When it was drawn out on a side track for inspection, the results of the builder's obstinacy were strikingly apparent.

The " Pioneer," as it had been named, was a foot wider and two and a half feet higher than any car that had ever been built. One of Pullman's railroad friends pointed out that the car could not be run on any railroad then in existence because it was so big that it would not clear the station platforms and bridges.

" I know it," said Pullman. " I suppose you'll

have to cut down the platforms and rebuild the bridges."

And that was precisely what happened. Since Pullman would not build his cars to fit the railroads, the railroads had to be built to fit Pullman's cars. Next they had to improve all their passenger equipment to fit the standard set by him. When enough track had been found on which to make a trip, Pullman invited a judicious selection of influential men, editors of papers with the best circulation, and railroad officials who would be most useful, to come and see his car and take a ride on it.

The guests found a car so very different from anything the world had ever seen that they were filled with wonder and delight. The Pioneer was not only of enormous size, but it rested on eight-wheeled trucks instead of four-wheeled, had a raised deck with ventilating transoms, and was a beautiful example of cabinet-making and decorative art. All were willing to believe that the Pioneer had cost eighteen thousand dollars. The best passenger cars of that period cost four thousand dollars. One thing that puzzled the guests was the lack of anything that looked like sleeping accommodations. They had understood that they had been invited to inspect a sleeping car. But where were the passengers to sleep?

Pullman smiled, and guessed they had better have something to eat before they talked about sleeping. At a word from him the first sleeping car porters brought out little tables, which fitted between the seats, just as do the tables in use in Pullman cars to-day, and furnished them with linen, silver, and china. The delighted guests sat down to a hot, well-served meal. After the cigars, Pullman requested all hands to step forward into a day coach for a few moments. When they were called back a short time later, they found that a complete transformation had been made. The seats and tables had disappeared, and in their places inviting looking beds, completely furnished with fine linen and blankets, could be seen through neatly parted curtains. This sleeping car bore no resemblance to the barren torture chambers they had known before. Again there was a round of applause. Then the guests undressed and went to bed. Half an hour later all rose and dressed and watched with keen interest while the porters transformed the sleeper back into a day car. The rest of the trip was spent in discussing the marvel and in examining its details over and over again.

The Pioneer caused a tremendous sensation. All the papers and magazines published descriptions of it. Everybody was talking about Pullman's sleeping car. All agreed that traveling in such cars would be delightful, but the verdict was equally unanimous that they were a commercial impossibility. Why, men would go to bed with their muddy boots on; they would expectorate on the carpets and upholstery; they would mar the beautifully finished cabinet-work, and—oh, well, it couldn't be done. Railroad men and personal friends redoubled their efforts to dissuade Pullman from inviting ruin. To all these objections Pullman made one comprehensive answer, which he had occasion to repeat many times in the course of his life:

" I have always held that people are very greatly influenced by physical surroundings. Take the roughest man, a man whose lines have always brought him into the coarsest and poorest surroundings, and bring him into a room elegantly carpeted and furnished, and the effect on his bearing is pronounced and immediate. I am not at all afraid people will go to bed with their boots on. I am convinced that if I devote all my energies to providing handsome cars the financial returns will take care of themselves."

Soon after the Pioneer was completed, it was used in the Lincoln funeral train. This necessitated cutting down the station platforms between Chicago and Springfield. A few months later the car was wanted to convey General Grant from Detroit to Chicago, so the Michigan Central stations and bridges were hastily adjusted to the standard fixed by Pullman.

Once the road was adapted to them the Michigan Central was ready to try Pullman cars. In pursuance of his lifelong policy, Pullman set out to make a great improvement in the new cars. When the second Pullman car was completed it had cost twenty-four thousand dollars. The first Pullman cars for the Michigan Central settled a question which has been a perennial source of worry to legislators; namely, the proper charge for a berth. Unfortunately, the legislators keep forgetting it and trying to settle it all over again. It was impossible to sell a berth in a car that had cost twenty-four thousand dollars for a dollar and a half, which was the rate in the Woodruff sleeping car then used on the Michigan Central. But when Pullman announced that he proposed to charge two dollars a berth, President Joy was horrified.

" My dear sir," he exclaimed, " that is not to be thought of. If you undertake to charge two dollars a berth when other roads only charge a dollar and a half between Detroit and Chicago, you will simply drive all the night travel to our competitors. It is no concern of mine that you have chosen to spend so much money for useless luxuries for people who will not appreciate them and do not want them."

" People are willing to pay for the best, if they get the worth of their money," returned Pullman. " But what is the use of spending time in useless argument over a subject which is so easily susceptible of demonstration? Run your cheap cars as usual at a dollar and a half a berth and put my cars on the same train at two dollars a berth, and let the public choose between them. If the traveling public thinks the beauty of finish, the comfort, and the safety of the new cars worth two dollars a night, there are the twenty-four-thousand-dollar cars; if, on the other hand, they are satisfied with the less attractive surroundings at a saving of fifty cents, the cheaper cars are at their disposal. We will submit the plain facts on both sides of the issue without argument."

This was such a practical suggestion that it was adopted without parley. Not only did the patrons of the road utterly refuse to look at the old cars so long as any two-dollar berths were available, but those who were crowded out of the Pullman complained so loudly at being compelled to put up with dollar-and-a-half berths, that within six weeks the cheap cars were taken off altogether. Instead of driving traffic away, the more expensive palace cars drew travel from the other roads, so that competing lines were forced to make terms with Pullman. Instead of a leveling down to the cheaper prices, there was a leveling up to the higher.

When the Union Pacific and Central Pacific were opened, through trains, equipped with Pullman cars, made the run between Omaha and San Francisco. This was a practical demonstration of the convenience of the Pullman system of operation that was convincing.

Soon after the Pullman Company was organized, in 1867, parlor cars were introduced on day runs. Then in the same year the first hotel car, the " President," a sleeping car with kitchen and pantry, a buffet car it would be called now, was introduced on the Great Western Railway, of Canada. It was the first car in the world built to serve meals en route. In 1868 the first regular dining car, the " Delmonico," was placed in service on the Chicago and Alton.

The Pullman idea was not based on beauty of surroundings and comfort alone, but also on safety. The " Pioneer," and every Pullman car that followed it, were so much heavier and stronger than the ordinary coaches in the train that in case of accident they almost always escaped injury. Pullman wanted something better than a strongly built car; he wanted a solid train. In 1886 he began working on a scheme for continuous trains. As early as 1852 patents had been granted for canvas diaphragms between cars. They were adopted on the Naugatuck Railroad, in Connecticut, in 1857, but were discontinued after four years. They were flimsy and practically useless, for they did not attempt to hold the cars in position, but were merely intended to keep passengers from falling off in passing from one platform to another while the train was in motion.

In 1887 the modern vestibule was patented. By means of this an entire train was made into one solid yet sinuous whole by elastic diaphragms faced with heavy steel frames, held in place by strong springs. The wide vestibule made it possible for the passenger to go from his sitting-room to his dining-room or his bedroom under one roof, just as he would in his own home. Vestibuled trains required less power to pull them, because the air-pockets between the cars were reduced to a minimum. They also reduced the danger from collisions to a very considerable extent. Several vestibuled trains have collided at a speed of forty miles an hour without injury to passengers. No safety appliance, with the possible exception of the air-brake, has yet been devised which has proved more valuable for the protection of travelers than this apparently simple device. An exhibition vestibuled train made the rounds of the principal cities in 1887, and then, with three others, was placed in service on the Pennsylvania road. The result was an increase of seventy per cent in travel on the limited trains.

But to return to the New York railroads of early days: On reaching Albany the passenger for New York was obliged to continue his journey by river in summer and by stage in winter, for the connecting rail link was not built for several years.

A railroad from New York to Albany was first chartered in 1832. The capital was fixed at three million dollars, and the State, as usual, reserved the right to purchase the road. The idea was pretty general in the early days that the State should own the highways, including the railroads. But nothing came of this scheme, and the time for construction was extended to 1838.

In 1842 the people of Poughkeepsie, weary of waiting for the building of the promised road, employed an engineer to survey a route along the Hudson from New York to Albany. He reported that the route was feasible. There the matter rested for three years. Then a convention was held at Poughkeepsie, at which a re-survey was decided upon, but still nothing happened.

Finally, on January 23, 1846, Mayor Havemeyer called a meeting in New York City to consider the desirability of building the road to Albany. The New York and Harlem Railroad Company had been chartered to build such a line, but it was not yet completed. The result of this meeting was the granting of a charter to the Hudson River Railroad on May 26, 1846. One month later the entire capital stock of three million dollars had been subscribed, most of it being taken in New York City.

Work was begun promptly, and on October 1, 1851, the entire line was opened for business. The first passenger station in New York City was at Chambers Street and College Place, to which point the cars were drawn by horses from Thirteenth Street and Eleventh Avenue. The Hudson River Bridge at Albany was not opened until February 22, 1866.

In 1850 the alarming discovery was made that the railroads, which had been intended merely for passenger traffic, were becoming formidable competitors of the Erie Canal. When this discovery was made the whole commonwealth was agitated by the problems presented. There was a strong sentiment in favor of legislation that would prohibit any such competition.

As late as 1858 the people of the State were still holding mass-meetings and resolving that the railroads had no right to compete with the canal.

It was strenuously urged that canals had a natural right to carry heavy freight, and that it was suicidal folly for railroads to try to handle such business. Managers who were trying to develop their roads into heavy freight carriers were denounced for ruining themselves and the stockholders. But the march of progress could not be delayed; the canals had to cut rates to meet the competition of the railroads.

Tolls were levied on railroad freight the same as on canal traffic. Some of the roads in the chain from Albany to Buffalo were limited by their charters to the carrying of passengers; and they had a hard time getting permission to include the transportation of freight in their business.

The outcome of the agitation was the first important railroad consolidation in history. On May 17, 1853, ten independent railroads, including the seven forming the route from Albany to Buffalo, with their branches and feeders, having a total of five hundred and forty-two miles of track, were consolidated under the title of the New York Central Railroad.

The charter was to run for five hundred years, and the capital was fixed at twenty-three million eighty-five thousand dollars, which was the aggregate amount of the capital of the consolidated companies.

The New York Central began business with 187 first-class passenger coaches, 55 second-class, 65 baggage, mail, and express cars, and 1,702 freight cars. There were 298 miles of main line, 236 miles of branch line, and 29 miles of leased road.

The average speed of passenger trains, including stops, had increased from an average of twelve to fifteen miles in 1840 to twenty-five miles an hour, express trains forty miles an hour, and freight trains fourteen miles an hour. Although the first-class passenger rate was only two cents a mile as compared with five cents a mile in 1840, the passenger earnings for the first year after consolidation were $3,151,514, as compared with $2,479,820 freight earnings. The business was extremely profitable, for the company paid in dividends that year $1,125,506.

Notwithstanding the advantages which resulted from this step, consolidation did not become fashionable for some years. The first act in the railroad drama, the period of construction, having now been played out, the scene shifts to Wall Street.

Cornelius Vanderbilt, having amassed a modest competence of a dozen millions from the operation of his steamship lines, selected Hudson River Railroad stock as a suitable investment in 1863. Wall Street, discovering this fact, prepared a nice little surprise for him by selling Hudson River short.

Vanderbilt obligingly absorbed all offers until he had the entire stock of the road in his hands. Then he invited the shorts to step up and settle at his own price.

The New York and Harlem Railroad already being in his hands, Vanderbilt had a bill introduced in the legislature for the consolidation of the two roads—the second consolidation in the present New

York Central system. Wall Street tried the same game on him after " seeing " certain legislators who were supposed to know how to do things at Albany.

The result was the same as in the first attempt, except that the shorts sold twenty-seven thousand more shares than had ever been issued, which obliged Vanderbilt to fix the low figure of 283 as the price at which the associated shorts might settle in order to avert a panic.

About the time this little affair had blown over, the New York Central Railroad directors thought it would be only neighborly to invite the newcomer in the railroad world to take a ride over their road. Mr. Vanderbilt took great pleasure in accepting the invitation. He did not communicate his impressions of what he saw, but an idea of them may be formed from what followed.

The New York Central management, having its eastern terminus on the Hudson River, felt pretty secure, and, consequently, independent, for its growing traffic could be sent by water to New York. But they had forgotten that navigation was interrupted for several months during the winter.

Consequently, when at the close of navigation in 1865, Commodore Vanderbilt, without any notice, withdrew the terminus of the Hudson River Railroad to the eastern bank of the river at Albany and refused to receive freight from the New York Central, the stockholders of the latter road were taken completely by surprise. There was a rush to sell, and down went the price.

Vanderbilt, by a strange coincidence, had been selling New York Central short, and his friends, oddly enough, had been doing the same thing. When no-body else wanted New York Central stock, after its communication with New York City had been cut, the Vanderbilt party obligingly took it off the hold-ers' hands at greatly reduced prices.

No one knew the extent of the clean-up until the next annual meeting of the stockholders. The polls were opened at Albany, as usual, for the election of a board of directors. Not a vote was cast all day long until just a moment before the polls were to close.

Then Commodore Vanderbilt walked into the room and deposited a single ballot. On opening the ballot-box immediately afterward it was found that this lone ballot represented eighteen million dollars out of a total capital stock of twenty-four million dollars. The new board of directors, who had been brought up from New York, was thereupon called into the room, and proceeded to elect Cornelius Vanderbilt presi-dent.

The consolidation of the New York Central and the Hudson River Railroads followed soon after.

These interesting events were celebrated with a quiet little melon-party at the home of Horace V. Clark one Saturday evening in December, 1868. The melon-cutting took the form of an eighty per cent stock dividend distribution of twenty-three million dollars.

The certificates were equal to stock in every par-ticular except the right to vote. New York Central had closed at 133 Saturday. It opened at 155 Mon-day, and sold up to 159.

The spectacular changes in the financial history of

the New York Central were immediately followed by a physical transformation even more extraordinary. Commodore Vanderbilt was no speculator. He wanted railroads that would earn dividends, and to achieve this end, to his way of thinking, it was absolutely necessary to have nothing but the best in both men and materials.

Staffs were reorganized, bridges rebuilt, heavier rails laid, curves straightened, grades reduced, better and heavier engines and more of them provided, the best cars the builders then knew how to turn out purchased, improved methods introduced, and rates reduced.

The net result was that less than a century after the Mohawk & Hudson "Rail Road" was opened for traffic it had become a part of a great railroad system, "The New York Central Lines," consolidated from 560 predecessor companies, with 12,095 miles of main line in twelve states having more than half the population of the United States, and in two provinces of Canada having 60 per cent of the population of the Dominion.

While the New York Central Lines had less than 5 per cent of the total mileage, less than 10 per cent of the total number of employes and only $8\frac{1}{2}$ per cent of the total railroad capitalization they then carried about 10 per cent of the freight traffic and more than 12 per cent of all the passenger traffic in the United States.

CHAPTER VI

INCUBATOR RAILROADS

"GOING at ten thousand, going, going—gentlemen, are you all done? Going at ten thousand once, going at ten thousand twice——"

The auctioneer was the sheriff of Sangamon County, Illinois. He was standing on the steps of the Capitol on the 26th of April, 1847, facing a little knot of idlers, who lounged in the warm spring sunshine, watching him as the most engaging diversion that offered at the moment.

The least interested man in sight, so far as outward appearances went, was N. H. Ridgley, of Springfield. He had made the only bid offered for all that remained of a section of the Northern Cross Railroad, the property of the State of Illinois.

This bit of railroad, twenty-four miles long, had cost the taxpayers $406,233. It was the sole asset left to show for a debt of $4,107,746. Even at that it wasn't much to speak of as railroads go.

Its only locomotive had been broken up for scrap-iron, its cars were falling to pieces, the iron had been used for sled-shoes and similar purposes by the farmers along the route, and the ties for fence-posts and firewood. But the right-of-way was as sound as a dollar.

Across the street in a little barber shop an elderly gentleman, with a pronounced waist-line, bearing upon his swelling waistcoat circumstantial evidence that he chewed tobacco, dozed in the chair while the barber leisurely wrestled with his wiry beard. The elderly gentleman was aroused by the sound of his own snoring.

His glance wandered through the window to the little group of idlers and then to the capitol steps to ascertain the object of their curiosity. Suddenly he sat upright as if he had just recalled something important.

" Here; wipe me off quick, Joe," he commanded.

" All right, Colonel Johnson, there you are, sir," replied the barber, whipping off the towel.

Colonel Johnson ambled across the street. Just as the auctioneer was in the act of opening his mouth to knock down the railroad to Ridgley, Colonel Johnson bawled:

" One hundred dollars."

The sheriff looked up in surprise. Ridgley turned toward the colonel with an aggrieved air and fairly gasped with astonishment, while the idlers almost stood erect in the intensity of their excitement.

The bidding was fast and furious until the price had been run up to twenty thousand dollars. The affair was growing serious for Ridgley. He walked up to Colonel Johnson.

" See here, colonel," he inquired, " are you bidding for yourself or somebody else? "

" I'm bidding for some parties in St. Louis," was the reply.

At the same time there was just the trace of a flutter in the colonel's left eyelid; or it might have been an optical illusion on the part of Ridgley.

" Well, wouldn't you just as soon accept a commission from people in Springfield as in St. Louis? "

" Oh, certainly," said the colonel, shifting his quid and walking nonchalantly away. Thereupon the road was knocked down to Ridgley for twenty thousand dollars.

Next day the enterprising Colonel Johnson sauntered into Ridgley's office, where he was handed a check for one thousand dollars. That check was the nearest approach to real money involved in the sale of the Northern Cross Railroad, for Ridgley paid the twenty thousand dollars in State bonds which he had bought for nine cents on the dollar and turned over to the State at par.

The bang of the auctioneer's gavel closed the first chapter in the history of the first railroad built in the country inclosed by the Alleghanies, the Ohio, and the Mississippi, and opened another which led up to the foundation of what is now the Wabash Railway system. Also it ended a most curious era in the development of the Middle West.

To begin at the beginning of that first chapter, it may be said that in the early thirties the whole region from the western slope of the Alleghanies to the Mississippi had become one vast incubator for railroad schemes. If money had been as abundant as exuberant optimism, every man would have had his own private railroad long before the nineteenth century was half completed.

True, these brothers of Colonel Sellers had exceedingly vague ideas of what a railroad was; but they were unanimous in their abiding faith that the word was a synonym for " highway " to untold millions which danced in the iridescent air before their enraptured eyes.

The incidental fact that none of them had any money troubled them not at all. What was more simple than to call railroads into being by legislative fiat and then let the State government foot the bills? Few of these fiat railroads ever progressed beyond the stock-selling stage, the majority did not live even that long. It was a time of rosy dreams of opulence and of weird financial jugglery, in which nothing multiplied by nothing equaled whatever the promoters chose to say it did. Yet, oddly enough, out of these disordered phantoms have been evolved some of the great railroads of to-day.

To Illinois must be awarded first honors in the art of building railroads by statute. The people had been building towns on paper, until the industry had begun to pall upon them. Then Governor Joseph Duncan, in a message to the special session of the legislature in 1836, diverted attention from towns to railroads. The suggestion caught the popular fancy at once.

Agitation for a bewildering scheme of canals and railroads was taken up by a certain type of patriots and statesmen who, having nothing to lose, could afford to be sanguine to the point of certainty, if not beyond. A great internal improvement convention was held, at which the immediate execution of a stupendous program was demanded.

From the time the first internal improvement schemes, an act passed January 28, 1831, for surveying a route for a canal or railroad in St. Clair County, and for the Illinois and Michigan Canal from Chi-

cago to the head of navigation on the Illinois River,
sanctioned on February 15, 1831, were formulated
up to 1835 opinion was about equally divided in Illinois on the relative merits of canals and railroads.
Then the railroads began to forge ahead in popular
estimation. The Chicago and Vincennes Railroad
was incorporated in 1834, but nothing further was
done in the matter for years.

The legislature, by an act to which the Governor
affixed his signature February 27, 1837, appropriated $10,237,000 to launch the internal improvement
scheme. This imposed a debt of $34.10 per capita
upon the scanty population of poor, hard-working
pioneers at a time when the State was already in debt
and without revenues sufficient to meet current expenses. Chicago, then a village with a population
of 1,470, had to have a garrison to protect it from the
Indians. The temptation to achieve sudden opulence by statute, however, was too strong to be
resisted.

Every man who had a railroad scheme secured for
it from thirty thousand dollars up to one million
eight hundred thousand dollars, according to the
amount of influence he could command. As a beginning, one thousand three hundred and forty miles of
railroad were to be constructed in the State, and
every river was to be made navigable. To allay
jealousies and heartburnings the sum of two hundred
thousand dollars for roads and bridges was distributed among the back counties which could not command the influence necessary to secure a railroad.

A board of fund commissioners was created and
ordered to commerce operations forthwith. In order

to avert local jealousies and assure every community an equal chance, the commissioners were instructed to begin work simultaneously at both ends of every road, and in the middle, too, if it could be reached by a navigable stream.

The legislature of 1838 appropriated five million dollars more, and authorized the issue of additional bonds to the amount of four million dollars.

Of the score of railroads planned in Illinois, none was carried far enough to admit of laying rails except the Northern Cross, which was to run from Quincy on the Mississippi to the Indiana line. Ground was broken for this road at Meredosia, on the east bank of the Illinois River, late in August, 1837. The ceremony occupied the entire day, and the undivided attention of all the inhabitants for many miles around.

The contractors having failed to gather a working force by offers of twenty dollars a month and board, James Harkness, who was employed as master carpenter to build the bridges, went to Louisville to get men. His offer of nineteen dollars a month and board, with eight jiggers of whisky a day as a clincher, soon secured a full force. Robert Reynolds and Joseph Williams, expert whip-sawyers, were engaged to saw the bridge timbers.

Harkness, as engineer, had also to lay out the road from Meredosia. He got on swimmingly until he ran his line straight through a cabin on the prairie belonging to C. E. Lazenby, an Englishman. Mrs. Lazenby, who was famed for her flow of language, came out and berated poor Harkness until he was glad to go back and change his line so as to leave the cabin some distance to one side.

Thereupon Mrs. Lazenby made peace with the railroad. Harkness taught her how to make egg-nog and milk punch. She bought another cow to increase the milk supply, and made enough money from the patronage of the railroad builders to pay for a good two-story frame house.

Strap-rails from the East were brought up the river to Meredosia in the spring of 1838, and on May 9th track-laying was begun. The track was of the customary construction of the day. Longitudinal wooden sleepers a foot square were laid on the ground.

On these ties were laid, and on the ties were wooden rails or stringers three inches wide at the bottom, tapering to two and one-quarter inches at the top. On these the strap-iron rails, five-eighths inch thick, two inches wide, and fifteen to twenty feet long, were spiked with ordinary twenty-penny nails.

November 8, 1838, the first puff of a locomotive was heard in Illinois. It was not much of a locomotive. It had a single pair of drivers, two feet in diameter, no cab, no pilot, no whistle, no bell, no spark arrester, but it made a great hit. Crowds swarmed into town clamoring to ride on the " thing," and audibly wondering what made the thing's wheels go round.

The " thing " hauled a select party, including the oldest inhabitant, Daniel Waldo, to the end of the eight miles of track and back again, to the unbounded astonishment of the natives. The trip was somewhat delayed owing to the fact that the engineer was so overcome by the frequency of hospitable invitations to take something in honor of the auspicious event that he had to be carried to a hotel to recover.

During the winter this first locomotive did occasional service in hauling ties and rails on four-wheeled cars ten feet long. The local papers of July 1, 1839, carried the first railroad advertisement printed in the Mississippi Valley, announcing that three " pleasure cars " had been received and that " extensive arrangements will be made for the entertainment of pleasure parties desirous of witnessing a railroad in actual operation."

Two trips a day were made between Meredosia and Morgan City, the distance of twelve miles being covered in two hours. The train would stop anywhere for freight or passengers. There were frequent races between the train and the stages, in which the stages won as often as they were beaten. By winter the track had been laid to Jacksonville. The engineers planned to build the road north of town; but the citizens were so eager to revel in the possession of a real railroad that in obedience to public clamor the rails were laid right down the principal street to the public square.

In the first snowstorm the " pleasure car " came to grief. After struggling slowly along until within a mile and a half of Morgan City, the train stuck fast, and the passengers, to their intense disgust, had to continue their journey on foot. For the rest of the winter the movements of the train were extremely uncertain.

Construction east of Jacksonville was pushed throughout 1840 and 1841, and on February 15, 1842, the first train entered Springfield. Three round trips a week were made. The train was an " accommodation " train literally. The need of business was so urgent that the company could not afford to stand on dignity or make conditions with its patrons. Any one who had any freight to offer dumped it alongside the track wherever it suited his convenience, and the trainmen loaded it when they came along. Freight for delivery was put off opposite the nearest house, and the charges were collected at some future date. At Jacksonville the merchants sent draymen, who unloaded their goods and returned with the money when convenient.

But no amount of coddling could make this pioneer railroad fifty-seven miles long pay. The engineer finally ran the locomotive off the track on the prairie east of Jacksonville, burning out some flues and inflicting so much other damage that the discouraged management let it lie there for nearly a year.

General Semple, of Alton, then purchased it, and undertook to make a traction engine out of it by putting tires two feet wide on the wheels. But he had to take a yoke of oxen along to pull it out of the mud, and after a journey of a score of miles across the prairies it was once more abandoned, this time to lie until it was broken up for old iron.

The broad tracks across the prairie left in this journey were the cause of fearsome wonderment among the natives, being taken for the trail of a monster serpent. Two venturesome settlers plucked up courage to follow the trail with guns and dogs " to see what the critter mout be like."

After the locomotive had been abandoned, mules were used for motive power. One man had sole charge of the train, which now hauled only freight, when it could get any to haul. The roadbed was allowed to go unrepaired, the strap-rails were stolen by farmers for sled-shoes, and the whole outfit finally fell into hopeless wreck, when it was sold as already described. The other sections of the line were bought in by Ridgley and his associates, James Dunlap and ex-Governor Joel Mattison.

The track was repaired, new bridges built, U rails laid, three locomotives and larger cars procured, the track through the main street of Jacksonville taken up, to the infinite relief of the good citizens who had demanded that the railroad should pass their doors, and in the fall of 1849 daily trains were operated from Springfield to the river, making the trip of fifty-seven miles in five hours.

Further improvements were made in 1850 and 1851, including the laying of T rails. In 1855 the road was finished to the Indiana line, where it was joined to the track building west from Toledo by the Toledo and Illinois River Railroad Company in Ohio, and the Lake Erie, Wabash and St. Louis in Indiana. The companies were subsequently merged and later became the Wabash.

Another Illinois road which was hatched about the same period as the Wabash, and ultimately developed into a great system, was what is now known as the Illinois Central. The road was incorporated January 18, 1836, to be built with State aid and under State supervision.

But the company became insolvent without having accomplished anything, its affairs were wound up, and on March 6, 1843, the Great Western Railway Company was incorporated to build the Central road. This charter was repealed March 3, 1845, and renewed February 10, 1849, but still no actual progress was made.

In December, 1849, Stephen A. Douglas introduced a bill for a land grant which became a law in January, 1850. Under the terms of the law 2,595,000 acres of land in Illinois, Mississippi, and Alabama were granted to aid in building a railroad from Chicago to Mobile. This was not the first land given by the National Government to aid in building a railroad, but it was one of the most important grants.

The land was given to the State, and the Great Western Company was induced to surrender its charter. January 15, 1851, Governor A. C. French sent a communication to the legislature transmitting an offer from Eastern capitalists to take the land grant and build the road by July 4, 1854. An act incorporating the Illinois Central Railroad accordingly became a law on February 10.

Never before had so vast a work as the construction of seven hundred miles of railroad been undertaken by one company. The Illinois papers hoped it could be done, but they were pretty sure it never would be. However, on March 22, 1851, the board of directors, at a meeting held in New York, chose Roswell B. Mason, of Bridgeport, as chief engineer, and told him to see what he could do about it.

The route was separated into divisions, a surveying party was assigned to each, and the entire line was located and under construction by fall. For one hundred and thirty miles south of Chicago the country was unbroken wilderness in which large herds of deer roamed. Indeed, there were not a dozen towns along the route of sufficient importance to be designated on the maps.

The first construction work done was between Chicago and Calumet, to enable the Michigan Central to enter Chicago. The main line between Cairo and La Salle, 301 miles, was completed January 8, 1855. Large numbers of slaves in Kentucky promptly showed their appreciation of the advantages of the new railroad by escaping over it.

The Galena branch, from La Salle to Dunleath, 146 miles, was finished June 12, 1855, and the branch from Chicago to the junction with the main line, 249 miles, September 21, 1856. Next day Chief Engineer Mason sent a despatch to the board of directors announcing that his task of building 705 miles of railroad was finished. Then he resigned. Not long afterward he was elected mayor of Chicago.

One year later the company was obliged to assign. Richard Cobden, the famous British statesman, who had almost his entire fortune invested in the road, came over, and by his advice helped the board of directors to get the company on its feet again. By October 31, 1882, the seven per cent of the gross receipts which under the law had to be paid to the State, had yielded $9,087,835, or more than enough to pay for all the public institutions in the State. This rich and ever-increasing source of income is permanent, for the State constitution provides that the law can never be repealed. In the long run Illinois ventures in railroad hatching turned out to be very profitable.

Chicago's first railroad was the Galena and Chicago Union, now part of the Chicago and Northwestern system, which was chartered January 16,

1836, by Ebenezer and T. W. Smith, real estate men, who wanted something to boom their holdings. It was then an open question whether Galena was not destined to become a greater city than Chicago.

James Seymour began the survey, February 19, 1837, at the foot of Dearborn Street, and managed to run a line due west ten miles to the Desplaines River, by wading waist-deep in cold water part of the way. Next year some piles were driven along Madison Street and stringers placed upon them. But it was a difficult matter to build a railroad without money, and as no one in that new country had any money worth mentioning, the project languished for years. Finally, in 1845, a convention made up of delegates from all the counties through which the proposed railroad was to run was held at Rockford. A further struggle of nearly two years followed before the charter could be amended and the company reorganized, when it was found that a New Yorker named Townsend and a Springfield man named Mather had contrived to buy up practically all the stock at one cent on the dollar, but were willing to part with it if they were suitably rewarded for their trouble. The company was finally reorganized in 1847 with William B. Ogden, another real estate dealer, as president. The real survey was begun in September of that year by Richard P. Morgan, late of the Hudson River Railroad, as engineer-in-charge at the munificent salary of $2.50 a day.

In due time Mr. Morgan reported to the directors that the distance from Chicago to Galena by the route he had selected was 182 miles, and that the road would cost $2,648,727, or $14,553 a mile. The engi-

THE "PIONEER,"

A second-hand bargain purchased on credit by a company that afterward became part of the Chicago and Northwestern Railroad. It was the first to run west of Chicago.

neer gave it as his opinion that the probable earnings for the first year after the road was completed would be about $393,000. He thought 50,000 passengers at an average fare of $3 each would equal all of the travel from every source, as there were but 200,000 people in all the country to be traversed, or who could use the road when built. Still, even with this modest traffic, the engineer was of the opinion that the net earnings would pay dividends of 8 per cent.

The survey progressed so rapidly that the first seven miles west of Chicago were put under contract in the fall of 1847. Actual grading, however, was not begun until June, 1848, near what is now the corner of Kinzie and Halstead Streets, then outside the city limits. The first rails laid were the old strap-iron affairs, which were purchased solely because the Eastern roads were taking them up to make room for the more modern T rails, and hence would be glad to sell their strap-rails very cheap. Even these second-hand strap-rails cost $50 a ton on board the boat at Buffalo. They were bought on credit and were to be paid for in two and a half years.

The first locomotive, the "Pioneer," was also a second-hand bargain, bought on credit from the Buffalo and Attica Railroad, which was furnishing the strap-rails. Being the first locomotive that ever ran west of Chicago, the Pioneer deserves more than passing mention. It was built by M. W. Baldwin, the Philadelphia watchmaker whom Fate turned from his chosen calling to found the world's greatest locomotive works. It had cylinders ten by eighteen inches, a single pair of driving wheels four and a half feet in diameter, and weighed ten tons. After long service it

was retired. It was exhibited at the World's Columbian Exposition at Chicago in 1893 in charge of John
Ebbert, its first engineer, who ran it for many years,
and was also exhibited at the Louisiana Purchase
Exposition at St. Louis in 1904. It can now be seen
at the Field Museum in Chicago. The Pioneer arrived at Chicago on the brig *Buffalo* October 10,
1848, and was unloaded next day, which was Sunday.
October 31 a hundred persons, including the stockholders and newspaper men, were invited to make a
trip over the entire system of ten miles. All the company's rolling-stock, consisting of one locomotive and
six box cars, was turned out in honor of the great
event.

On the return trip a load of wheat was transferred
from a farmer's wagon to one of the cars, and hauled
in triumph back to town. This was the first shipment of wheat by rail into Chicago. The event made
a great sensation. The farmers were eager to experience the novelty of shipping wheat by rail, and the
company was quick to take advantage of the situation.

One week later the city was electrified by the an-
nouncement that as much as thirty loads of wheat
were awaiting purchasers at the Desplaines Station.
To boom the passenger traffic the railroad management announced that wheat buyers would have to go
to Desplaines instead of awaiting the arrival of grain
at the foot of Randolph Street Bridge.

The first railroad depot in Chicago was a one-story
wooden affair built by the Chicago and Galena Union
Railroad, near the junction of the present Canal and
Kinzie Streets, in the fall of 1848. In the following

year the building was enlarged and a portion of it was set aside for freight, while the east end was used for passengers. A second story, surmounted by an observatory, was added for the general offices. Here President John B. Turner and his associates planned the extension of the road and controlled its destinies. President Turner occasionally left his more pressing duties to ascend to the observatory, where with an old-fashioned marine telescope he swept the open prairies that extended from his office to the horizon watching for the first signs of smoke from his approaching trains. On clear days the smoke could be seen when the trains were six miles distant. The use of the telegraph was not yet dreamed of on any Western road.

In August, 1853, the road, for the construction of which the president and directors had had to borrow money on their individual credit, paid a dividend of eleven per cent, and six months later another of ten. September 4, 1853, the road was opened for traffic to Freeport, 131 miles from Chicago. Two passenger and three freight trains each way daily were required to care for the traffic.

This heavy traffic necessitated something better than a marine telescope and time card rules for handling it, so the company in 1854 installed a telegraph line and used it for the operation of its trains. This was the first use of the telegraph for the movement of trains in the West. In the same year the company bought two locomotives adapted to burning soft coal with the stipulation that they were not to be paid for unless they were " successful with Illinois soft coal." Prior to this experiment all Western locomotives burned wood exclusively at an average cost of $2.13 a cord.

The prosperity of the pioneer line was of short duration. The great panic of 1857 not only put a stop to railroad building, but it also cut off dividends and very seriously crippled all Western roads. The Galena and Chicago Union was obliged to reduce its working force from 1,904 in August, 1857, to 722 in January, 1858. The same panic put a summary end to work on the Chicago, St. Paul and Fond du Lac Railroad, organized to build to St. Paul and the copper regions on the shores of Lake Superior, with the result that the company was absorbed by the Chicago and Northwestern Railroad Company, organized June 6, 1859. Although this company was so desperately poor that for some time it could not pay interest on its bonds, and the officers had to make up part of the pay-rolls out of their own pockets, it contrived to absorb the 545 miles of owned and leased lines of the Galena and Chicago Union in 1864, when it owned but 350 miles of its own. The consolidation was a nine days' wonder from the Atlantic to the Missouri River.

The period of active railroad construction in the Central West began in 1851. First of all the railroad contractors to attract the world's attention by the miracles they wrought in rapid construction were Sheffield and Farnam, who took the contract to build the Chicago and Rock Island, now a part of the Chicago, Rock Island and Pacific Railway.

Beginning at Chicago, April 10, 1852, the road was opened to Rock Island, 181 miles, February 22, 1854. The road, the first from the Great Lakes to the Mississippi, was turned over to the company July 10, 1854, a year and a half before the date specified in the contract.

The internal improvement mania seems to have broken out spontaneously all over the West about the same time. While the people of Illinois were committing themselves to extravagant and impracticable plans for railroads and canals, Indiana, which was no better able to pay the bills than her neighbors, planned a ten-million-dollar system of railroads.

In 1833, when the Territory of Michigan had a population of only thirty-five thousand, the Erie and Kalamazoo Railroad, the first fragment of which ultimately became a part of the Lake Shore system, was chartered to build from Toledo to the headwaters of the Kalamazoo River. At the same time the Detroit and St. Joseph Railroad, which in the process of evolution became a part of the Michigan Central, another Vanderbilt line, was also chartered to build from Detroit to St. Joseph on Lake Michigan. Before these two roads entered upon the placid prosperity of a common management they were pitted against each other in a long and spectacular contest for supremacy.

Not having capital or the means of obtaining it, the Detroit and St. Joseph could not be completed. In 1836 the State government determined to take over the property, finish it, and name it the Central Railroad. By an act approved March 24, 1837, the internal improvement program was expanded to include three railroads across the southern end of the southern peninsula, where all the scanty population of the State was gathered. The law authorized a loan of five million dollars to finance the undertaking. Governor S. T. Mason and Theodore Romeyn were appointed a committee to negotiate the loan. Mason was honest, but a poor business man. The sequel seems to indicate that Romeyn, also, was no match for Wall Street financiers.

After considerable difficulty the commissioners sold the bonds to the Morris Canal and Banking Company, of New Jersey, on most unfavorable terms. The Banking Company paid five hundred thousand dollars in its own paper on account, and, after taking the precaution to sell the Michigan bonds in Europe, failed. The State of Michigan was thus saddled with a debt of five million dollars, for which it had received no value whatever. The affair came near bankrupting the new State, and earned for it the odium of a repudiator; for the taxpayers were not willing to redeem bonds for which they had never received an equivalent.

After this disastrous experience the State was not in a position to build railroads. Nothing whatever was done on the northern line. In the course of eight years the Central was completed to Kalamazoo. The Southern road, now a part of the Lake Shore system, was finished to Hillsdale, sixty-seven miles from Monroe, in October, 1843, at a cost of one million four hundred thousand dollars. It was the usual flimsy wooden structure with strap-rails. The State charged twelve cents a bushel to haul wheat from Hillsdale to Monroe in cars that held a hundred bushels, provided the grain was in bags. The warehousemen got three cents a bushel for storing and shipping, one cent for buying, and another three cents for storing at Monroe, making a total of nineteen cents for moving the grain from the farmer's wagon at Hillsdale to the vessel at Monroe, sixty-seven miles away.

In 1845, James F. Joy, a young lawyer of Detroit, in the absence of clients, devoted a portion of his superabundant leisure to writing letters to the local papers advocating the sale of the State railroads to private corporations. A paper containing one of these letters by the merest chance fell into the hands of John W. Brooks, superintendent of the Syracuse and Rochester Railroad. Brooks was only twenty-seven, and he was burning to get into something big; so he hurried off to Detroit, where he and young Joy quickly agreed to pool their capital of nothing apiece and buy one of the State railroads. Joy was to draw up the charter and inveigle the legislature into selling out, while Brooks went to Boston to try to raise some capital with which to put their prospective purchase in operating condition.

Local jealousies made so much trouble for Joy that he was barely able to squeeze his measure through the legislature on the last day of the session. But the State was bankrupt and simply had to get rid of the railroads, even if no cash was received for them. And of course no one would think of disbursing real money for railroads when they could be paid for in State bonds obtainable at almost any price from fourteen cents on the dollar up, but which the State was obliged to accept at par. The Central road was sold to Brooks and Joy for two million dollars. The Southern road went to E. C. Litchfield, of Detroit, and John Stryker, of Rome, N. Y., for five hundred thousand dollars, payable in ten years on the instalment plan.

Getting capitalists to invest was more difficult than overcoming local prejudices in Michigan; but at last the Central was organized with John M. Forbes, a New York tea merchant, who had made a fortune in Hong Kong, as president. Then Brooks returned to Michigan as general superintendent, and in two years had the line completed and in operation to New Buffalo, on the eastern shore of Lake Michigan, from whence steamers plied to Chicago, then a town of ten thousand inhabitants, situated in a quagmire.

As the rails approached New Buffalo it dawned upon Joy and Brooks that the water route would never do, but that they would have to lay their rails into Chicago. The only difficulty was that they could get no charter to build through Indiana. A railroad had been chartered by the Indiana legislature in 1835 to build from La Porte to Michigan City. This project for a railroad twelve miles long was designated as the " Atlantic and Pacific Railroad Company " when it was brought before the legislature; but this grandiloquent title aroused so much ridicule that its sponsor contracted it to the " Buffalo and Mississippi." As he would not yield another mile, the road was finally incorporated under that title.

A beginning was made at La Porte June 14, 1837, with the customary celebration, and a mile of the road was partly graded. The panic and the epidemic of 1838 killed the Buffalo and Mississippi so dead that for ten years even the formality of an annual election was not observed. In October, 1847, W. B. Ogden, who, in default of a successor, still regarded himself as president, called a meeting of stockholders to revive the project. One man, the holder of two shares, responded to the call. Two years later, when there were indications that the franchise was about to become valuable, the company was at last reorganized under the name of the Northern Indiana Railroad.

Meanwhile Joy had arranged in 1848 to buy the charter for fifty thousand dollars. Brooks was delighted. He wrote a letter to Joy in which he formally commended the purchase and ventured the extravagant prediction that in twenty years Chicago would have two hundred thousand inhabitants.

Armed with this letter, Joy went to New York to secure the ratification of his great bargain. Everything went off beautifully until the directors read Brooks's prediction about the two hundred thousand inhabitants in Chicago in 1868. In great disgust they declared that any man who could make such preposterous prophecies was so obviously lacking in common sense that they would have nothing to do with anything he proposed. The charter deal was repudiated.

The Southern road, which up to that time had been in a bad way, and could have been bought cheap by the Central, snapped up the charter which the Central's board of directors had rejected as worthless, and began laying track from White Pigeon through Elkhart toward Chicago.

To retrieve this lost opportunity Joy hurried to Indianapolis to try to obtain a charter from the legislature. The Southern road, which wanted to monopolize the Chicago business, blocked his efforts.

He retaliated by introducing a bill in the Michigan legislature to forfeit the Southern's charter because its terms had not been fulfilled. The Southern called on the northern Indiana towns for help, and engaged Schuyler Colfax, afterwards vice-president of the United States, to manage its campaign. Then ensued one of the hottest fights in the history of railroad lobbying. It ended in an agreement that both sides should leave Indianapolis.

Joy observed the treaty faithfully, but found time before leaving to slyly lay the wires for amending the charter of a north and south line in Indiana to enable the company to build branches from points on the main line before the main line itself was completed. For a suitable consideration the Indiana company was to build a " branch " that would enable the Michigan Central to cross the State and then lease the " branch " in perpetuity to the latter road. Joy again went to New York with a charter that would open the way to Chicago, but the directors refused to believe it would answer the purpose until Judge Benjamin R. Curtis, of Massachusetts, who, as justice of the United States Supreme Court, afterward wrote the dissenting opinion in the famous Dred Scott case, assured them that it was all right. Then the directors paid half a million dollars for a privilege that Joy had tried a short time before to get them to buy for one-tenth of that sum.

Joy then went to Illinois to get a charter that would enable the Central to build from the Indiana line to Chicago. He employed Abraham Lincoln, a rising lawyer of Springfield, to get the measure through the legislature; but Lincoln was not a good corporation lobbyist, and he failed. The difficulty was finally solved after a sharp struggle by diverting the route of the Illinois Central to the Indiana line so the Michigan Central could get into Chicago over it.

Under its new management the Southern road had been making haste slowly. Upon taking possession in 1846 the first act of the new board of directors was to decide that no more credit should be allowed for freight charges or passage, which would seem to indicate that the former management had been more easy-going than is usual at the present time. At the same meeting the directors elected two conductors, or " captains of trains," at salaries of forty dollars a month, thus manifesting an attention to detail which is not kept up under the present management. Little further was done until August 1, 1849, when a perpetual lease of the Erie and Kalamazoo was secured. This road had had a stormy and uncertain existence, managed part of the time by a commission representing the board of directors and part of the time by a receiver appointed by the court, and still another part of the time by both together, until it was finally sold under accumulated judgments to Washington Hunt, of Lockport, N. Y., and George Bliss, of Massachusetts, who seized the first opportunity to get rid of it.

When the Southern secured control of the Northern Indiana a great construction race with the Central ensued. It was won by the Southern, which ran its first train into Chicago February 20, 1852. The first train over the Central did not reach Chicago until May 21 of the same year. Two years later it was possible to make the journey from New York to Chicago in thirty-six hours, or exactly the time now required for the round trip by the fastest trains.

While straining every nerve to get into Chicago, the Central underwent a singular experience in Michigan, an inheritance resulting from State management, that for a time threatened disaster.

Under political management the railroad officials were especially considerate of the sensibilities of the voter, just as the State railroad management in Pennsylvania had been. If a hog or a cow chanced to be killed by a train on the State lines, settlement was promptly made for about three times the value of the animal. The farmers along the road were not slow to perceive the advantages of the home market which Providence had thus brought to their doors. They began feeding their old, decrepit, and diseased stock on the railroad track, where it would stand a good chance to meet an untimely but profitable fate.

The business acumen of the farmers was robbed of its just return to some extent by the caution of the railroad men. In those days of strap-rails and light equipment the little locomotives and cars were pretty certain to fare badly in any encounter with a cow or even with a hog. So while the engineers may not have had any compunctions about killing the troublesome stock, they had a wholesome regard for their own safety, which prevented them from taking unnecessary chances. In spite of all precautions, though, a good deal of stock was killed.

When T rails and larger engines were introduced under private management, the slaughter of stock, long accustomed to yarding on the track, was appalling. At first the company attempted to pay a fair valuation for stock killed by its trains; but upon investigating the causes of such extraordinary mortality, fenced the track and announced that thereafter only one-half the value of any animal killed while trespassing upon the company's property would be paid.

The farmers showed their resentment of this ungenerous attitude of the railroad company by starting a systematic campaign of petty annoyances which in the aggregate became serious. Stations and all other accessible property were damaged, journal boxes were filled with sand so they would heat and delay trains, switches were tampered with, and the rails were frequently greased for long distances. This always brought trains to a standstill until the trainmen got off and sanded the greased rails.

This soon became too tame for the farmers, who began placing obstructions on the track. Matters reached such a pass that a hand-car had to be sent out just ahead of every train to remove ties and logs and old strap-rails placed on the track by would-be wreckers. If the hand-car got too far in the lead the lurking miscreants would dodge in behind it and place fresh obstructions on the track before the train came along.

Next, trains were stoned as they passed through the woods at night, and finally volleys were fired at them repeatedly. It became a matter of common report that the enemies of the road had sworn to kill some passengers. Naturally enough, under such circumstances, passenger traffic ceased almost entirely. Even some of the engine and train men quit the road rather than take further risks of being shot from ambush or killed in a wreck.

With ruin staring it in the face unless this baseless persecution could be stopped, the railroad company engaged a corps of amateur detectives in October, 1850, to secure evidence against the ringleaders. It did not take long for the detectives to ascertain that the chief trouble makers were Abel F. Fitch, a leading citizen of Michigan Centre, who cherished a grudge against the railroad company because he had been unsuccessful in getting a contract, and Amos Filley, the keeper of a tough saloon. These two had taken advantage of the hostility of the farmers to square accounts with the railroad for their own grievances.

The detectives ingratiated themselves into the confidence of the conspirators so completely that one of them was actually selected to set fire to the depot at Niles. He carried out this duty conscientiously after he had secretly notified the company to have men handy to put out the fire. By the end of March, 1851, the detectives announced that they had all the evidence needed for conviction of the chief conspirators.

A special train carrying some seventy-five detectives and deputy sheriffs was sent to Michigan Centre on the night of April 10, 1851. Divided into squads, this large force made a swift and stealthy round-up of the town and its vicinity. The raid was a complete success. One after another thirty-six prisoners were brought in, the majority of whom made damaging admissions to save themselves under the impression that full confessions had already been made by the leaders. On returning to Detroit, Henry Gay, a member of the gang who had burned the new freight depot at that point five months before, was arrested.

This remarkable raid and the ensuing trial, which lasted from the first of May to the end of September, created a tremendous sensation throughout the State. Although W. H. Seward, ex-Governor of New York, was engaged to lead the defense, twelve of the gang were convicted and sentenced to the penitentiary, from which they were soon pardoned, while two others died in jail before the trial was ended.

In April, 1855, the Michigan Southern and Northern Indiana were consolidated. Soon after a dividend of ten per cent was declared, and for a time the company was very prosperous and aggressive, building branches and improving equipment. But there was such a thing as being too enterprising, as the Southern found out when the crash of 1857 caught it with a heavy floating debt. Then its fortunes underwent an eclipse so total that the board of directors had to borrow chairs to hold a meeting, the sheriff having seized every stick of furniture for debts.

Meanwhile the other component parts of the present Lake Shore system had come into existence and were slowly gravitating toward the inevitable consolidation. Nehemiah Allen, a Quaker, was the first to propose a railroad along the shore of Lake Erie. But the idea of a railroad presuming to compete with the large, luxurious, and swift steamers plying between Buffalo, Cleveland, and Detroit seemed so preposterous that he was regarded as a crank. No move was made to build a road east of Cleveland until July

4, 1849, when books were opened for subscriptions for the stock of the Painesville, Ashtabula and Geneva Railroad, which was opened for traffic November 20, 1852. In spite of all predictions that a railroad could never compete with the lake, this road paid dividends of five to ten per cent every six months for the next twenty years. A small stock investment reluctantly made by the city of Cleveland formed the principal part of that city's famous sinking fund.

The building of this road completed a rail route to Buffalo one hundred and eighty-three miles to the east; but right in the middle was the Erie and Northeast Railroad of six-foot gauge, twenty miles long. This necessitated two transfers of passengers and freight at Erie and at State Line, the termini of the broad-gauge road. This was an intolerable condition of affairs, yet business was actually done that way for a year. As traffic increased the double transfer grew too burdensome to be endured; so on November 16, 1853, a contract was signed to change this twenty miles of track to standard gauge, so that trains could be run through between Cleveland and Buffalo.

This seemed to be the logical, if not the inevitable, thing to do; but, strangely enough, the people of Erie resented this as an invasion of their personal and private rights, which they determined to resist. They announced that they would prevent the change of gauge at all costs. The result was an episode which was certainly unique.

In 1846 the Erie and Northeast Railroad was organized in Erie to build a railroad to the New York State line, where connection was to be made with the lines of two companies organized in New York State: the Dunkirk and State Line, which proposed to build from Dunkirk, which was to be the terminus of the Erie, to the State line, and the Buffalo and State Line, which was to build from Buffalo, the western terminus of the series of little roads forming a route across New York, to the State line. As the Erie was a broad-gauge road, the people of Erie hoped to get a through route to New York City by building their road of the same gauge. But as it would obviously be unprofitable to build parallel competing lines, the two New York companies got together and agreed to build but one line, which was to be of standard gauge.

The transfer of baggage, mail, express, freight, and passengers necessitated by the different gauges of the Erie and Northeast and its connections was extremely profitable to the hotels, omnibuses, and draymen of Erie. They feared if through trains were run their town would become a " Helmit by the Wayside," as the local orators expressed it. Attempts to intimidate the railroad by revoking its right to lay tracks through the streets or to cajole it by proffers of municipal assistance in laying a track to the dock proving equally unavailing, Mayor Alfred King called a public meeting on July 19, 1853, to devise means to prevent the change of gauge which had been determined upon by the Erie and Northeast management on the preceding day. The whole population of the town in response to the call assembled in the park, where excited orators delivered inflammatory harangues urging the people to resort to arms if necessary to prevent the railroad company from

adapting its property to the requirements of its rapidly growing traffic.

Immediately afterward the town council met and
passed an ordinance forbidding the company to
change the gauge of its tracks under severe penalties.
A continuous series of ordinances and resolutions by
the town council and daily meetings at which the
speeches grew more and more incendiary, wrought the
town into a frenzy.

Accordingly when Erie was alarmed early on the
morning of December 7, 1853, by the violent ringing
of the courthouse bell, practically every able-bodied
man in the place rushed to the courthouse square.
Upon learning that a force was actually at work
changing the gauge, a procession led by Mayor King
marched to the railroad, drove away the construction
gang with a shower of stones and rotten eggs, and
tore up the track. A similar mob at Harbor Creek,
seven miles east, tore up the track at that point.
Guards were posted to prevent the track from being
relaid.

This made a gap of seven miles, across which all
passengers and baggage had to be transferred
through deep snow in bitterly cold weather. This
seven-mile march came to be known as " Crossing the
Isthmus." Many passengers had feet, hands, and
faces frostbitten in crossing the Isthmus. Women
and children in particular suffered severely.

Freight traffic was almost entirely suspended. The
result of all these unnecessary hardships was to arouse
the bitter hostility of the traveling public and shippers. Erie soon found herself without a friend.
Loud appeals were made by the people of other sec-

tions to the Federal Government to put an end to the outlawry at Erie and thus raise the embargo on commerce, while the railroad company sought redress in the courts.

When a United States marshal attempted to serve an injunction on the leaders of the mob, the document was trampled under foot in token of contempt of the courts, and the marshal and his deputies were imprisoned. Five separate attempts by the railroad company to relay its tracks and resume traffic were thwarted by the mob, which came to be known as the " Rippers " in recognition of its prowess in ripping up track. The small minority who believed the railroad had a right to manage its own affairs in its own way were derisively dubbed " Shanghais."

On one occasion the Rippers attempted to capture a train, but were thwarted by the quick-witted engineer, who began backing toward the New York line. The Rippers were so disconcerted by this unexpected move that they all tumbled off into the snowdrifts the best way they could, with the exception of Old Bill Cooper, their leader. Old Bill, being afraid to jump, was taken captive by the trainmen, who took him some distance beyond the State line, then delegated the most muscular one of their number to kick him every step of the way back into Pennsylvania.

With a total lack of humor, Major Fitch, the poet laureate of the Rippers, made the kicking of Old Bill Cooper the subject of a stirring ballad, which did not a little to keep the martial spirit of the Rippers alive.

Finally Governor Bigler, of Pennsylvania, went to Erie and persuaded the people to permit the railroad company to relay its tracks and resume traffic on

February 1, 1854, when the first train ran through from Buffalo to Cleveland. This truce, however, did not end the strange Erie war. An incredible bitterness and animosity had been engendered, which demoralized business, disrupted churches, and led to frequent assaults. At all hours of the day and night the courthouse bell called the citizens together to listen to harangues which grew ever more incendiary.

Matters finally reached such a pass that martial law was required to restore order. Discussion of the railroad question was forbidden under severe penalties, and special constables were appointed to enforce this ordinance. More than a year after traffic was resumed a mob summoned by the courthouse bell tore up the railroad track and burned the bridges in Erie. After that the railroad was disturbed no more, but the ill-feeling engendered by the episode only died out with the generation involved in it.

After the war was ended the career of the Erie and Northeast was prosaic enough. It was consolidated with the Buffalo and State Line to form the Buffalo and Erie on May 15, 1867, and on June 22, 1869, by another consolidation with the Cleveland, Painesville and Ashtabula, the Cleveland and Toledo, and the Michigan Southern, and Northern Indiana, each of the companies being a consolidation of two smaller roads, became a part of the Lake Shore and Michigan Southern.

Ohio was in an even greater hurry than Illinois to acquire a railroad system. The people of Sandusky held a meeting in 1825 to plan a railroad to Dayton. This was a year before a charter was issued to the Mohawk and Hudson, the first link in the chain that afterward became the New York Central. But the scattered settlers in the woods had not then learned the potency of the legislative fiat in building railroads, and as the Sandusky crowd had no money, nothing came of the scheme.

The agitation was kept up, however, until it resulted in the most remarkable feat in railroad building ever recorded. On the evening of April 25, 1836, seven men, who by their united efforts could not have raised twenty-five thousand dollars, met in the Mansion House, at Painesville, O., and organized the Ohio Railroad Company, to build a line from Pennsylvania across the northern tier of Ohio counties to Manhattan, then a rival of Toledo, now a part of it.

By means of the wonderful " plunder law " of Ohio, which obliged the State to furnish one-third of the capital of railroad companies when the stockholders had furnished the other two-thirds, these seven men, by simply writing their names as subscribers for six hundred thousand dollars' worth of stock, obtained two hundred and nineteen thousand dollars in State bonds, which they sold, thus obtaining the only capital they had.

Having decided to build their railroad on piles instead of grading a roadbed, they were ready for the services of a chief engineer. Cyrus Williams presented himself as a ready-made engineer, and was given the job. Williams had been a barn-builder in central New York until he was crippled by a glancing blow from his adze.

Then he turned shoemaker until he was cured of his lameness through the skill of an Indian friend and the marvelous efficacy of " Seneca Oil," better known now as plain petroleum, when he again became a barn-builder, and by easy gradations developed into a house-builder, and finally a bridge-builder. As the Ohio Railroad was to be one continuous bridge, he was evidently the man for the place.

The construction outfit was the most wonderful traveling railroad circus ever seen. First came a curious framework with two pile-drivers at the front end. Following this was a portable sawmill on the track, with the engine coupled direct to the saw shaft.

This mill furnished the timbers for the structure as they were needed. Back of the sawmill, also on the track, was a traveling boarding-house for the men.

The piles were nine to twenty-five feet long, according to the irregularities of the ground. After they were driven they were cut off to grade by a circular saw on a swinging arm. The pile-drivers were moved forward, holes were bored in the tops of the piles, and a handful of salt poured in to preserve the wood.

Stringers were fastened to the piles by wooden pins, wooden rails were laid on these, and finally strap-iron, weighing twenty-five tons to the mile, was nailed down. Fifty-two miles of this structure, from Fremont to Maumee, were finished by the spring of 1843. Then the continuous quarrels of the directors became so violent that they put an end to the work. No train was ever run over the road.

The first railroad actually operated in Ohio was the Mad River and Lake Erie, now part of the Indianapolis, Bloomington and Western, the first earth on which was turned at the end of Water Street, Sandusky, September 7, 1835, with great festivities.

THE "SANDUSKY,"

The first locomotive with a whistle, which fixed the gauge for early Ohio railroads.

J. H. James, of Urbana, president of the road, happened to be in New York early in October, 1837. Hearing that Rogers, Ketchum & Grosvenor, founders of the Rogers Locomotive Works, were to make a trial trip with their first locomotive on the 6th, he obtained permission to go along.

This first Rogers engine had cylinders eleven by sixteen inches inside the frame, with eccentrics outside, and a single pair of drivers four feet six inches in diameter. These drivers were of cast iron, with hollow spokes and rims—a great novelty then. There was a four-wheeled truck in front, but no cab, pilot, nor headlight.

However, the new engine gloried in a whistle, the first ever attached to a locomotive. On the trial trip from Paterson to New Brunswick and back the whistle was so overworked that there was scarcely steam enough to run the engine.

President James was so entranced with the new locomotive, and particularly with the whistle, that he insisted on buying it, notwithstanding that it had been built for a New Jersey road. It was forthwith shipped to Sandusky, arriving November 17, 1837.

Not a foot of track had been laid, but the arrival of the locomotive inspired immediate efforts in that direction. By the time Thomas Hogg, who had accompanied the locomotive as engineer, had his machine set up, enough track had been laid to give the delighted Ohioans an opportunity to see, and particularly to hear, a locomotive in actual operation. That whistle made itself heard all over the State.

Admiring legislators were so impressed with the merits of a locomotive with a whistle that they passed a law at the next session that all railroads built or to be built in the State of Ohio should be of the same gauge as the locomotive at Sandusky, which happened to be four feet ten inches. On the completion of the road to Bellevue, sixteen miles from Sandusky, it was opened for business.

A letter in a newspaper led to the building of the present Cleveland, Columbus, Cincinnati and St. Louis Railroad, just as a similar cause led to the development of the Michigan Central. The letter was written by J. H. Sargent, the noted civil engineer, and was published in the Cleveland *Plain Dealer* early in 1846. It opened the eyes of Cleveland business men to the dangerous rivalry of Sandusky, which was pushing a railroad south to Cincinnati. A company was formed, and Sargent was sent out to make a survey in 1847.

At the farther end of the State railroad development was proceeding more rapidly. The Little Miami Railroad, from Cincinnati through Xenia to Springfield, eighty-three miles, which was begun in 1841, came to be known all over the country as the "Model Road." General Superintendent William H. Clement earned this reputation for his road by his recognition of the necessity of developing the character of his employees and enforcing discipline.

Clement's power was never so well shown as in the unprecedentedly severe winter of 1856-1857, which brought on a fuel famine as bad as that in the Northwest in the winter of 1906. Coal advanced from fourteen to sixty cents a bushel in Cincinnati. The Little Miami was the only road reaching a coal-field. Axles and wheels became as brittle as glass in the intense cold, frequently breaking and demoralizing the train service.

People became so clamorous for coal that they threatened to tear up the tracks because the road could not supply their needs at once. In this emergency train-crews were kept doubling the road almost continuously, with little chance to eat and still less opportunity for sleep, until at last the fuel famine was relieved.

No set of railroad men was ever called upon to endure more severe service than the Little Miami men that winter. Brakemen in those crude days had to get out and stay on top of their trains often for hours with the temperature twenty degrees below zero. Yet no one complained.

Kentucky was five years ahead of Ohio in getting her first railroad in operation. Henry Clay was the leading spirit in this enterprise, the Lexington and Ohio River Railroad, the first west of the Alleghanies and south of the Ohio. It was to run from Louisville to Lexington, and was begun in 1831. Mules furnished the motive power at first. The cars had accommodations for four passengers, provided two of them did not object to riding backwards.

In 1833 a Lexington mechanic made a curious contrivance which he called a " steam motive power." One bleak November day the steam motive power with half a dozen cars attached went out on a trial trip, while all Louisville stood around and envied the fortunate few who could get aboard. The passengers put on rather more airs than the occasion seemed to warrant, until the train got about four miles from town, when snow began falling. At this the steam motive power came to a stop and refused to go any farther. The passengers had to foot it back to town, to their own great humiliation and the intense enjoyment of those who had been left behind.

The colored population felt greatly relieved when the steam motive power was condemned as impracticable, and horses were substituted. The colored sages had said all along that horses were much the safest when the great speed of eight miles an hour was to be attained.

In 1835 a locomotive was obtained from the East and kept in use until the owners, becoming convinced that a railroad would pay, rebuilt the line and ordered more locomotives. The stage companies and wagoners had thought the railroad a great joke at first, but when they realized that it really would become a competitor, they covered the track with gravel and invited any one who wanted his head blown off to step up and try to remove the gravel.

It is curious to find that Abraham Lincoln and Jeff Davis were first arrayed against each other over the affairs of one of these Western incubator railroads. The road which, starting February 27, 1847, as the Rock Island and La Salle Railroad, ultimately developed into the Chicago, Rock Island and Pacific, was the first road to connect the Great Lakes with the Mississippi. The contract for the first railroad bridge across the Mississippi was let by the Rock Island September 26, 1853. The bridge, which was at Rock Island, was finished April 21, 1856. Jeff Davis, as Secretary of War, used all his influence in behalf of the steamboat interests to prevent the building of the bridge, even directing the United States

District Attorney to seek an injunction to stop the work. Judge McLean, however, refused to grant the injunction.

Fifteen days after the bridge was opened one span of it was burned by the steamboat *Effie Afton,* which was on fire, drifting against a pier. The owners of the boat sued the railroad for obstructing navigation and causing the loss of their boat. But Lincoln, as counsel for the railroad company, convinced the jury that the bridge was not an obstruction to navigation, thus retrieving the prestige he had lost as a railroad lawyer in the Michigan Central charter affair, and demonstrating for the first time that he was more than a match for Jeff Davis.

To attempt to follow even a material portion of the formidable flock of railroads hatched by the ardent optimists of the central West would be as profitless as it would be wearisome. In Illinois alone no fewer than 789 distinct railroad organizations were formed between 1835 and 1882, and neighboring States were not far behind.

After 1855 the most ambitious schemes of the " Internal Improvement " era began to be realized, for railroad building then went on with great rapidity. Illinois, which had only 110 miles of railroad in 1850, had 2,799 in 1860. Ohio's mileage grew from 575 in 1850 to 2,945 ten years later; Indiana's from 228 to 2,163; Michigan's from 342 to 779; and Wisconsin's from 20 to 904.

The twin brothers of Colonel Sellers had only mistaken their cue, and appeared on the stage twenty years too soon.

CHAPTER VII

THE FIRST TRANSCONTINENTAL RAILROAD

VIEWED through the perspective of years, the building of the first transcontinental railroad seems less a commercial enterprise, stimulated by political considerations, than a great melodrama in which the stage was a continent and the audience a nation. Like many another prosperous production, the first act of this episode in real life was swamped with talk and skimped in action. But thereafter the thrills came thick and fast in an ascending scale of climaxes, culminating in a grand finale which earned a world's applause.

Taking all the circumstances into consideration, no railroad project so daring has ever been proposed. Bearing in mind the small population and the poverty of the Nation, the half-developed state of the practice of railroad building and operation, and of the myriad other sciences upon which it depends, the immensity of the wilderness to be crossed, the distance from the base of supplies, the crudeness of transportation facilities, the number and implacable ferocity of the savage foes to be encountered, it must be conceded that the building of the Union Pacific and Central Pacific must forever remain unparalleled in the annals of the railroad.

Until the rails met on that fateful day at Promontory the Union was incomplete. It was but a geographical dogma, a mere political theory, which an attempt to materialize the proposed Pacific Empire, or other contingency, might readily have changed. The driving of that last spike riveted the bonds that made the East and the West one grand whole as surely as it held the rail in place. All the magnificent achievements of after years have been possible to the great Nation then made a virile fact: whether they would have been possible otherwise may well be doubted.

Less than six months after the De Witt Clinton, the third locomotive built on American soil, had made its initial trip from Albany to Schenectady, when there were less than a hundred miles of railroad in the country, Judge S. W. Dexter, of Ann Arbor, Mich., proposed, in an editorial in his paper, the *Weekly Emigrant,* of February 6, 1832, that a railroad should be built from the Great Lakes, across more than two thousand miles of unbroken, almost unexplored, wilderness, to the Pacific Ocean.

In the winter of 1836-7 John Plumbe, a Welsh civil engineer who had worked under Moncure Robinson in surveying a route over the Alleghanies for the State of Pennsylvania in 1831-2, and who had afterward acted as superintendent of the railroad between Richmond and Petersburg, Va., asked a few friends and acquaintances to meet him at his home in Dubuque, Ia., to discuss privately the building of a railroad to the Pacific coast. Plumbe, who acted as correspondent for papers in New York, Boston, Philadelphia, Baltimore, and Cincinnati, had long been advocating the building of a transcontinental railroad. Pursuant to a call issued by him, the first pub-

lic convention ever held to discuss the Pacific railroad project, met in Dubuque March 31, 1838. Resolutions asking Congress to appropriate funds for a
survey were adopted and in due time were laid before
Congress by Territorial Delegate George W. Jones.
In response Congress set aside funds with which a
survey for a railroad was made from Milwaukee to
Dubuque. In the winter of 1839-40 Plumbe induced
the legislature of Wisconsin to address a memorial to
Congress asking that the survey be continued west of
the Mississippi. He took the memorial to Washington himself and devoted a good deal of time to advocating his project, but he was too far ahead of time,
and nothing came of his efforts.

Then came Asa Whitney, a New York merchant,
who, while on a business trip to China, became filled
with the idea of a railroad across the continent as the
means of securing for America the rich trade of the
Orient. Returning to New York in 1840, he gave
up business, and with the fanaticism of a Mad Mullah
preaching a holy war devoted ten years of his life and
all of his fortune to advocating the immediate building of a transcontinental railroad.

In 1845 he submitted to Congress a proposal to
undertake the building of the road in consideration
of a grant of land sixty miles wide for the length of
the route. For the next five years he bombarded the
national legislature with memorials and addresses,
carrying on, at the same time, a vigorous publicity
campaign.

Whitney's plan was coldly received in the East.
Six months' hard work was required to get enough
signatures of well-known citizens of Philadelphia to

justify a call for a meeting, which was finally held in that city December 23, 1846. Whitney's eloquence made few converts.

Going to New York City, he fared even worse. Although Mayor John Swift was induced to preside at a meeting January 4, 1847, a mob broke up the meeting, and Mayor Swift, the vice-presidents, and Whitney were glad to escape by the back door.

Whitney's bill was killed in Congress in July, 1848, chiefly through the efforts of Thomas Benton. The project was revived in another bill, only to be summarily slaughtered in January, 1849, through the efforts of Benton. Then Whitney made a canvass of the State legislatures, and in 1850 was back in Congress again with a new bill for his project, backed by memorials from the legislatures of fourteen States and from public meetings in eight cities.

At the first session of the Thirty-first Congress committees of both Houses made exhaustive reports favoring Whitney's transcontinental railroad project; but sectional feeling killed the bill a third time, and that was the end of Whitney's efforts. Worn out with his exertions, and his money all gone, he had no choice but to give up the struggle. His remaining years were eked out on the proceeds of a small dairy in Washington.

An interesting estimate of Whitney's character, which may explain why Congress looked with so little favor upon his scheme, may be found in the following extract from an editorial in the *American Railroad Journal* of April 5, 1851:

" We freely admit that Mr. Whitney possesses some qualities which eminently fit him to head a great enterprise. He is enthusiastic and possessed to a remarkable degree with the capacity for inspiring others with his own views. He is deterred by no obstacle and discouraged by no defeats. But here his qualifications for conducting to a successful issue a work of such immense magnitude as that of a railroad from the Atlantic to the Pacific end. He is self-confident without experience or training, arrogant in his opinions, and over-bearing toward all who differ from him. He has a hearty contempt for the whole engineering profession and loses his temper the moment that one of that class talks about tunnel-ing, bridging, excavation, etc., which are certainly great an-noyances in railroad construction and which have made others, besides Mr. Whitney, lose their temper. He can never toler-ate the introduction of such disagreeable topics as these, but is never tired of poring over maps and enlarging upon the grandeur of his scheme. So long as his mission was confined to the matter of arousing the attention of our people to the importance of the proposed work, his success was remark-able. The moment he came to the question of construction his plans failed to receive respectful attention. Congress, in fact, refused the courtesy of printing extra copies of his bill for circulation and turned the cold shoulder upon the whole scheme. As far as the railroad to the Pacific is concerned the public voice is unanimous in its favor; but in reference to the plan of construction, that of Whitney has hardly a de-fender. We are sorry for his disappointments and heartily wish he would adapt his scheme to the practical ideas of the present day, of which he appears to have not the least appreciation."

When Whitney made his final exit, Josiah Perham, of Boston, took up the rôle of prophet to carry on the crusade for a transcontinental railroad. To Per-ham his efforts were literally in the nature of a cru-sade, for he believed he had a divine mission to bring about the building of the road.

Perham was a Maine woolen manufacturer, who lost all his property by unwise plunging in land speculation. Going to Boston in 1842, he started a wool commission business, in which he prospered for a time, but was again a bankrupt seven years later. He was about to start for California during the great excitement of 1849 over the discovery of gold, when he chanced to make the acquaintance of an artist who had just completed a panorama of Niagara Falls, the St. Lawrence, and the Saguenay. He saw a chance to make some money out of this, so he abandoned his contemplated trip to California.

Perham's plan was to go to nearby towns and organize cheap excursions to Boston to see the " Seven Mile Mirror," as the panorama was called. This gave country people a chance to spend a day in the city at small cost, which they were quick to accept, making Perham's scheme a great success for him and for the railroads.

At first the railroad managers were astonished at the way Perham's plan caught the popular fancy; but they soon recovered and did everything they could to help it along. It was in this way that the cheap excursion business originated.

Perham quickly extended his field of operations to include all New England and Canada. In 1850 he brought more than two hundred thousand excursionists to Boston. Then he began sending parties to New York, Niagara, Quebec, and other points of interest. In twelve years he had made another fortune, and had become one of the most widely known men in the country.

While busy with his popular excursions, Perham

found time to become an enthusiast on the subject of the Pacific Railroad, to evolve a scheme for building it that certainly had the merit of originality, and to convince himself that he had been inspired to execute it. Perham's plan, perfected in 1853, was to apply the popular idea to the financing of the Pacific Railroad. He thought he could collect a million subscriptions of a hundred dollars each from the general public, which, he imagined, was eager to make such an investment from patriotic motives. The People's Pacific Railroad was incorporated in Maine, March 20, 1860.

In Congress Perham received scant encouragement, even though he was able to secure the support of the omnipotent Thad Stevens. Finally a bill was drafted which met the views of Congress, but not until after the Union Pacific and Central Pacific had been launched. The measure was signed by President Lincoln July 2, 1864.

The People's Pacific Railroad became the forerunner of the Northern Pacific; but Perham did not live to see the work under way. His last fortune was frittered away on this Pacific Railroad propaganda, and, like Whitney, he died a poor man.

The first soil actually moved in the attempt to build a transcontinental railroad was turned July 4, 1851, on the south bank of Choteau pond, on the outskirts of St. Louis, by Mayor Luther M. Kennett, who then expressed the eloquent hope that the spade with which he did it " would not rust until it was finally burnished by the golden sands of the Pacific." St. Louis, then a city of 90,000 inhabitants, with a commerce of fifty million dollars a year, had had the railroad fever ever since the first railroad convention was held April 20, 1836. Yet nothing was accomplished until the Pacific Railroad Company, of which Thomas Allen was president, was incorporated January 31, 1850. The track of the company, which ultimately became the Missouri Pacific, did not reach Kansas City until October, 1865. The spades of its builders have not yet been " burnished by the golden sands of the Pacific."

Meanwhile, in the decade from 1850 to 1860, Congress devoted a large and steadily increasing proportion of its time to discussion of the Pacific railroad project. As the idea grew, no Congressional orator considered an address on any topic complete without a fulsome peroration devoted to the Pacific railroad. Senator Butler, of South Carolina, declared:

" The Pacific railroad project comes nearer being a subject of deification than anything I ever heard in the Senate."

The net result of all this talk was an appropriation of one hundred and fifty thousand dollars in 1853 to defray the expenses of six surveys to ascertain the most practicable route for the proposed road. An additional appropriation, later on, paid for four more surveys. There was scarcely a town or a hamlet from Canada to the Gulf and the Atlantic that was not only willing to be benefited to the exclusion of other towns by being made the terminus of a railroad built at government expense, but was also determined to see that the road was not built on any other terms.

Charleston, S. C.; Memphis, New Orleans, Corpus Christi, Tex.; Fulton, Ark., and Independence, Mo., were among the insistent candidates for the terminus, backed by the Southern statesmen, who were resolved that the road should not benefit the North, whatever happened.

The war with Mexico had added California to the Union. A year later the discovery of gold, followed by the rapid development of agricultural and other resources, capped, finally, by the finding of the great Comstock lode, built up sources of traffic which demanded better facilities than were afforded by a sea voyage of nineteen thousand miles. Lastly, there appeared at the proper time, as he always does, the Man.

To Theodore D. Judah belongs the credit of making the actual beginning of the first transcontinental railroad. Judah was educated at the Troy Engineering School. He was resident engineer of the Connecticut River Railroad, surveyed and built the railroad from Niagara Falls to Lewiston, and served as engineer on the Erie Canal, and on the Rochester and Niagara Falls Railroad.

He gave up a lucrative position in 1854 to go to California to build the Sacramento Valley Railroad, the first on the Pacific coast. Twenty-two miles of that road were completed in 1856.

Judah was not only almost as much of a fanatic on the subject of a Pacific railroad as Asa Whitney, but he combined with the enthusiasm of the promoter the practical knowledge of the engineer and the executive capacity which gets things done. In the fall of 1856 he went East to raise funds for extending the Sacramento Valley Railroad from Marysville to San Francisco.

The winter of 1856-1857 he spent in Washington

trying to secure a land grant for the railroad scheme. Returning to California, he took a prominent part in the railroad convention held in San Francisco September 19, 1859. He was sent as the accredited agent of this convention to Washington to lobby for the transcontinental road.

His room became the headquarters for advocates of the Pacific railroad, and he himself was the recognized authority on everything relating to the subject. He was made secretary of the Pacific Railroad Committee of the House, and was accorded the privileges of the floor of both Houses.

So effectively did Judah labor that he returned to California in the summer of 1860, confident of success when the new administration came in, to solve a problem which was the bugbear of timid Congressmen. This was to find a pass through the Sierras.

Judah had no money to pay for surveys, and the business men of San Francisco had borne his expenses to Washington that he might induce other people to foot such bills, not to earn the privilege of doing it themselves. So the engineer went to his friends in the mountains.

They hadn't much to spare, but what they did have they gave freely. Dutch Flat, Illinoistown, Grass Valley, and Nevada City, among them, raised the money to buy the outfit for Judah's trip into the Sierras and the men to help him.

Mrs. Judah accompanied the party. While her husband was out with the men she caught trout for their meals. When the larder was supplied she laid aside her rod and sketched the magnificent mountain scenery. Two of her sketches were used on the stock certificates of the Central Pacific Railroad; others went to enlighten outsiders regarding California.

Judah was as successful with his transit as his wife was with rod and pencil. He found a pass by which the Sierra Nevadas could be surmounted 128 miles east of Sacramento on a maximum grade of 105 feet to the mile at a maximum cost of $150,000 a mile, a saving of 184 miles in distance and $13,500,000 in money over the route proposed by the government engineers.

Returning to Dutch Flat, he made the first profile of the new pass on the counter of his friend D. W. Strong's drug-store. Armed with this, he proceeded to Sacramento. He had been in the habit of dropping in at the hardware store of Huntington & Hopkins, No. 52 K Street, where he was always sure of finding sympathetic spirits with whom he could discuss his hobby.

Calling together C. P. Huntington and Mark Hopkins, the proprietors of the store; the Crocker brothers, dry goods merchants down the street, and Leland Stanford, wholesale grocer, Judah told of the practicable pass he had found. They were quick to realize what it meant, and warmly urged him to go to San Francisco and raise the capital; then they would help him to form a company and take care of the profits. The uniform willingness to let some one else foot the bill for the Pacific railroad was as spontaneous and as cordial west of the Sierras as east.

Judah went to San Francisco with the profile of his practicable pass and figures showing that two hundred eight-mule teams passed over the Placerville road to Virginia City daily, and half as many over the

Henness road, which traffic alone would make a very respectable local income for a railroad. But the San Francisco capitalists laughed at him.

Once more Judah traveled the dusty road to the hardware store in Sacramento. What he said when he arrived there no outsider will ever know, but it must have been very much to the point, for in June, 1861, the Central Pacific Railroad Company, with a capital of one hundred and twenty-five thousand dollars, was organized.

Leland Stanford, who had just been elected Governor, was president of the company; C. P. Huntington, vice-president; Mark Hopkins, the other member of the hardware firm, treasurer; James Bailey, secretary, and Judah, chief engineer. The Sacramento merchants didn't object to putting their names down for fifteen thousand dollars each, or even to contributing enough actual cash to send Judah East again after the necessary capital.

In October, 1861, Judah set out for Washington once more, as agent of the Central Pacific Railroad, to secure government aid in bonds and land to build the road. He drew up a bill embodying substantially the plan upon which the road was finally built, and intrusted it to A. A. Sargent, newly elected Representative from California.

The House passed the bill May 6, 1862, the Senate June 20, and President Lincoln affixed his signature July 1. Judah was able to start back to Sacramento ten months after he left there with his object accomplished.

Even with government aid assured, the San Francisco bankers still refused to put up the ready money needed to make a beginning. Orders had been given for plans for an office building. Just as a final and more than usually emphatic negative had been received to the last appeal for funds, the architect walked into the hardware store and with pardonable pride exhibited his designs.

Huntington, senior partner in the hardware firm and the actual executive of the railroad company, glowered at the plans in silence. At last he blurted out:

" How much is that thing going to cost? "

" Only twelve thousand dollars."

" Twelve thousand dollars! Why, man, do you know we'll have to pay the bill ourselves? Here, I can beat that to a frazzle."

Taking up a piece of chalk, Huntington rapidly drew on a door the plans for the first general offices of the Central Pacific Railroad. The building was completed that same afternoon, at a cost of one hundred and fifty dollars. Finding that they really would have to make a beginning with their own scanty means, the Central Pacific directors decided that they would only undertake what they could pay for.

Grading was begun January 1, 1863, when Governor Leland Stanford shoveled some sand from a cart into a mudhole at the foot of K Street, Sacramento, in the presence of the members of the legislature, the State and city officers, and a mixed crowd which was highly amused by the idea of a bunch of local storekeepers trying to build a railroad across the continent. But once the work was begun it never stopped until it was completed.

The first shipment of rails arrived in Sacramento in October, 1863. By June 1, 1864, the track had been laid to Newcastle, thirty-one miles from Sacramento, and nine hundred and thirty feet above the sea.

Although the legislature authorized San Francisco, Sacramento, and Placer counties to issue bonds to a total amount of one million one hundred and fifteen thousand dollars in aid of the road, this action had no effect whatever upon the adamantine hearts of the coast capitalists. In desperation the hardware store crowd scraped the till and managed to get together enough money to send Judah East once more— this time to try to sell their franchise.

But he caught the fever in crossing the Isthmus of Panama, and died in November, 1863. He was only thirty-seven years old, but he had laid the corner-stone of a mighty monument to himself.

Fortunately for the hardware store crowd, the Eastern capitalists preferred government bonds to railroad securities. The only way to get back the small amount they had invested was to put in more and keep putting in more. Accepting the inevitable at last, they went at the task in dead earnest, and by a succession of miracles raised money enough to meet the pay-rolls and other bills while they worked with desperate energy to finance the enterprise. Also, they took care to retain control of the situation.

Not until September, 1866, three years and eight months from the date of beginning, did the rails reach Alta, seventy miles east of Sacramento, at an elevation of 5,625 feet. Two months later the line had been extended twenty-three miles farther to Cisco, overcoming an elevation of 2,286 feet in that distance. The road was now in the very heart of the Sierras, only thirteen miles from the summit.

By this time the Union Pacific Railroad, which had been organized to build the eastern end of the line, stimulated by the example of the Central Pacific, was under way. Although the former did nothing for eighteen months after the latter began operations, by the time the Central Pacific was ninety-three miles into the mountains, where the maximum government subsidy was only half the cost of construction, the Union Pacific had extended its rails two hundred and forty-seven miles out on the plains, on an average grade of thirteen and a half feet to the mile, where the minimum subsidy more than paid for the road.

The Union Pacific Company had seen quite as much of trouble as the hardware store crowd. Under the act of 1862, the Union Pacific was duly organized, with General John A. Dix as president, and T. C. Durant as vice-president. By heroic exertions the company contrived to raise money enough to pay the expenses of celebrating the breaking of ground at Omaha, December 2, 1863, eleven months after ground was broken on the Central Pacific.

That was all that was done for many a day. Nobody wanted Union Pacific Railroad securities or land. The Mississippi and Missouri Railroad, which later became the Rock Island, had sent General G. M. Dodge out across the plains on a survey ten years before, but the company didn't think it worth while to push on beyond the Missouri River.

Neither could the Northwestern, then building across Iowa, see any money in a railroad across the lonely plains. No one would have anything to do with the Union Pacific on any terms whatsoever. The company got into such desperate straits that it was obliged to sell part of its material and cars.

No one coming to the rescue of the Pacific railroad project, Congress, in 1864, had doubled the subsidy, making the amount $16,000, $32,000, and $48,000 a mile in bonds, according to the nature of the country, and twenty sections of land per mile instead of ten. Altogether, the government aid offered lacked but $4,000,000 of the estimated cost of the road.

In spite of everything that could be done the Union Pacific remained a financial outcast until the fall of 1867. Capitalists knew the road could never be completed, and that it could not possibly earn expenses if it was built. When it seemed as if the whole affair was doomed to become a humiliating fiasco, Congressman Oakes Ames, of Massachusetts, a wealthy manufacturer whose shovels had become favorably known wherever such implements were used, was asked by the administration to undertake the building of the Union Pacific. By the influence of his great wealth and business connections, aided by the attraction of the increased subsidy, he was finally able to finance the enterprise through the medium of a construction company, the notorious Credit Mobilier, the cause of the greatest legislative scandal in American history.

As the government assumed all risks under this plan, and the profits promised to be enormous, capital at last took up the project, though timidly. So grudgingly was money advanced that the work would have come to a stop even then, and the completion of the enterprise would have been delayed for years, if Oakes Ames had not sacrificed his personal fortune, saying:

" We must save the credit of the road. I will fail."

But as soon as it became a certainty that the Union Pacific would be completed, and that the builders would make immense profits from its construction and operation, blackmailers, stockjobbers, and plunderers of every degree pounced upon it like a pack of famished wolves. Cornelius Wendell, a government commissioner whose duty it was to examine a completed section, refused to approve it until he was paid twenty-five thousand dollars. As delivery of the government subsidy was dependent upon his approval, he got the money.

James Fisk managed to gain control, and then held up the company in the most approved style, threatening to ruin it unless paid his price. When more legislation was needed influential Congressmen required to be " seen," and Oakes Ames made the crowning mistake of his career by taking three hundred and seventy-five shares of Credit Mobilier stock to Washington, where, in his own phrase, which has become a classic, he " put it where it would do the most good."

Those who could find no leverage by which to extort money busied themselves with criticising financial and engineering methods and everything else connected with the project. It seemed as if there were as many foes in the rear as at the front.

Besides all this the physical obstacles to be overcome were immense. Omaha for all practical purposes was almost as inaccessible as San Francisco. The nearest railroad was the Northwestern, one hundred and fifty miles to the east, and in no hurry to reach Omaha. Every pound of supplies had to be brought overland by wagon or up the Missouri River in steamboats.

As a sample of the expense of railroad building under these circumstances it may be mentioned that ties cost two dollars and fifty cents each when they were finally in place. The workmen had so little confidence in the solvency of the concern that they demanded and received their day's pay before beginning work.

While the white men, who had been so ready to applaud the abstract idea of a transcontinental railroad, and so reluctant to facilitate its realization, were giving the Union Pacific so much trouble, the Indians rendered the company an invaluable service. This they achieved through an earnest effort to lift the scalps of General G. M. Dodge and his escort.

In the winter of 1864-1865 the Indians had declared war by way of varying the steady round of unofficial outrages, which had begun to pall upon them. General Dodge, who had made the survey for the Rock Island in 1853, was sent out to conduct the campaign against them.

Repeated efforts had failed to reveal a pass by which the road could be taken over the mountain range in southern Wyoming. General Dodge, being keenly interested in the Union Pacific survey, took advantage of every opportunity to pick up topographical points.

One day the general took an escort of six cavalrymen, and, arranging to meet the main body of troops at a certain point, set out to have a look at the country. About noon he discovered a large body of Indians trying to corral him and his escort. Being a good Indian fighter, he rode hard for the nearest ridge, where there was no cover to enable the scalp-hunters to stalk him, and started along its crest toward his command, stopping occasionally to beat off the Indians whenever they became too eager.

After a long ride the little party reached the main body of the troops. The ridge upon which the Indians had herded them all afternoon had led them down a gentle slope without a break to the plain. The pass through the mountains had been found.

One year later General Dodge returned to the spot where the ridge blended into the plains and laid out the city of Cheyenne, Wyo. While he was at work the Indians raided a party of Mormon emigrants on the trail over which the general had just passed and killed a couple of men, thus enabling the cemetery of the new town to be started without delay.

By the beginning of 1867 the Union Pacific was in operation to a point three hundred and five miles west of Omaha. The completion of the Northwestern to Omaha, in December, 1866, opened up a line of communication which very greatly reduced the cost of supplies.

The Union Pacific being now extended to a point most convenient for the Indians, all the tribes of the plains united their forces for the avowed purpose of exterminating the whites. Fifteen thousand warriors took the field, devoting especial attention to the railroad.

Everything had to be done under armed guard. The engineers laid out the line within musket-range of a strong military escort, dividing their attention between their instruments and their rifles. Even then numbers of them were killed and their stock run off by thousands.

One party of ten men was " jumped " by Indians in Wyoming. Not being skilled in Indian fighting, they did the worst thing they possibly could have done—they undertook to conceal themselves in a clump of sage-brush, some five hundred feet in diameter, which was commanded by a little bluff at a distance of two hundred yards.

The sage-brush afforded no protection, and simply provided a cover under which the Indians could creep up on them without risk of being seen. Whenever a white man moved or made a sound a volley of bullets would come in his direction. When darkness came three white men, the only ones left alive, crept from that sage-brush and contrived to reach safety.

Not satisfied with murder and robbery, the Indians pulled up the surveyors' stakes and destroyed them, so that much of the work had to be done over.

At first the Indians had not known what to make of the locomotive; but soon they gathered courage to try to stop a train by stretching a lariat across the track held by thirty braves on each side. After it was all over the red man had a new grievance against his pale-faced oppressor, which he sought to redress in the usual way. A station near the scene of the disastrous hold-up was raided next evening.

One man was caught before he could reach the shelter of the building. Him the Indians took to a little depression, where they would be out of range of the guns of the few men in the station, staked him out on the ground, built a small fire on his breast, and then gathered about it to warm themselves and enjoy the agonies of the victim. His cries could be heard by the men in the station for several hours, but they dared not venture out in the darkness to attempt a rescue.

The Indians soon learned how to wreck trains. One night in the summer of 1867 they placed an obstruction on the track near Plum Creek, Neb., and ditched a freight train. The engineer, fireman, head brakeman, and conductor were killed. The hind man, named Johnson, was shot in the back.

The bullet knocked him down, but did not render him unconscious. He had presence of mind enough not to utter a sound or move a muscle, even when an Indian seated himself astride his body and with an extremely dull knife proceeded, with great deliberation, to scalp him. This operation completed to the Indian's entire satisfaction, he stripped Johnson of everything but shirt and shoes and left him.

Next morning another train was flagged about a mile from the scene of the wreck by a hideous object, which, upon examination, proved to be Johnson, covered from crown to sole with blood and dirt. His scalp was found where it had been dropped by the Indian in the excitement of plundering the train, but it wouldn't grow on again, although an obliging surgeon gave it every encouragement.

On another occasion the Indians made the unforate mistake of sacking a train when General Dodge was close at hand. The General was on his way back from the front one day, when he was notified at Plum Creek, two hundred miles west of Omaha, that the Indians had captured a freight train a few miles east of the station. Dodge's private car was merely an arsenal on wheels, with enough space left for a berth and a table, which served alternately as a dining table and a desk. On the train were some twenty men, who had had enough of railroad construction on a war footing, and were bound for civilization.

On hearing of the capture of the train, General Dodge immediately called for volunteers to help punish the Indians. Every man on the train immediately fell into ranks like veterans, as, indeed, they were. The engine was coupled on to the private car, the volunteers hastily climbed aboard, and as the engineer coaxed the utmost possible speed out of his machine, they were given arms and instructions. So quickly was the scene of the wreck reached that the Indians were still busy with the plunder without a thought of danger.

In perfect order the volunteers sprang to the ground and deployed. So brilliantly was the maneuver executed that few of the red wreckers escaped.

At Sedgwick the Indians made an exceptionally successful raid, capturing the entire outfits of two sub-contractors and killing such a large number of men that the survivors fled to civilization. It was only after considerable difficulty that others were induced to take their places.

The construction gangs fought off Indians with one hand and wielded pick and shovel with the other. No one will ever know how many men were killed by Indians in the building of the Union Pacific.

Vice-president Durant didn't like to have such things made public.

The only settlements west of the Missouri, with the exception of Denver and a few other mining camps in Colorado and Nevada, were those of the Mormons in the vicinity of Great Salt Lake. Ogden was a village of a few hundred inhabitants.

An exception might be made to this statement if the community of something like three thousand inhabitants living in tents and shacks at the end of the track could be called a settlement. As fast as the road was finished to a convenient point it was operated to that point, which then became temporary headquarters from which the work of construction was managed. The town always moved with headquarters, and so came to be known as " Hell-on-Wheels," and the title was appropriate.

Aside from the railroad employees and a few storekeepers the population consisted chiefly of gamblers and desperadoes and the very worst class of women. The chief article of commerce was vile whisky, and the principal industry was robbery, either thinly disguised as gambling, or by more elementary methods whenever convenient. Only by the frequent application of lynch law were the murders kept down to an average of one a day the greater part of the time.

There was a ceaseless orgy of the lowest debauchery and the grossest crime in this Hell-on-Wheels that has left a stigma which will last as long as the Union Pacific itself. That such shameful conditions are not necessarily a part of railroad building was conclusively demonstrated in the construction of the Canadian Pacific.

At one of its stops, six hundred and ninety-eight miles west of Omaha, in August, 1868, " Hell-on-Wheels " assumed the dignity of a " city," which was divided into five wards and christened " Benton," in honor of the Senator who had taken such a conspicuous part in the fight on Whitney's project for a Pacific railroad. A mayor and full city government were elected, and ordinances to safeguard the public health were adopted. Being the end of the freight and passenger division, and the beginning of the construction division, Benton was an exceedingly lively place. Twice a day enormous trains arrived and departed, and stages left for the end of the Central Pacific track and other points in Utah, Montana, and Idaho. All goods for the front and for points on the plains and in the mountains had to be reshipped.

The streets were beds of alkali dust eight inches deep, which blinded and strangled all passers-by, and floated away in dense irritating clouds to settle in dirty white drifts on the wretched tents and shanties. There were one daily paper, five dance houses, and twenty-three saloons. The chief public resort was known as " The Big Tent," a canvas structure a hundred feet long and forty feet wide, at one side of which was a gorgeous bar lavishly set forth with plate-glass mirrors, cut-glass goblets, glasses, and ice pitchers. Brass bands brayed continuously day and night, while monte, faro, roulette, and chuck-a-luck games never closed.

When railroad headquarters moved, Benton moved also. In a few weeks not a shack was left standing.

While the Union Pacific was struggling with uncompromising Nature, bad Indians, and worse white men, the Central Pacific was also waging a great contest, though of a totally different character, against the Storm King of the Sierras.

To build a railroad through mountains where the slope is one foot rise in each foot of distance, and where winter is an almost continuous series of snowstorms accompanied by high winds, is no trifling matter. To cross the Sierras, fifteen tunnels were driven by the expenditure of a million dollars' worth of blasting-powder, the longest being 1,659 feet. Work on the tunnels had been stopped entirely during the winter of 1865-1866.

To avoid another such delay, Engineer John R. Gilliss kept three shifts of men at work day and night on the approaches to the tunnels in the summer of 1866. One night in the autumn he stumbled over two miles of rough mountain trail and laid out the east end of tunnel number twelve by the light of a bonfire. Before midnight the men were at work.

When winter began the headings were underground, so that the work could go on uninterruptedly, though it was necessary to dig snow tunnels two hundred feet long to keep the entrances open. That winter there were forty-four snow-storms, in some of which ten feet of snow fell. As the usual temperature was about thirty-two degrees above zero, the snow was wet and heavy.

During the storms the wind blew so violently that the drifting snow hid a warehouse thirty feet from the cabin of the engineers. One man was lost in going a short distance in a straight line between rock walls, and came in exhausted. In running lines outside it was necessary to dig deep cuts and tunnels in the snow to get at the original transit points. Yet the tunnel-headings met only two inches out of alignment.

All summer the Central Pacific was pushed on with a force of ten thousand men, principally Chinese, and one thousand three hundred teams. By December 1, 1867, all the tunnels were pierced, and trains were running across the summit to Truckee, one hundred and forty miles east of Sacramento.

The spring of 1868 found the two companies on equal terms. While the Central Pacific had been crossing the Sierras the Union Pacific had surmounted Evans Pass, the highest point on the line, at an elevation of 8,242 feet. Both had ample funds at last, and both were almost equally distant from Monument Point, at the head of Great Salt Lake, the Union Pacific being 522 miles away and the Central Pacific 545 miles.

As soon as the weather permitted a construction campaign was begun which has never yet been equaled. From twenty thousand to twenty-five thousand men, and from five thousand to six thousand teams were employed, and from five hundred to six hundred tons of material were used daily. At one time the Central Pacific had no fewer than thirty vessels loaded with supplies at sea, on the long voyage of nineteen thousand miles from New York around the Horn to San Francisco. Twenty-five sawmills around Truckee worked up timber for the use of the Central Pacific, while a dozen mills in the Black Hills and the Rocky Mountains did a similar work for the Union Pacific.

Money was no object now. Speed, not economy, was the great desideratum. In their eagerness to earn as much as possible of the subsidy the rival companies pushed their grades ahead until they overlapped more than two hundred miles. In an attempt to get beyond Promontory Point, where there was a section of the most intricate alignment, heaviest grades, and sharpest curves on the entire line, the Union Pacific took the work out of the contractors' hands and put on day and night shifts to finish the job in a hurry.

The result was that at the finish it cost $618,000 to move 178,000 cubic yards of material, whereas it had cost but $623,000 to move 800,000 yards under the contract system. The track-layers followed the graders as closely as the delivery of material would permit. In 1867 the Union Pacific laid 240 miles of track; in 1868, 425 miles, and to May 10, 1869, when the tracks met, 125 miles. The Central Pacific laid 94 miles through the mountains in 1867, 363 miles in 1868, and 186 miles to May 10, 1869.

General Jack S. Casement and his brother, D. C. Casement, directed the Union Pacific forces, which were handled like an army. In fact, the force on the Union Pacific was largely composed of former army men. Operations partook somewhat of the nature of military maneuvers. The men marched to work to beat of drums, with outposts as a precaution against surprises by Indians. As expressed in one of the popular songs of the day, it was:

> " Then drill, my Paddies, drill;
> Drill, my heroes, drill;
> Drill all day,
> No sugar in your tay,
> Workin' on the U. P. Railway."

The engineers were the skirmishers, and the tie-makers, of whom there were fifteen hundred employed in the mountains, were the advance guard. The ties had to be sent to the railroad in large wagon trains, under strong military escort. Two thousand graders prepared the line. Back of these came the tie-layers. Bridges were framed and the pieces numbered at the mills, ready to be put together immediately on reaching the front.

Twenty miles back of the tie-layers were the construction trains, and still back of these half a dozen miles were the supply trains. Cars were loaded with the proper proportion of rails, chairs, bolts, and spikes, so that there should be no delay in putting down the iron.

First of all was the boarding train of rough sleeping, kitchen, dining, and office cars, that the men might lose no time between their meals and their work. The boarding train would be pushed up to the end of the track while a supply train was run up behind it and unloaded. Then the boarding train would be pulled back, to allow the material to be loaded on little dump-carts, which two horses would take to the front at a gallop.

Arriving there, four men on each side would seize the rails, run forward, and drop them in place, in an average time of thirty seconds to the rail. A gang following them would half drive eight spikes to the rail and place the bolts. A second gang drove home the spikes and put in the rest with an average of three blows of the sledge to each spike and tightened the nuts on the bolts.

Lastly came the surfacing gang, which threw in the

ballast, leveled the track, and tamped the ties in place. On many a day the construction gangs of the two companies laid more miles of track than an ox team averaged in a day's travel on the old overland trail. Such performances as these attracted the attention of the newspapers in the East, which began to send their star correspondents to the front and to announce the number of miles of track laid each day, as baseball scores are announced nowadays.

All this notoriety spurred the rival construction gangs to renewed exertions and made them boastful. One day the Union Pacific laid six miles of track. The Central Pacific thereupon laid seven miles in one day. Upon hearing of this feat the Union Pacific laid seven and a half miles.

The Central Pacific authorities declared that their men could lay ten miles in one working day if they wanted to. Vice-president Durant, of the Union Pacific, offered to bet ten thousand dollars that they couldn't do it. The money was covered, and April 29, 1869, was set as the day for the race.

A large party of distinguished guests assembled to see the bet decided. Four thousand men, trained by the discipline of four years to the precision of a machine, began their mighty task on the stroke of seven o'clock. Most of the working force was composed of Chinamen, but the Chinamen were not heavy enough to lay the rails.

For this work there were eight stalwart Irishmen, whose names have been handed down to posterity— Michael Shay, Pat Joyce, Thomas Daly, Mike Kennedy, Fred McNamara, Ed Killeen, Mike Sullivan, and George Wyatt. They handled the rails at the rate of one minute forty-seven and a half seconds to each two hundred and forty feet.

In six hours they had laid eight miles of track, so they nailed a board with the word " Victory " on it to a stake, and stopped for dinner on the boarding train, which was now run up.

After the usual noon rest of one hour, work was resumed. At exactly 7 P.M. ten miles and two hundred feet of track had been laid. To do this required the bringing up and placing in position of 25,800 ties, 3,520 rails averaging 560 pounds each, 55,000 spikes, 7,040 plates, and 14,080 bolts, a total weight of 4,362,000 pounds.

Durant acknowledged himself ten thousand dollars poorer and returned to his own camp. Then, to prove that the job was well done, Campbell, the boarding boss, got on the locomotive and ran the heavy train back over the ten miles of newly laid track in forty minutes.

Ten days after this great track-laying feat, which has never been equaled, all was ready for the driving of the last spike which would unite the two roads, making a continuous line from the Missouri River to San Francisco Bay.

When the two roads met the grades overlapped some eighty miles. The Union Pacific had wasted a million dollars in its reckless race to seize the lion's share of the fat government subsidy. The Central Pacific was too crafty for its rival, for it had induced the Secretary of the Treasury to advance it two-thirds of the bond subsidy on its graded line to Echo Summit, forty miles east of Ogden, before the track was completed to Promontory Point, while the Union

Pacific had actually laid its rails to Ogden. There was a pretty row over this incident, which waxed so virulent that Congress interfered; but the companies concluded it would be the better part of discretion to compromise, which they did; and Congress ratified the agreement by a joint resolution which was adopted April 10, 1869.

A space of a hundred feet had been left between the ends of the two tracks on May 9, 1869. Early on the morning of the following day Leland Stanford and his party arrived at the end of the Central Pacific track in a special train drawn by the locomotive " Jupiter." Soon after the Union Pacific official train, drawn by engine No. 116, bringing Vice-president Durant, Directors Dillon, Duff, and others, arrived.

A strangely mixed crowd of Mormon saints, Mexicans, Indians, Chinese, negroes, Irish laborers, army officers and their wives, Eastern bankers, bullwhackers, muleskinners, frontiersmen, and camp followers had assembled to watch the proceedings with varying degrees of interest, curiosity, or ennui. Mrs. S. W. Strowbridge, wife of the Central Pacific's superintendent of construction, who, by the enthusiastic interest she had taken in her husband's work, had earned the title of " Heroine of the Central Pacific," was given a place of honor.

After the Rev. Dr. Todd, of Massachusetts, had offered prayer, a Chinaman carefully smoothed the spot on which the last tie was to be laid. The tie, of California laurel, beautifully polished, was brought up by the two superintendents of construction, Strowbridge, of the Central, and Reed, of the Union Pacific. In the center of the tie was a silver plate bearing this inscription:

> THE LAST TIE
> LAID IN THE COMPLETION OF THE PACIFIC
> RAILROAD, MAY 10, 1869.

A spike of gold, silver, and iron from Arizona, and one of silver from Nevada were handed to Durant, of the Union Pacific, who stood on the south side of the track. When he had driven these Dr. Harkness handed the last spike, of California gold, and a silver sledge to Leland Stanford.

Then, at 12.45 P.M., the man who six years before, amid the jeers of a knot of street loafers in Sacramento, had tossed the first shovelful of sand turned in the building of the first transcontinental railroad, drove the last spike which completed that splendid achievement.

The motley crowd of six hundred which saw the blows struck was but an insignificant part of the audience which participated in the ceremony. Through connections between the sledge and the telegraph wires the whole Nation heard the strokes that drove home the last spike. Cannon boomed and bells rang out in response to those taps in every city in the land. At Chicago there was a procession four miles long and an address by Vice-president Colfax. At New York the mayor ordered a salute of one hundred guns, and a " Te Deum " was chanted in Trinity Church while the chimes pealed forth the solemn notes of the " Doxology."

San Francisco was delirious with joy. The celebration began there on May 8 and continued uninterruptedly until the night of the 10th. The buildings and the shipping in the harbor were decked with flags and bunting, cannon boomed, bells rang, and whistles tooted for hours; there were speeches and processions, and every one kept open house for all comers.

The completion of the Pacific railroads did more than anything else to put an end to organized outlawry in the West, and to curb hostile Indians, who up to that time had cost the government one hundred thousand dollars each to kill. It developed a traffic which earned for the Central Pacific alone, in the first three months, $1,703,000. Also, the construction of the Union Pacific netted its builders the neat profit of $16,710,432, or twenty-seven per cent on the cost. Finally, it created one of the greatest scandals this country has known when the people who had lacked the nerve to invest their money in the enterprise undertook to get even with the men who had risked and won.

CHAPTER VIII

THROUGH TRIBULATION BY RAIL

IF the uses of adversity are as sweet as the proverb makes them out to be, then the corporate existence of the Atchison, Topeka and Santa Fé Railway Company has been one long rapture. For if there is any conceivable form of trouble which can befall a railroad that has not beset the Santa Fé, no one who was ever connected with the company has been able to name it. Man and Nature separately and in combination seem to have done their honest best to prevent the development of the road.

The fact that in the face of all these difficulties it has grown into a vast system of ten thousand miles, tapping the chief centers of traffic from the Great Lakes to the Gulf and the Pacific, is an eloquent tribute to the genius of its builders.

The builders of the Santa Fé were a remarkable lot of men, as, indeed, they had need to be. Their talents covered a wide range, for the obstacles they had to overcome ran all the way from poverty and prejudice to military strategy. For, be it known, the Santa Fé and its adversary, the Denver and Rio Grande, enjoy the unique distinction of being the only railroads that ever levied war and maintained armies in the field.

First of these builders, in point of ability as well as chronologically, was Colonel Cyrus K. Holliday, the dreamer, the enthusiast, who saw before any other man could the golden future of the great Southwest. Colonel Holliday was one of the founders of Topeka. As early as 1859 his vision of a transcontinental railroad following the old Santa Fé trail into the Southwest took form. As a member of the Kansas Territorial Senate he secured a charter for his project. That was the only easy step in the building of the Santa Fé.

For the next nine years Colonel Holliday wore out his shoes tramping from office to office of Eastern capitalists in quest of means to finance his vision. He reaped a rich harvest of rebuffs and ridicule, but no money. But he had the true spirit of the pioneer; that is, he never knew when he was defeated.

He kept at it until, in 1867, George K. Beach, of New York, was induced to enter into a contract to build the entire road as then planned. But Beach lacked the courage to carry out the contract, so he assigned it to T. J. Peter, of Cincinnati.

Peter also developed alarming symptoms of cold feet when he went to Kansas to look the ground over, and realized from observation that the Southwest was then inhabited almost entirely by buffalo, prairie-dogs, and Indians, whose principal industry was raising hair. On reflection, however, it occurred to Mr. Peter that a country which could support countless millions of buffalo was capable of supporting civilized men also.

So, the contracting firm of Dodge, Lord & Co., of Cincinnati, was organized, which built the first thousand miles of the road. Twenty-eight miles were built in 1869 between Topeka and Burlingame, Kan.

Once the beginning was made, the end of the track crept steadily westward. In 1863 Congress granted three million acres of land in Kansas to aid in the building of the Santa Fé Railway, which was to become the property of the road only on condition that it was completed to the Colorado line within ten years.

Congress was as free with land grants then as legislatures were with charters.

Probably there never again will be towns as tough as those which punctuated the progress of the Santa Fé across Kansas. Law there was none, and human life was lightly esteemed.

Yet, after all, the men killed were nearly always those who needed killing. Those who attended to their own business were usually permitted to do so in peace.

At Newton, where the road crossed the Texas cattle trail, at Abilene, and at other points it was considered an exquisite bit of humor for a party of drunken cowboys to ride their cayuses up and down the wooden sidewalks at full gallop, yelling at every jump, creating a deafening clatter, the chorus to which was a fusillade of revolver shots.

If any man got in the way of the bullets, that was his affair. There were more saloons than anything else, and each saloon had a dance-hall and a gambling outfit in connection. Everything was wide open—day, night, and Sunday.

But for all-around cussedness the palm must be awarded to Dodge City, which was founded in 1872, on the advent of the Santa Fé. This place was in the very heart of the buffalo country. The face of the earth fairly swarmed with the huge creatures.

A good hunter could make one hundred dollars a day slaughtering them. Every one had money to throw at the birds. A paper of pins, a shave, or a drink cost twenty-five cents. No smaller coin was recognized.

But even in Dodge City there came, by and by, to be a limit to the excesses that could be committed with impunity. Murder was a trivial incident of every-day life for a time. But when Bill McGeachie began to swagger from barroom to barroom boasting, with loud oaths, that he had a jury in hell, meaning that he had sent a dozen men to the nether world with his own pistol, the more respectable part of the community thought it would be a nice thing to send Bill before his jury.

So, there was a quiet little necktie party one evening, at which Bill was the star guest. After that things began to simmer down in Dodge.

The Santa Fé was fixed as a deadline, to the north of which bad men must not venture. On the south side, gamblers and all the scum of that wild civilization rioted for a long time afterward. On the north side, considerable pains were taken to insure freedom from molestation for the peaceably inclined.

A woman was treated with chivalry decidedly militant. If a drunken man accidentally jostled a woman he was promptly knocked down by the nearest bystander, with a profane adjuration to be more polite in future.

The first calaboose in Dodge was a well fifteen feet deep, into which drunks were lowered until they sobered off. Sometimes this unique prison contained half a dozen inmates.

The Santa Fé Railway conducted its business at Dodge City in a box-car for a long time, and it was a very flourishing business, too. Dozens of carloads of buffalo hides and meat were shipped out daily from the very beginning, and other dozens of carloads of merchandise came in to be distributed throughout the Southwest by the long wagon trains which crowded the streets.

As an indication of the extent of the business done in the canvas and clapboard town at the end of the track, it may be noted that Charles Roth & Co., of Dodge City, a few weeks after the town came into existence, ordered by wire two hundred cases of baking powder from Long Brothers, of Kansas City.

The latter firm, thinking there must be some mistake, inquired if the Dodge people really meant two hundred cases.

Back the answer came: " Yes; double the order and rush it."

The public sense of humor was even more fully developed at Dodge than elsewhere. Baiting tenderfeet was a very common form of diversion for a time. Many a snipe hunt was organized, in which the credulous one from the East was inveigled out to a swamp to hold a bag all night, waiting for his new-found friends to drive the snipe into it, while these same friends slipped quietly back to their favorite barroom, where they went into ecstasies of mirth while they waited for the bag-holder to realize that he had been sold.

The favorite joke, though, was an Indian hunt. The tenderfoot would be induced to go out on a buffalo hunt with half a dozen local wits, who would ride by his side and fill his receptive mind with blood-curdling accounts of Indian atrocities until they caught sight of a party dressed in Indian finery which had ridden out ahead. The supposed Indians would ride toward the hunters, emitting the most frightful whoops of which they were capable.

At this the tenderfoot would turn and ride for his life back to the town, to the gratification of the jokers. At last, however, the jokers picked out the wrong tenderfoot.

When the time came for him to exhibit abject fear, instead of carrying out his part of the program he held his base and began pumping lead into the make-believe Indians as fast as his rifle would work. While none of the wounds he inflicted were fatal, they were numerous enough and serious enough to discourage that form of humor thereafter.

At Dodge there was an Irish justice of the peace named Flannery. Two Irish section hands on the Santa Fé got into a quarrel. One attacked the other with a spike-maul, and was promptly killed by his intended victim with a shovel.

Duly penitent, the survivor surrendered himself to the authorities. An investigation showed that he had acted in self-defense. Thereupon he was arraigned before Mr. Justice Flannery.

" Guilty or not guilty? " he was asked.

" Guilty, yer onner."

" Shut your dom mouth. Ye don't know what ye're talkin' about. I discha-arge ye for want av ividence," roared the justice.

The completion of the road to the Colorado line, at the close of 1872, marked the end of the first period in the Santa Fé history. The great problem to be solved in this first period was to inspire capitalists with faith enough in the future of the West to advance money to build the road and earn the valuable land grant.

The next hard nut to crack was to convert the land grants into cash, which was merely incidental to creating traffic that would support the road by peopling the wilderness. This difficult task fell to A. E. Touzalin, who at the age of thirty-three was called to fill the position of general passenger agent, general freight agent, land commissioner, and a few other things.

He was a terrific worker. Soon after he took hold things began to happen in Kansas. Mr. Touzalin was the originator of many of the modern methods of railroad development work. Booklets were prepared and distributed, large advertising contracts placed, and an army of land agents was organized.

One of the most interesting features of this work was that furnished by C. B. Schmidt, who was appointed foreign immigration agent. Mr. Schmidt was the son of the architect to the King of Saxony, who had wandered out to Kansas and had taken up newspaper work. His first trip to secure immigrants was to Russia, after the Mennonites, who were something like the Quakers.

The Russian government heard of Mr. Schmidt's mission, and promptly sent a numerous delegation from the police department with a pressing invitation to him to get out and stay out. But by fast driving and night journeys, enlivened by some rather exciting adventures, he contrived to elude the police and do his work so well that he was followed to Kansas, in 1875, by a first detachment of one thousand nine hundred Mennonites, who brought two million two hundred and fifty thousand dollars in gold with them.

The call of this entire body of men, women, and children in their picturesque costumes on the Governor at Topeka is one of the spectacular incidents in the history of the State.

The energy and originality displayed in this colonization work disposed of the entire land grant in a few years, at an average price of four dollars and seventy-one cents an acre, with expenses and commissions averaging eighty-four cents an acre. Of course, government land tributary to the railroad was also settled at the same time, so that in the ordinary course of events the faith of Cyrus K. Holliday and his co-laborers would have been abundantly justified in a heavy volume of traffic.

But there were drawbacks which no man could foresee. One of these was the great grasshopper raid of 1874. No man who has never seen a grasshopper raid can form any conception of what it is like. For three days the flight of the insects spread a haze over the sun like smoke from a forest fire. They settled down until they covered the face of the earth.

They flew up in such countless swarms against the noses, eyes, ears, and bodies of horses that they ran away, and they covered the railroads so thick that the wheels ground them into a slimy pulp in which the drivers spun impotently around while trains stood still. What was more serious, the grasshoppers ate every green thing within twenty-four hours after their arrival, leaving the new settlers face to face with famine. Many colonists left the country never to return.

That grasshopper year was a severe blow to Kansas, and an even more serious one for the struggling Santa Fé Railway, which started from nowhere and also ended there. The earnings of the five hundred and eight miles in the grasshopper year were two thousand four hundred and sixty-two dollars a mile. But a worse setback was experienced in the drought of 1879-1880. Destitute settlers left the country by thousands, carried free by the railroads. Those who remained had to be supplied with free seed wheat and corn by the railroads. Railroad earnings went down like mercury in a blizzard.

Under these pleasant conditions, Thomas Nickerson undertook, as president of the Santa Fé, the simple task of extending the road. He must have been a wonder, for under such discouraging circumstances he raised the necessary money to push the road steadily to the westward for six years, from 1874 to 1880. Mr. Nickerson's genius was solely as a financier.

Nevertheless, he was immensely popular with the men. He never felt it necessary to put on any frills. When he went out on a tour of inspection he didn't need a private car. He just swung himself aboard the little red caboose at the tail end of a way freight with his lunch wrapped in a newspaper, in his coat pocket, and chummed with the crew.

Stories about these trips in the little red caboose reached the ears of the investing public, and profoundly impressed all hearers with the rigid economy of the Nickerson régime, thus stimulating the drooping price of stock.

The latter part of Mr. Nickerson's administration was not marked by that serene repose which is supposed to be agreeable to financiers. When the road got into Colorado it also got into an entirely new set of difficulties. William B. Strong, a young man who had been brought up in the way he should go on the Burlington road, was made vice-president and general manager.

Now, Mr. Strong was the antithesis of Mr. Nickerson in temperament, taste, and training. Strong was a cyclone which never ran down, to whom strife, difficulty, and discouragement were the breath of life. Whereas Nickerson maneuvered by the gentle arts of diplomacy, Strong greatly preferred, figuratively speaking, to knock his adversary down first and argue with him afterward.

The result was that Nickerson was obliged to spend a good deal of time roosting on the safety-valve of Strong's enthusiasm when he would have preferred a more congenial occupation, while Strong expended a great deal of nerve force in fretting because he was not permitted to tear the Rocky Mountains up by the roots.

Events seem to demonstrate that a judicious blending of these diverse temperaments and talents was exactly what was needed to work out the destiny of the Santa Fé. Unfortunately, the management erred at first regarding what that destiny was to be.

The Santa Fé people had been under the impression that they were to have Colorado for their own. Leadville's palmy days were beginning, and, in fact, the whole State held out alluring promise of rich traffic. But Nature, most unfortunately, had created the Rocky Mountains without regard to the limitations of railroad engineering.

There is only one way through the front range near enough to be of use to the Santa Fé, and that is a mere crack in the granite something less than three thousand feet deep, with sides so straight up and down that a fly attempting to walk upon them would probably fall and break his neck.

Through this crack roars a mountain torrent which becomes the Arkansas River. Several thousand dollars had to be expended in blasting footholds in this granite fissure before the engineers could be sure they could find room to squeeze a line of rails through.

The Santa Fé prepared to build through this tremendous chasm regardless of the fact that the Denver and Rio Grande Railroad Company had been organized some years before to do this very thing, and had made a survey through the cañon, but had been prevented by their poverty from building. The Denver and Rio Grande then had less than four hundred miles of narrow-gauge road in operation.

At the same time the Santa Fé prepared to continue on toward the Pacific coast by way of Raton Pass, which the Denver and Rio Grande also had planned to use in its business.

It is a pretty well established fact that two material bodies cannot occupy the same position in space at the same time. When the bodies which attempt this impossible feat happen to be as substantial as railroads, under the protection of numerous guards of determined Western men whose religion is to shoot before the other fellow does, interesting developments may be looked for.

As a preliminary to the extension through New Mexico, Mr. Strong was sent to Santa Fé to get the necessary legislation and whatever financial aid could be obtained from the Mexicans, as his first task after joining the Santa Fé Railroad, at the close of 1877. On reaching the Territorial capital he found that the Southern Pacific had thoughtfully endeavored, a few days before, to save him the work and worry of building a railroad through the lonely mountains by securing the passage of a certain law.

This law provided that a majority of any board of directors operating a railroad should be residents of the Territory, that they must have ten per cent of the cost of construction on hand before beginning work, and there were other interesting details that would make it impossible for the Santa Fé to raise money to build five hundred miles through that remote region. Moreover, the Mexican natives were decidedly hostile to the proposed American invasion.

But the Southern Pacific forces had made a fatal error. They had neglected to insert in their measure a clause repealing the old law or providing that the new should take immediate effect. The old law was therefore still in force.

With characteristic energy, Strong organized a corporation to build his line through the Territory, and prepared and secured the passage of an innocent little bill relieving his new company from all the objectionable features of the new railroad law. This measure was signed by the Governor before the leisurely hostiles awoke to what was going on.

Strong hurried back to headquarters, and after much urging secured permission to make the surveys in the spring. As this was in the last week of February, 1878, Strong interpreted " spring " as meaning that moment. He immediately sent a rush message to Chief Engineer A. A. Robinson, who, by the way, achieved the remarkable record of building every mile of the Santa Fé system not acquired by purchase, to go to Raton Pass and take possession.

When Mr. Robinson stepped on the Rio Grande train at Pueblo to go to El Moro, the nearest railroad point to Raton Pass, he found J. A. McMurtrie, the chief engineer of the Rio Grande, on board. Each guessed the other's business.

On reaching El Moro, McMurtrie instantly set about organizing and arming his force, while Robinson hurried to Trinidad, five miles away, as fast as horseflesh could carry him. The Denver and Rio Grande company in the beginning instituted the disastrous policy of avoiding established towns and building up towns of its own. This policy quite naturally embittered a good part of the people of the State, and endangered the existence of the road.

Trinidad was an old town, which had been passed by in favor of El Moro, a creation of the railroad. Consequently, Robinson had no difficulty in recruiting a little army with shovels and rifles, enthusiastically willing to thwart the Rio Grande company and to shoot up its cohorts if opportunity offered. McMurtrie, on the other hand, found it easy to gather a strong force of equally eager partisans of his own road at El Moro.

Robinson's men proved to be the best sprinters, for they reached Raton Pass at four o'clock in the morning, just thirty minutes before the McMurtrie forces appeared. There was a good deal of loud talk, but as neither leader was Western bred, they didn't know where to leave off talking and begin shooting. The baffled Rio Grande forces finally withdrew and left the Santa Fé in possession of the pass.

It was by the narrow margin of thirty minutes, therefore, that the Santa Fé missed being cut off from the coast and left a mere local road, to be gobbled up by a stronger system, for if McMurtrie had reached the pass first he would unquestionably have held it for the Rio Grande.

The first car passed into New Mexico over Raton Summit, December 7, 1878, by means of a switchback three and a quarter miles long, with six switches and maximum grades of three hundred and sixteen feet to the mile. A Baldwin mogul, weighing one hundred and ten thousand pounds, the largest locomotive ever built up to that time, was ordered especially to do the work on this switchback.

A year later a tunnel two thousand feet long pierced the summit at an altitude of seven thousand six hundred and twenty-two feet, reducing the maximum grade on Raton Mountain to one hundred and eighty-five feet. Even that was enough to make things interesting for the train crews before air-brakes came into general use. That same season the grading was completed to Las Vegas, one hundred and ten miles beyond.

While the main line was being pushed over the Raton Mountains, a spectacular struggle was going on for possession of the Grand Cañon of the Arkansas. Strong began making arrangements early in the spring for a *coup*. Being in possession of the telegraph wires, the Rio Grande was able to get hold of cipher dispatches which revealed to them what was going forward.

Strong, who was at El Moro, heard, on the 19th of April, 1878, that General W. J. Palmer, president of the Rio Grande company, had arranged to cut him out of the Grand Cañon. Accordingly, he wired to Engineer William R. Morley, who was at La Junta, to take an engine and proceed with all possible speed to Pueblo, sixty-three miles away, and there take a Denver and Rio Grande train to Cañon City, to organize a force with which he was to take possession of the Grand Cañon and hold it against the Rio Grande. Morley carried out his instructions until he got to Pueblo.

No train to Cañon City being available, he tried to get a narrow-gauge locomotive on the Rio Grande to take him up, but he was refused. He immediately hunted up the best horse procurable in Pueblo, and started late at night on the forty-mile ride to Cañon City. About the same time that he left Pueblo a Rio Grande train also left that place, bearing a force of one hundred men to take possession of the Grand Cañon for General Palmer.

It was a pretty race between horse and locomotive. A narrow-gauge mountain locomotive has to turn its wheels over a good many times to cover a mile, and besides, the track being new and rough, the engineer was not trying to make speed records. Also, the Rio Grande commander didn't know Morley.

It was an unequal race. The horse was good for a spurt, but a forty-mile run against a locomotive was too much. Toward the last he failed under Morley's lash, and something more than a mile from Cañon City he dropped dead.

Without a moment's pause Morley struck a dog-trot, and kept it up till he reached the office of the local company which had been organized to build the road for the Santa Fé. With all possible speed he gathered a force of one hundred and fifty men and started for the mouth of the cañon, two miles away, on the run.

Precious little time was lost in this, for Cañon City was bitter against the Rio Grande for seeking to build a rival town near by, and citizens were never very widely separated from their guns.

Arriving at the mouth of the canon, part of the force began digging wherever they could find any loose dirt. The construction of the Santa Fé road through the Grand Cañon had begun. The rest selected nice cozy nooks behind bullet-proof bowlders, arranged their rifles and six-shooters so they would be real handy, and waited as if they were expecting some one.

They didn't wait long. The Rio Grande people were so sure they had the advantage that they had not exhibited undue haste; therefore, on a second momentous occasion they arrived thirty minutes too late.

Knowing only too well that the arrangements made for their reception were no idle bluff, the Rio Grande forces withdrew after a brief parley. Work was pushed on the grading with all possible despatch.

Strong was so delighted with Morley's achievement that he presented him with a repeating rifle elaborately mounted with gold. While making a survey for the Santa Fé near Guayamas, Mexico, some time

THE ROYAL GORGE, FOR POSSESSION OF WHICH THE RIO GRANDE
WAR WAS WAGED.

At the point where the hanging bridge is seen in the background the canyon is
thirty feet wide at the bottom, while the walls rise almost vertically 2,627 feet
above the track.

later, Morley attempted to take this rifle out of an ambulance muzzle foremost.

The gun was discharged, killing him instantly. His name has been given to a station on the main line near the southern border of Colorado.

Possession of the Grand Cañon was necessary to the existence of the Rio Grande. The company, therefore, never for a moment considered the possibility of giving up the struggle for it. A working force, guarded by a small army of fighting men, took possession of the cañon some distance above where Morley was at work, erected forts, and began the construction of the road.

Thereupon the Santa Fé obtained an injunction to restrain the Rio Grande forces from any further action, and also had Chief Engineer J. A. McMurtrie and Treasurer R. F. Weitbrec, of the Rio Grande, arrested.

Both sides continued to seize and fortify all available points in the cañon above and below. There were numerous arrests every day, and events were hurrying forward as speedily as possible to a bloody encounter, when, on April 26, the Rio Grande secured an injunction to stop the Santa Fé's work. Ten days later the Rio Grande had the injunction proceedings transferred to the Federal courts, alleging that it could not get justice in the local courts, which was strictly true, as the feeling against it at Cañon City was intense.

Judge Hallett, of the Federal Court, enjoined both parties from doing anything in the cañon until their rights could be decided in the courts. Each party was placed under twenty thousand dollars bond. The matter was taken to the United States Supreme Court.

For a while it looked as if the guns were to be put aside while the contest was fought to a finish with the less romantic check-book. President Nickerson was continuing his achievements in raising money for construction, the system had grown to a total of eight hundred and sixty-eight miles, and the earnings for 1878 were three million nine hundred and fifty thousand eight hundred and sixty-eight dollars, while the Rio Grande was growing more hopelessly involved every day. General Palmer grew discouraged, and on the 19th of October, 1878, leased his road to the Santa Fé. Possession of the road was given at midnight, December 13, 1878.

This move by no means allayed the ill-feeling between the rival companies. The Santa Fé's first act intensified the feeling, aroused the antagonism of the people of Colorado, and played into the hands of the Rio Grande company. A part of the agreement under which the lease was made provided that the lessee should not discriminate against Denver.

In defiance of this agreement, rates from Denver southward were immediately raised, which had the effect of cutting off Denver's jobbing trade and throwing it to Kansas City. In other ways the Santa Fé gave indications of an intention to wreck the Rio Grande road; at least, so the Rio Grande people said.

Almost immediately after the lease was executed the Rio Grande company, alleging that the instrument had been broken in letter and spirit by the lessee within twenty-four hours after taking possession of the road, set about getting its property back again.

General Palmer renewed his efforts to raise money for construction to Leadville, and at last was successful.

As time went on the Rio Grande people became exasperated to the fighting point. The sentiments of the management were cordially shared by its old employees in the train and engine service. W. W. Borst, superintendent for the Santa Fé, had to issue a circular admonishing his men to take orders from no one but the Santa Fé authorities.

Armed detachments began to slip into the Grand Cañon and fortify advantageous positions in March, 1879, in anticipation of the decision of the United States Supreme Court, which was expected soon. April 19, Mr. Strong went to Denver to prepare for the war in the Grand Cañon which seemed inevitable, and also for the impending legal struggle.

Early in June, 1879, the Rio Grande people procured from Judge Bowen, at San Luis, an order restoring the road to them. This order was placed in the hands of the sheriffs of the various counties, to be served simultaneously all along the line at 6 o'clock on the morning of Wednesday, June 9. The Rio Grande saw to it that the sheriffs had plenty of armed men to enforce the mandate of the court.

The spectacular feature of the day was the raid of ex-Governor A. C. Hunt, an enthusiastic Rio Grande partisan, who is described as a " whirlwind of energy and indiscretion." He lived up to his characterization in a raid, on that memorable 9th of June, which makes the exploits of Mosby's guerrillas seem tame.

Starting from El Moro, bright and early, with a train carrying two hundred armed men, he swept everything before him as he went up the line to Pueblo. Station agents were captured and taken on the train. There was a good deal of shooting, and at Cuchara two Santa Fé men were reported killed and two wounded. At Denver, office doors were battered in with a cross-tie handled by husky section men. At most points there was an easy victory for the Rio Grande.

At Pueblo, things looked squally for a time. The Santa Fé had recruited a select band of fighting men at Dodge City, under the command of Bat Masterson, who as marshal of that interesting town had achieved a reputation for skill and celerity in disposing of bad men who expressed a desire to shoot him up.

This formidable force was posted in the roundhouse at Pueblo on that 9th of June. The Rio Grande army did not attempt to take the fortress by storm, but threw up fortifications commanding it and prepared for a siege. Doubtless there would have been another Sebastopol if it had not been for R. F. Weitbrec, the practical-minded treasurer of the Rio Grande.

On the theory that the dollar is mightier than the six-shooter, Mr. Weitbrec sent a flag of truce to the roundhouse. In due time he transacted a little private business with the valiant defenders of Pueblo, and the siege was ended.

One last stronghold in Pueblo remained in the hands of the Santa Fé, and that was the despatcher's office. This was taken late in the evening by an assault in which there was a great deal of shooting, but no list of killed and wounded. Ex-Governor

Hunt's victorious army then made a dash upon Cañon City, where some Santa Fé fugitives had fled with four locomotives. The place was captured without resistance.

On taking possession of the road, Mr. Strong had allowed the old Rio Grande men, with the exception of a few station agents, to retain their places. This may have been good railroad management, but it was mighty poor military strategy.

When war broke out the whole operating department not only became willing captives, but on reaching Colorado Springs, which was then headquarters of the Rio Grande, each crew received arms and ammunition to defend its train from recapture.

Vanquished in war, Mr. Strong appealed to the United States Circuit Court at Denver, where Judges Miller and Hallett, on the 23d of June, ordered the road restored to the lessee within three days. They added an emphatic warning that it would be well if the mandate of the court were obeyed, but intimated that legal proceedings might be begun to cancel the lease.

Great was the wrath of the Rio Grande men over the order of restitution. Santa Fé engineers were pulled from their cabs and beaten; threatening notices, decorated with skulls and cross-bones, were sent to agents, brakemen, and every one connected with the Santa Fé. A word of sympathy for the Santa Fé was a bid for a broken head.

Blood flowed freely, and the authorities were powerless. Judge Hallett ended the disturbance by appointing Colonel L. C. Ellsworth receiver, on the 24th of June, who managed the road until it was restored to the Rio Grande company, which has remained in undisturbed possession ever since.

During the war the United States Supreme Court had rendered a decision in the contest for possession of the Grand Cañon favorable to the Rio Grande. The Santa Fé had not thought it worth while to wait for this little formality, and had rushed work with such energy that twenty miles of road had been completed, and the rest of the line to Leadville nearly all graded.

To show that there was no hard feeling, the Rio Grande sent Engineer De Remer to carry news of the decision to the Santa Fé construction gang. Mr. De Remer, for company's sake, took fifty men with him on the journey to the end of the track; also fifty repeating rifles. Hunting up the Santa Fé engineer in charge, he ordered him to stop work instantly.

" By whose authority do you give that order? "

" By the decision of the United States Supreme Court and these fifty men behind me."

Work was stopped.

Jay Gould, having through heavy purchases of Rio Grande stock, acquired the right to act as mediator, a protocol was signed, December 20, 1879, which put an end to the Rio Grande war, the most extraordinary episode in the annals of the railroad. For months each belligerent had maintained an army of three hundred to five hundred men in the field, had laid sieges, built fortifications, captured trains, cut telegraph wires, kidnaped public officials, purloined court seals, kept a whole State in a ferment, and done many other picturesque things which are now regarded as foreign to railroad operation.

By the treaty of Boston, signed February 11, 1880, all possibility of further hostilities was obviated. By the terms of the treaty the lease was canceled, the receivership ended, all litigation was stopped, the line to Leadville became the property of the Rio Grande on payment of one million four hundred thousand dollars to the Santa Fé, and the Rio Grande's projected line from Pueblo to St. Louis was abandoned. The Santa Fé had now grown to one thousand one hundred and eighty-one miles, and its earnings in 1879 were six million three hundred and eighty-one thousand four hundred and forty-two dollars.

Having abandoned its Colorado plans, the Santa Fé was free to devote all its energies to building on to the Pacific. They were needed. While New Mexico is generally regarded as a desert, the face of the country shows unmistakably that it is visited by rainstorms of extreme violence. The engineers consulted old inhabitants at great length, studied the topography of the country, and constructed the road in accordance with the information thus obtained.

But after they had built an impregnable culvert at one point to carry off the surplus waters, they would go out after a storm to find that not a drop of water had flowed through it, while some miles of track they had regarded as safe from the possibility of washout would be scattered promiscuously over the landscape for miles around.

The Rio Grande River was also extremely troublesome. One day it would be on one side of the track, the next day on the other. As late as 1884 Superintendent George L. Sands and his men might be seen wading, swimming, and diving in efforts to find a section of main line over which trains had been running a few hours before.

In 1880 the Santa Fé entered into an alliance with the St. Louis and San Francisco Railroad to build at once that part of the old Atlantic and Pacific line west from Albuquerque, and thus gain an entrance into California independent of the Central Pacific influence. As a precaution against this hostile influence it was provided that the control of the road was to be in the hands of three trustees, two of whom were to be from Boston, where Santa Fé stock was chiefly owned, and that seven of the thirteen directors were to be Santa Fé men.

Late in 1881 the expenditure of sixteen million five hundred thousand dollars was authorized, and the stockholders were jubilant over the prospective speedy completion of the road. Early in January the astounding fact became known that Jay Gould and C. P. Huntington had purchased the St. Louis and San Francisco, and were in a position to prevent the extension of the road. Gould wanted the Southwest for his own roads, and Huntington was interested in protecting his California monopoly. Both insisted that the Santa Fé should stop at the Colorado River.

Other troubles followed thick and fast. Between 1885 and the beginning of 1888 the Missouri Pacific, a Gould line, built one thousand and seventy-one miles of road, and the Rock Island built one thousand three hundred miles paralleling the Santa Fé. The payment of dividends ceased, the price of stock went down to almost nothing, and the road lost the confidence of shippers and the respect of competitors.

The panic of 1893 put on the finishing touches. There was a receivership and a reorganization, and then prosperity.

Cyrus K. Holliday lived to see his dream fulfilled. The road of which he was a director for twenty years, and which one of his cheerful fellow members of the board predicted would never pay operating expenses, now runs through trains over its own rails from Chicago to Denver, Galveston, Los Angeles, and San Francisco.

Its hoodoo has at last been laid, its rifles have been traded for coupon scissors, and the competitors who once treated it with contumely now respectfully request the loan of its recipe for boosting net earnings. The hopes of its founders have been realized.

CHAPTER IX

ROMANCE OF A GREAT RAILROAD

TO speak of the building of the Canadian Pacific Railway as a " work," sounds almost pedantic. Think of men toiling month after month through almost impenetrable forests, seeking a way across a mountain range, and when at last it seemed as if they must be forced to admit themselves defeated, being led by an eagle to the only pass in the entire range!

Think of a vast wilderness turned as if by enchantment into a populous and thriving empire by the magic of the steel highway, built on the route the eagle revealed! Think of an enterprise which involved the expenditure of one hundred and forty million dollars which the breath of scandal never tarnished, which met every obligation when it was due, and many even before they were due; and which voluntarily pensioned those dependent upon the pioneers who lost their lives in its service!

Think of the poor Scotch boy, who began life in the desolation of the Labrador wilderness in the hardest of all services, that of the Hudson Bay Company, at a salary of one hundred dollars a year, winning vast wealth, a peerage, and about everything else that men prize, as one of the prime movers in this great enterprise!

Think of the many other men who won wealth and titles and fame in executing this same magnificent

DRIVING THE LAST SPIKE ON THE CANADIAN PACIFIC AT CRAIGELLACHIE, B. C.,

At 9.30 A.M., November 7, 1885. Donald Smith, later Lord Strathcona, is driving the spike. Behind him, wearing a top hat, stands Sir Sanford Fleming, the engineer who surveyed and built the road. To the right of Sir Sanford is Sir William C. Van Horne, General Manager, later Chairman of the Board.

325

conception, and then say if " Romance " is not a more
fitting term with which to characterize the building of
the Canadian Pacific Railway.

The sheer audacity of the project when it was first
broached was fascinating. Here was a colony, not an
independent nation, a mere appanage of the British
crown, with fewer than five million inhabitants scattered in a narrow fringe along the eastern end of the
boundary line between Canada and the United States,
proposing to build a railroad three thousand miles
through an unknown wilderness to reach four or five
thousand other colonists in the lonely forests of the
Pacific coast.

But as the four thousand would join the newly
formed confederation on the Atlantic seaboard only
on condition that they be provided with a railroad
over which they could travel whenever their advice
was needed by their four million brethren, there was
nothing to do but build the road.

The proposal to build the Canadian Pacific encountered the usual derision and the usual demonstrations
that it could never be done common to all great enter-
prises. But gradually the scheme took shape. As
it seemed obvious that no private corporation would
consider three thousand miles of railroad through a
wilderness a profitable investment, it was proposed to
have the government build the road.

Immediately the transcontinental railroad became
a political issue. The Conservative party wanted the
road built; the Liberals took the position that it would
be a scandalous waste of public money, since such a
road could never earn enough to pay for its axle
grease. Here, then, was a subject for dissension

abundantly capable of keeping the Dominion in a ferment for years, and it did it. Government after government went down in the effort to get the railroad under way.

In March, 1874, two years after the surveys had been instituted, the Liberals, more than ever appalled by the formidable undertaking, sent J. D. Edgar as envoy extraordinary to the unreasonable British Columbians to try to persuade them to be content with a wagon road across the mountains to be maintained at an annual expenditure of one million five hundred thousand dollars. Instead of receiving the Liberal envoy graciously, and talking the matter over with him, the indignant British Columbians rushed their Premier, George A. Walkem, straight to London to lay their grievances before the Colonial Secretary. It is said that the obstreperous Westerner so disturbed the equanimity of the Colonial Office that it has not recovered to this day. Naturally this did not make friends of the Liberals; but in the end the British Columbians and the Conservatives had their way.

Each change of government contributed a little to the evolution of the magnificent project. Sandford Fleming, a Scotch engineer who had built the Intercolonial Railway, was engaged as chief engineer. In 1871 he made the preliminary arrangements for the surveys. As the whole territory, large enough to make a dozen States the size of Illinois, lying between Ottawa and the Pacific, was entirely uninhabited except by a few hundred persons around the silver mines near Port Arthur and a couple of thousand more at Winnipeg, and was practically unknown, this was a formidable undertaking.

In July, 1872, Fleming started from Montreal to take his first look at the country, and after traveling three thousand three hundred miles through the wilderness in ninety days, arrived in Victoria October 11. In the following year a great amount of surveying was accomplished.

Although there were no bloodthirsty Indians dogging their footsteps with tireless cunning, watching for a chance to massacre without danger to themselves, the task of the pathfinders was not without its perils. Sometimes death, swift and terrible, overtook those who sought to solve the riddle of the wilderness. On August 7, 1871, Alex. Sinclair, William Matheson, and five Indians, belonging to a surveying party assigned to the great woods north of Lake Superior, were surrounded by forest fires and burned to death.

Then there was Tom Clancy, who started alone to drag a load weighing four hundred pounds, lashed to some poles, across the ice on an arm of Lake Huron, November 13, 1872. His cap, found floating on the water in a hole in the ice, showed only too plainly what became of him.

May 20 of that same year A. Hamilton, engineer in charge, and E. J. C. Abbott, transit man, in that same wild region went to a Hudson Bay Company post on Lake Temiscamingue in a small canoe to settle an account and get G. Knaut and G. Rochette, chain and ax men, who had been laid up with scurvy.

The post trader wanted them to take a larger canoe on their return trip, but they refused. None of the party was ever seen again, but their canoe was found floating bottom up.

November 26 of that same disastrous year the

steamer *Mary Ward* was wrecked a few miles west of Collingwood, and three members of the survey who were on their way to a new field of operations were drowned. July 24, 1873, three men were drowned trying to get away from a camp on Whitefish Lake with a canoe-load of supplies.

The accident happened within two hundred feet of shore while the whole camp was looking on, but no help could reach them in time. Most of the deaths in this preliminary work were from drowning, though a few died from the effects of exposure.

Altogether thirty-four lives were lost in those seven years of adventurous toil and hardship. In each instance the government paid two years' salary to the family of the dead man. Sandford Fleming saw to that, often paying the money first and consulting the government about it afterward.

Camp equipment, instruments, and provisions usually had to be carried on men's backs, and supplies forwarded to parties in the field were transported by the same method, sometimes for hundreds of miles. It can readily be imagined, therefore, that camp life under such circumstances was not exactly luxurious.

Indians rendered valuable assistance in the surveys. Sometimes the difficulties of travel in the trackless mountains were so great that the white men sent to deliver messages turned back while their Indian companions went on and accomplished what they were sent to do, even if they did get in more dead than alive.

Surveying on the Pacific coast, where, owing to the wet climate, the forest growth is tropical in luxuriance, was particularly difficult. Marcus A. Smith, the resident engineer in charge of the work in British Columbia, set out early in the summer of 1872 to explore a possible route from Bute Inlet, which is far to the north of the location finally chosen.

He was provided with both pack-horses and canoes. But the ground was so covered with underbrush, matted together by aralea, a creeper armed with long thorns which made festering wounds wherever it touched the flesh, and so obstructed by enormous fallen trees, that the party could only cover five miles the first day, and the men with the canoes could not do even that well owing to the extreme crookedness of the Inlet.

As a result of three days' excessively hard work the party advanced eighteen miles. Then the horses were abandoned and Indians were engaged to carry the supplies. The fallen trees were so large that it was necessary to cut steps in them to enable the men to climb over.

But even this was nothing to the difficulties encountered in endeavoring to follow up the cañon of the Homathco River. Here there were cliffs of smooth granite rising vertically two hundred feet from the boiling torrent below. It was necessary to drill holes in the rock for iron bars to support a line of timbers to get through this cañon.

Chasms were bridged with single logs over which men had to crawl with heavy loads on their backs. The roar of the river and the boom of bowlders carried along by the torrent striking on the rocks in its bed were so deafening that men a few feet apart could not hear each other shout. Work had to be directed by signs. This was too " skookum " for the Indians, so they resigned.

The experience of Engineer E. W. Jarvis, who late in the autumn of 1874 received orders to explore a pass through the Rocky Mountains, is a fair sample of the life of the engineers who searched out the route for the railroad through an unknown mountain wilderness.

Jarvis left the mouth of the Quesnelle River on the Pacific coast, December 9, 1874, taking with him C. F. Hannington as assistant, Alec McDonald as dog-driver, and an Indian boy as cook. They went first to Fort George, a Hudson Bay Company post, where they were to get dogs and supplies.

On January 14, 1875, the expedition started. There were three white men, three Indians, and three dog teams of four dogs each, carrying provisions calculated to last two months. Some of the men and teams were to turn back after they had transported supplies well up into the mountains.

Their outfit consisted of a pair of snow-shoes and one pair of blankets to each man, with some extra moccasins and a piece of light cotton sheeting for a tent, canvas being too cumbersome to carry. This airy structure was to be their sole shelter, when they had any, throughout a winter in which the temperature averaged thirty-nine degrees below zero for the season, and often dropped to fifty-three degrees below. The provisions were bacon, beans, flour, and tea for the men and dried salmon for the dogs.

They were to traverse an unexplored country many miles to the northward of the present line of the road. Two men always had to go ahead to break

a trail by packing down the snow with their snow-
shoes to enable the dogs to get through.   Then came
the lightest team with the others following, with a
driver to each.

Lastly came Jarvis or Hannington to make a track
survey of the route.   Bearings were taken with a
pocket compass.   Distance was measured by pacing,
forty paces to the chain.   The whole weary distance
to Lake St. Anne, fifty miles above Edmonton, was
measured in this manner.

Noses and ears were frequently frozen in the intense cold.   There was no comfort in camp, for when
a roaring fire was built the men only succeeded in
roasting the side nearest the blaze while the other side
was rendered more susceptible to the cold.   The dogs'
toes were frozen so badly that it was necessary to
make moccasins for them.

On halting at noon on the third day out, Marquis,
the leader of one of the teams, lay down.   He tried to
rise, failed, gave a spasmodic wag of his tail, and
rolled over dead.   Upon examination, his legs were
found to be frozen stiff to the shoulder.   A thermom-
eter exposed to the sun on top of a sled at the time
registered forty-six degrees below zero.

Six days after leaving Fort George, a cache made
the previous summer was reached.   Here Hannington turned back with two of his teams to bring up
some dried fish for dog feed, while Jarvis, taking
McDonald with him, went on up the north fork of
the Fraser to explore and break a track.

Six days later the party reunited at the cache.
Three more teams from Fort George came up with
provisions and fish, swelling the party to eight men

and six teams of dogs, part of which were to turn back at the summit.

One day McDonald went to a small brook which tumbled down a rock into the river to get a drink. The water of the brook had kept the river ice thin so that when he stooped down to drink he suddenly dropped beneath the ice. Fortunately an Indian was near enough to grab him by the hair when he popped up to the surface.

The only damage was a soaking in ice water when the temperature was forty degrees below zero. In the next few days nearly all the rest had a similar experience.

Jarvis himself went down where the current was so swift that it caught his snow-shoes and tugged at him so desperately that it required the united efforts of the entire party to drag him back to safety. Had he not been fortunate enough to throw his arms out and get a support on firm ice he would have gone under for good and all.

About the 1st of February the snowstorms became almost continuous. The snow was so deep that when they shoveled down to the moss for a place to sleep they could not see over the edge of the hole.

In traveling, the snow-shoes would sink into the snow a foot and come up with a small avalanche on the toes at each step. This caused many blisters and frequent attacks of *mal de raquette,* which is a combination of paralysis and cramp in the legs, due to constant traveling on snow-shoes. When night came all hands were utterly exhausted.

Finally the valley took a sharp turn to the north, the stream divided, and the explorers were confronted by impassable barriers of rock. There was nothing for it but to return to the forks and try the south branch of the Fraser. They reached the forks February 12, where they rested a day.

Then sending two of the Indians with two teams back to Fort George, they set out to explore the south branch of the north fork of the Fraser, the object being to find a pass by which the Smoky River, flowing southeast from the eastern slope of the Rocky Mountains, could be reached. The woods here swarmed with moose and other game, but they had no time for hunting.

The party was hardly out of sight of the forks when the cañon closed in and the rocks overhung the trail so much that Hannington, who was in the lead, was obliged to take off his snow-shoes and crawl on hands and knees for fifty yards, where he was halted by a waterfall. Turning back, he started a snowslide, which thundered down to the river, leaving him clinging to the rocks like a fly on a wall. However, he crawled back in safety.

Going through the woods, they made a long portage, as every detour from the river was called. At the south end of the portage the descent to the river was so steep that Jarvis, though he turned the sled on its side and sat on the bow as the only way of applying brakes, was thrown off, and team and sled plunged into the open water. Fortunately no harm beyond breaking some traces was done.

Hannington took a hitch around a tree with his trail rope and lowered his sled in splendid shape until the end of the rope was reached. When he tried to pass the rope to a tree lower down, the sled and team shot down the mountainside until they came to a sapling.

The team went one side, the sled the other, bending the sapling down until the traces slid some twenty feet up its trunk, when it flew back, dangling the outfit in the air. A few blows with an ax ended this difficulty.

On finally reaching the river, the sight of a clear sheet of ice caused the men to shout and the dogs to bark with joy at the prospect of a stretch of easy traveling. There was a general scamper to get to it.

The first team promptly went down, for the ice was only a quarter of an inch thick, having evidently just formed. The water happened to be only two feet deep, so the team was fished out safely.

One evening they had just picked out a nice spot to camp when they were startled by the thunder of an avalanche above them. While they were discussing the chances of its passing near them, a bowlder of perhaps ten tons' weight, loosened by the avalanche, came hurtling down the mountain straight toward them.

By good luck a bunch of large pines turned it aside just before it reached the group, or that particular survey would have ended right there.

This valley, like the other, came to an abrupt end. By climbing two thousand feet a pass could be reached, so Jarvis decided to go on to Edmonton. The second morning, after crossing the divide to the eastern slope of the Rockies, they came suddenly to the brink of a fall two hundred and ten feet high.

There was no sound of falling water to warn them. If the morning had been misty, as the mornings usually were, they must inevitably have walked over the edge of the abyss. As it was, they discovered later, on looking up from below, that the whole party had stood on a projecting ledge of ice and snow only two feet thick.

A little farther on in this same cañon, in going down a precipitous descent, one of the sleds became unmanageable, and shooting down the mountain struck a log, crushing one of the dogs to death and splintering the sled.

By the time they were fairly out of the mountains the dogs were giving out. All six men had to go ahead and break track. Even then the dogs had to wallow up to their bodies in snow.

Their course in following the valley was northeast, instead of southeast as it should have been if the stream they had struck was the Smoky River. They began to fear that they were following the Pease River toward Hudson Bay and starvation.

Nearly every day the dismal howls of the dogs announced that another had dropped dead of hunger and exhaustion. It was now March 6, and their supplies were almost gone, and there was no game to be seen.

So they cached two of the sleds and the instruments and taking one sled struck across country in the direction they thought Jasper House, a Hudson Bay Company post, lay. Each man carried his blankets and share of the provisions, leaving the worn-out dogs only fifteen pounds of fish each to drag.

It was now a scramble for life over an exceedingly rough country, with the certainty of death staring them in the face if they failed to find, within a short time, the one place where there was help. Every morning one or more of the dogs was too weak to rise and had to be shot to cut his sufferings short.

One night the Indians gave up in despair and declared, with tears and great lamentation, that they were lost. It required all the eloquence of the white men to reassure them, particularly as the white men were by no means sure themselves that they would get out of the scrape.

On March 20 the exhausted party stumbled upon Fiddle River depot on Lac à Brûlé, which had been established by the survey and left in charge of some Indians. Here they found that Jasper House had been abandoned, and that Lake St. Anne, the nearest Hudson Bay Company post, was eleven days' travel away.

As the Indians were nearly out of provisions, and the dogs too exhausted to go any further, Jarvis and his party were obliged to struggle on with their outfits on their backs. The last three days before reaching Lake St. Anne they had to flounder through the snow without a morsel of food.

They became so exhausted that at times they were unable to push one snow-shoe before another, but stood still, feebly marking time. They finally reached the post in a dazed condition April 1, after a journey of nine hundred miles on snow-shoes in a temperature that averaged thirty-nine degrees below zero for the four months they were out.

There was a vast amount of work of this character to be done. To say nothing of the routes that proved to be hopeless upon first examination, every foot of the long route through the mountains which was finally selected had to be gone over six times before the graders arrived.

First there was the exploration. Next came the exploratory survey; then the revised survey; the trial location; the location survey; and lastly the revised location.

Seven years these surveys lasted, with twenty to twenty-five parties in the field, winter and summer. In that time the engineers examined forty-six thousand miles of territory, most of which had never before been seen by a white man, at a cost of three million five hundred thousand dollars.

When at last their great task was done, it was well done, for they had found passes through the mountains three thousand feet lower than those on any of the American lines. In only three places on the line were there heavy grades, and in each of these places they were compressed within twenty miles instead of being scattered over hundreds of miles as on the American lines.

Some idea of the difficulty of the work may be gathered from the fact that for a long time it seemed impossible to find a way across the Gold Range, the third range of mountains from the plains, until Major Rogers one day followed an eagle which led him to the only practicable pass in the entire range.

The news of this discovery seemed too good to be true. Chief Engineer Fleming would not believe it until he had been personally conducted through the pass by the triumphant Major Rogers. Afterwards the board of directors voted a present of five thousand dollars to the Major in recognition of the great service he had performed. A like reward was voted to

Engineer Sykes, who laid out a loop by which some steep grades and heavy rock cuts were avoided. Good work by other engineers was rewarded by a number of lesser bonuses.

Before the surveys were completed the work of construction was begun. Instead of undertaking a continuous line, though, the Mackenzie government pursued a makeshift, haphazard policy of building short stretches of railroad to connect lakes and navigable rivers. That did not suit the people, and the Mackenzie administration gave place to Sir John Macdonald, who was for building a transcontinental railroad without any more nonsense.

The Macdonald government accepted the offer of a syndicate composed of Donald Smith, governor of the Hudson Bay Company, who began life as an employee of the company in Labrador at a salary of one hundred dollars a year; George Stephen, his cousin, president of the Bank of Montreal; James J. Hill, with whom the two had been associated in the conversion of the abandoned streak of rust in the Minnesota woods into the vigorous and profitable St. Paul, Minneapolis and Manitoba Railroad; Duncan MacIntyre, the head of the Intercolonial Railway, who had been a Montreal mechant; R. B. Angus, and two other firms of bankers, one in London, and the other in Paris.

Under the terms of the contract which was signed October 20, 1880, the syndicate undertook to have a railroad in operation from Montreal to Vancouver ten years from that date in consideration of $25,-000,000 cash, 25,000,000 acres of land, and 712 miles of railroad in various stages of completion. No duty was to be levied on material imported, and the company was to be free from taxes and competition for twenty years.

Construction was begun by the company the following spring, but only one hundred and sixty-five miles were built that season. This was too slow for the syndicate, so they turned to the United States for help. W. C. Van Horne, of Illinois, who had risen from telegraph operator to the presidency of the Chicago, Milwaukee and St. Paul, then the largest railroad system in the country, was engaged as general manager.

An American firm, Langdon & Shepard, of St. Paul, was induced to undertake the contract for building the six hundred and seventy miles from Flat Creek, which is one hundred and seven-five miles west of Winnipeg, to Calgary, and another American, James Ross, was installed by the contractors as general manager of construction.

Then ensued the most spectacular bit of railroad building ever seen. March 11, 1882, the day the contract was signed, Langdon & Shepard advertised for three thousand men and two thousand teams. Sixty sub-contractors were set to work on sections of one mile or more, according to their means and ability.

By the time the grass was green an army of ten thousand men was at work on the great prairie. The work was done on the English plan; that is, the construction was solid and substantial as it was possible to make it, and not a rough temporary track. It was heavy work, averaging seventeen thousand cubic yards per mile of earth removal across the prairies.

As soon as a sub-contractor finished his job he

moved forward one hundred to one hundred and fifty miles, where he began on another section. In another six weeks he was pretty sure to hear the locomotive behind him. In advance of the track-layers were bridge gangs, as large as could work to advantage, divided into day and night shifts.

As every stick of timber had to be hauled from Rat Portage, one hundred and forty miles east of Winnipeg, the bridge-builders could not work more than eight or ten miles ahead of the track-layers. Timber was unloaded at night and hauled to the front so as not to interfere with other work.

Where not a sign of preparation or a stick of timber could be seen one day, the next day would show two or three spans of a nicely finished bridge, and on the second day trains would be running over it.

Following the bridge-builders came the track-laying gang, the most picturesque feature of railroad building. This gang consisted of three hundred men and thirty-five teams, working in as perfect accord as a fine machine. Floods in Red River Valley, the only route over which supplies could come, delayed work so much that by the end of June only seventy miles of track had been laid.

But in the next six months 349 miles were laid. Next year 376 miles were laid, making a total for the syndicate's three years of 962 miles of main line and 66 miles of siding. The record month was July, 1883, when 92 miles were laid.

The biggest day's work, 6.38 miles of track, was done on July 28, 1883. That day 2,120 rails weighing 604 tons were laid. To accomplish this feat required twelve men to unload rails, twelve to load them on dump cars, and ten men, five on each side, to lay the rails in place.

Two distributors of angle-bars and bolts handled 4,240 plates and 8,480 bolts. Following them fifteen bolters put in an average of 565 bolts each. Thirty-two spikers, with a nipper to each pair, drove 63,000 spikes distributed by four peddlers.

The lead and gauge spikers each drove 2,120 spikes with an average of four blows each, which required an average speed of 600 blows per hour for fourteen hours.

Sixteen thousand ties were unloaded, loaded on wagons, and hauled to place by thirty-two men and thirty-two teams. On the grade eight men unloaded and distributed the ties, four others spaced them, two spaced the joint ties, while still another two men adjusted the misplaced ties immediately ahead of the leading spikers.

Four iron-car boys and two horses hauled the iron to the front. The side track gang put in a siding 2,000 feet long that day.

To handle the commissariat for so large an army distributed over one hundred and fifty miles of territory and constantly on the move was no small task. The horses required 1,600 bushels of oats, and the men two carloads of provisions a day, all of which had to be unloaded and hauled where it was needed. The men were fed on the best that money could buy. There were ham, bacon, corned beef, and spiced rolls from Milwaukee, while a butcher's outfit supplied the camps with fresh meat at least three times a week. There were blacksmiths, wagon and harness makers, shoemakers, and tailors, a dispensary and five doctors to be supplied and moved forward with their outfits every time the camp moved.

In one important particular the building of the Canadian Pacific was very different from the building of any other railroad in the wilderness. There was no rowdyism, no drunkenness, no gambling, no daily murder. As one of the delighted American sub-contractors enthusiastically expressed it, this was due:

" Not to rough usage and old-fashioned Western lynch law, but to law made by the Queen and lived up to and enforced by her people. No liquor is allowed in the country, and under no pretext can any be smuggled in.

" There are none of the roughs and rowdies hanging around the camp so common on the other side of the line. There are no dance houses, no saloons, nothing to inflame and brutalize men and fleece them out of their money.

" When a man breaks the law here justice is dealt out to him a heap quicker and in larger chunks than he has been accustomed to in the States, and he has a small show when the guilt is once fastened home. All trains are examined, and every arrival is known. If a man's reasons for being in camp are not satisfactory, his stay is very brief.

" For the first offense of bringing in liquor there is a fine of fifty dollars and costs, and the liquor is destroyed. Next time he pays two hundred dollars and heavier costs; the third time he gets a fine of four hundred dollars, and, what is worse, six months in a fort with the inconvenience of a ball and chain riveted to his leg.

" The moment a complaint is made of a dealer having liquor under any of its aliases, three or four mounted police make their appearance at Mr. Dealer's shanty, and if there is any truth in the complaint he is provided with a conveyance to a fort, perhaps a hundred miles off, where in the absence of friends and free from outside influence or interference he takes his dose without fear or favoritism, and the medicine is generally a certain cure. I tell you there is a way to do it, and they are doing it right from the scratch."

Langdon & Shepard reached the summit of the Rocky Mountains in December, 1884. Their men were employed by another contracting firm, and the work went forward without interruption.

While the Langdon & Shepard forces were making their remarkable dash toward the Rocky Mountains, some extraordinarily difficult work was being done along the northern shore of Lake Superior. To get through this wild country, 2,500,000 cubic yards of the hardest rock known to engineers, syenite and trap, had to be removed.

To do this required the ceaseless efforts of 12,000 men and 2,000 teams working day and night, winter and summer, for three years.

The task of supplying this great force the year round in a region so nearly inaccessible was one of extraordinary difficulty. The severe cold of winter, which greatly increased the difficulties of transportation, also acted as a tonic which so sharpened the appetites of the men that they consumed an average of five pounds of food a day, or a total of four hundred and twenty thousand pounds a week for all the camps.

To supply current needs and to lay in a supply that would last through the seven months of winter, when communication with the outer world was cut off, twelve steamers were kept busy while navigation was open. The northern shore of Lake Superior is so wild and rough that it was impracticable to build good wagon roads; so small boats had to be used whenever possible to distribute supplies. Michipicoten would have been the most convenient point for a central depot, but it was so exposed that the wharf and warehouse were twice washed away. Then the landing was moved to a point four miles west.

In order to reach the line of the railroad it was necessary to make a portage road seven miles in length to a small lake six and a half miles long, which was navigated by a steamboat that had to be built on the spot. At the farther end of this lake the supplies were again transferred from a boat to wagons for a sixteen-mile haul over an extremely rough road, which had been made passable only by an immense expenditure of labor and dynamite. A second lake, eleven miles long, was navigated by another steamboat, then came a stretch of two and a half miles of exceedingly bad road to the third lake, which was traversed by still another steamboat that had to be built out in the heart of the wilderness. This third steamboat, by making a voyage of twenty-six miles, could land the supplies at a point from which they could be distributed to the camps. Every pound of provisions and other supplies required in building the road for a hundred miles east and west from this last landing had to be handled through this laborious routine of six transfers from boat to wagon and wagon to boat again. In the winter three hundred dog teams were kept busy distributing supplies.

A shelf twenty feet wide and eleven miles long had to be blasted through the living rock along the coast in one stretch of this difficult road. Five tunnels were driven, and ten rivers, one of them a stream one hundred and fifty yards wide, had to be diverted from their natural courses through rock tunnels.

This tremendous amount of blasting required one hundred tons of dynamite a month for fifteen months. It was all manufactured on the works with such care that not a single life was lost in the making or the handling.

When it was all over it was found that ninety miles of road had cost two million dollars. The worst mile cost seven hundred and fifty thousand dollars. But the work was so well done that the maximum grade was fifty-two feet to the mile, and there was no curve greater than six degrees.

The first use to which this stretch of road was put was to transport troops west to help put down the Riel rebellion in April, 1885. The road not being completed, the soldiers were hauled over the unballasted track in construction trains, and picked their way as best they could over the gap. Their unexpected appearance at the front did much to quell the uprising. On returning in the fall, the soldiers found sleeping and dining cars running regularly over as fine a road-bed as there was in the Dominion.

Still another army of 6,000 men, principally Chinamen, were working eastward from Kamloops, 250 miles east of Vancouver, the end of the Pacific section of government-built road, under Contractor Onderdonk. But the Chinamen spent most of their time around fires in cold weather. Only white men were of any use when real hard work was to be done.

Some wonderful engineering work was required to carry the road through the mountains. In the sixty-two miles from the summit of the Rocky Mountains to the valley of the Columbia River, the Kicking Horse River, which the line follows, falls two thousand seven hundred and seventy-eight feet. The river had to be crossed nine times, while there were three hundred and seventy thousand cubic feet of rock to be removed, exclusive of tunnel work. All drilling had to be done by hand, because it was not possible to get machinery over the long and difficult trail.

On the Pacific slope of the Selkirks the descent is two thousand three hundred and fifty feet in forty-two miles. The Cascade Range was passed by following narrow ledges along the Fraser River through an endless succession of tunnels and over some of the highest timber trestles ever constructed. One of these was two hundred and ninety-six feet high and four hundred and fifty feet long. All food, material, and supplies had to be transported long distances through a wilderness, and finally through mountains which Sir Edwin Arnold declared surpassed the Alps, the Himalayas, and the Andes in magnificence. And it must not be forgotten that the more attractive a mountain is to the æsthete, the more troublesome it is to the engineer and to the humbler mortals upon whom devolves the necessary duty of getting bags of flour and sides of bacon over it.

Some curious obstacles were encountered at various

places which worried the engineers and cost the company money. For instance, two hundred and seventeen miles east of Winnipeg the line crosses the Barclay muskeg, which is the Indian name for bog. This muskeg is a huge basin filled to a depth of two hundred feet with material dense enough to support the track, but which quivers like a bowl of jelly whenever a train strikes it. The surface is thrown into waves five or six inches high by the passage of a train. This jelly-like quivering caused the rails to creep, in some instances as much as two feet four inches under a single train. Track bolts were frequently sheared off by the creeping movement, and it was found necessary to station watchmen at the muskeg day and night with short pieces of rail to repair the gaps left by the creeping until the engineers could find a way to anchor the track securely.

Again, in going down the western slope of the Rockies, the engineers wanted to tunnel a mountain spur, but the mountain proved to be of quicksand which filled up the tunnel as soon as it was finished. After the third attempt the engineers decided to go around.

On the Thompson River, two hundred miles east of Vancouver, irrigation on some mountain terraces had caused a series of extraordinary landslides before the railroad was built. In the largest of these a mass of earth one hundred and sixty acres in area and four hundred feet in depth slid down into the river until it was stopped by the opposite mountain wall, damming the river to a height of one hundred and sixty feet and forming a lake twelve miles long. As soon as the river rose to the height of the dam it began flowing over the top, and in due time scoured out its bed again. There were a number of smaller slides in the same locality.

When the railroad builders came along they found to their astonishment that they could not make the track stay where they put it. The whole surface of the earth, lubricated by the continual seepage from the irrigating ditches, was steadily sliding toward the river over the slippery substratum of clay silt. One morning they found the track had moved toward the river eight feet and had sunk four feet below grade during the night. Watchmen had to be stationed day and night to watch the wandering track until the engineers could find a way to outwit the elusive mountainside.

Indeed, the building of the Canadian Pacific Railway was one long struggle with natural obstacles as formidable as they were unique. Like the pioneers who first grappled with the problems of the railroad, the engineers of the Canadian Pacific had no precedents to guide them, and not even any facts on which to base their plans, for the whole of the route lay through an unknown wilderness. It was evident, for example, that the precipitation in the Selkirk Mountains was enormous, and that snow-slides, or avalanches, were frequent and appallingly destructive. In order to learn just how formidable these snow-slides were and to determine the position, character, and extent of snow-sheds required to protect the line from them, parties of engineers, well provided with meteorological instruments, snow-shoes, and dog trains, passed a winter in the mountains.

The snowfall was found to be tremendous, amount-

ing in one winter to an aggregate of forty-three feet
six inches. In a single storm of six days' duration
eight and a half feet of snow fell. Owing to the
warm Chinook winds and winter rains the snow in
these mountains packs down into dense, heavy masses,
a cubic foot of it weighing from twenty-five to forty-
five pounds. The slightest disturbance, such as a
man or an animal walking across the lower edge of a
steep slope, or even the vibrations of the atmosphere
caused by talking in a loud voice, was sufficient to set
a slide, sometimes amounting to a quarter of a million
cubic yards, in motion. Usually the slides started by
their own weight. With a crash and a roar the great
mass, weighing from a hundred thousand to a hundred and fifty thousand tons, would dart down the
mountainside in a great white flash, sweeping trees,
loose bowlders weighing several tons, and everything
else down to the solid granite of the mountain core,
with it. So great was the force of these slides that
they would cross the valleys and be carried up the
opposite slope a hundred feet or so.

The most remarkable effects were caused by the
cyclones induced by the tremendous velocity of these
enormous masses. These cyclones, extending for a
distance of a hundred yards on each side and in front
and for a hundred feet above the slides, were called
" flurries." Huge trees, several feet in diameter, that
happened to be caught in the vortex of these flurries,
would be uprooted; others outside the vortex would
be cut off as by a chain shot. A man who had the mis-
fortune to be caught in a flurry was picked up and
whirled and twisted spirally and finally dropped, a
limp mass, without a bruise or break in skin or cloth-

ing, yet with every bone in his body broken or dislocated.

The information gathered by the observers led to the building of seven miles of snow-sheds, in which 26,000,000 feet of timber was used, at a cost of $3,000,000, to protect the tracks. The sheds were built of large square timbers, with their roofs on a level with the mountain slope, so they would offer the least possible resistance to the snow-slides. As a further precaution magazines of provisions, oil and coal for the coaches were established at intervals of ten or twelve miles, throughout the Selkirks, so that if a train should have the misfortune to be detained by snow blockades it would never be more than six miles from supplies. These magazines have proved, however, to be of little use except for such moral support as they may provide, for the engineers who planned the snow-sheds did their work so skilfully that the Canadian Pacific has experienced even less trouble from snow blockades than lines farther south.

Nor were the engineers and the contractors the only ones who were having a hard time building the Canadian Pacific. The men behind the engineers were ensconced in comfortable offices away back in Montreal, where they never had to give a thought to the chances of the next instalment of bacon and beans getting through in time to keep them from starving to death; but they had to study very hard upon problems scarcely less vital. In 1884, when the great work was well along toward completion, there came a crisis that cost the officers and directors some sleepless nights, and very nearly swamped the undertaking with all hands involved in it.

All the money obtained from the government and from sales of stock had been spent. Stephen, Smith, and the other members of the syndicate had pledged all their earthly possessions upon which money could be raised, and the Bank of Montreal was deeply involved. It should have been easy to raise money since so much of the road had been built, and the management had been energetic and economical, but it wasn't. The somewhat numerous class which had known all along that the road could never be built now had the public ear, and all attempts to raise money were viewed askance. The fate of the Dominion, as well as of the railroad company, hung in the balance for a time.

As a last resort the government was asked for a loan of twenty-two million five hundred thousand dollars. It hesitated. Public opinion was intensely wrought up, and the government could not count on its stanchest supporters. Finally a secret loan was advanced by the government, and the crisis was passed. The syndicate proved itself worthy of this mark of confidence by repaying every dollar of all the government loans before they were due.

All obstacles, natural and financial, were overcome at last, however, and on the 1st of November, 1885, a train bearing some of the directors and railroad officials left Montreal while the eastern and western ends of the road were still several miles apart. When the train reached Craigellachie, 2,553 miles from Montreal and 351 miles from Vancouver, only one rail remained to be put in place in the track.

The celebration attending the driving of the last spike on transcontinental lines across the border had always been an elaborate and expensive one. The admitted cost of the ceremony on the Northern Pacific was one hundred and seventy-five thousand dollars; the real cost was probably more. But in Canada they managed it differently.

" The last spike," said General Manager Van Horne, " will be just as good an iron one as there is between Montreal and Vancouver. Any one who wants to see it driven will have to pay full fare."

Such inhospitable terms as these had the effect of limiting the party who witnessed that historic event to barely a dozen railroad officials and the workmen who finished the job. On November 7, 1885, Donald Smith, a Scotchman who had begun life in the wilderness at a salary of one hundred dollars a year, drove the last spike which completed the Canadian Pacific five years before the time specified in the contract.

There was no speechmaking, no banquet, no anything. When Smith had delivered the last blow he threw down the spike maul and then the little party went fishing.

OTHER BOOKS FROM CGR PUBLISHING AT CGRPUBLISHING.COM

1939 New York World's Fair: The World of Tomorrow in Photographs

San Francisco 1915 World's Fair: The Panama-Pacific International Expo.

1904 St. Louis World's Fair: The Louisiana Purchase Exposition in Photographs

Chicago 1933 World's Fair: A Century of Progress in Photographs

19th Century New York: A Dramatic Collection of Images

The American Railway: The Trains, Railroads, and People Who Ran the Rails

The Aeroplane Speaks: Illustrated Historical Guide to Airplanes

The World's Fair of 1893 Ultra Massive Photographic Adventure Vol. 1

The World's Fair of 1893 Ultra Massive Photographic Adventure Vol. 2

The World's Fair of 1893 Ultra Massive Photographic Adventure Vol. 3

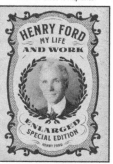

Henry Ford: My Life and Work - Enlarged Special Edition

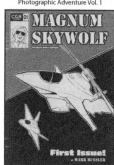

Magnum Skywolf #1

Ethel the Cyborg Ninja Book 1

The Complete Ford Model T Guide: Enlarged Illustrated Special Edition

How To Draw Digital by Mark Bussler

Best of Gustave Doré Volume 1: Illustrations from History's Most Versatile...

OTHER BOOKS FROM CGR PUBLISHING AT CGRPUBLISHING.COM

Ultra Massive Video Game Console Guide Volume 1

Ultra Massive Video Game Console Guide Volume 2

Ultra Massive Video Game Console Guide Volume 3

Ultra Massive Sega Genesis Guide

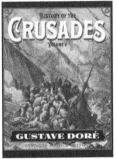

History of the Crusades Volumes 1 & 2: Gustave Doré Restored Special Editions

Chicago's White City Cookbook

The Clock Book: A Detailed Illustrated Collection of Classic Clocks

The Complete Book of Birds: Illustrated Enlarged Special Edition

1901 Buffalo World's Fair: The Pan-American Exposition in Photographs

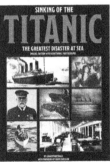

Sinking of the Titanic: The Greatest Disaster at Sea

Gustave Doré's London: A Pilgrimage: Retro Restored Special Edition

Milton's Paradise Lost: Gustave Doré Retro Restored Edition

The Art of World War 1

The Kaiser's Memoirs: Illustrated Enlarged Special Edition

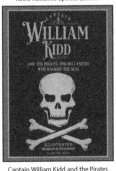

Captain William Kidd and the Pirates and Buccaneers Who Ravaged the Seas

The Complete Butterfly Book: Enlarged Illustrated Special Edition

- MAILING LIST -
JOIN FOR EXCLUSIVE OFFERS

www.CGRpublishing.com/subscribe

Made in the USA
Monee, IL
19 December 2023

50069796R00197